D0742295

JUSTICE IN YOUR COURT

JUSTICE IN YOUR COURT

What would it look like?
50 real-life cases for you to decide

Tom Borcher

Illustrations by Simon Goodway

Copyright © 2022 by Tom Borcher.

Library of Congress Control Number:		2022908471
ISBN:	Hardcover	978-1-6698-2405-3
	Softcover	978-1-6698-2404-6
	eBook	978-1-6698-2406-0

All rights reserved. No part of this book may be reproduced or transmitted in any form or by any means, electronic or mechanical, including photocopying, recording, or by any information storage and retrieval system, without permission in writing from the copyright owner.

Any people depicted in stock imagery provided by Getty Images are models, and such images are being used for illustrative purposes only.
Certain stock imagery © Getty Images.

Print information available on the last page.

Rev. date: 06/20/2022

To order additional copies of this book, contact:
Xlibris
844-714-8691
www.Xlibris.com
Orders@Xlibris.com
840780

CONTENTS

To Sanford M. Gage

Preface

The battle between parties in a court of law has always fascinated me. I bought my first book of case decisions at a flea market when I was in my early teens. Later, following a period I call my "hippie" stage, I went to law school in Atlanta, Georgia. After passing the bar exam in 1979, I practiced there for three years as a trial attorney litigating on behalf of plaintiffs (the ones bringing the lawsuits). In 1982 I moved to Los Angeles, where I continued to represent plaintiffs in civil matters. I loved being a trial lawyer and facing the challenges of the courtroom.

Now that I am retired—since 2014—presenting cases to the public for discussion has helped to fill the void created by my no longer arguing in court on behalf of a client. I created a program for student and adult groups called "You Be the Judge" in which I give an audience the facts of real cases. I then afford time for the participants to discuss the cases and to ask questions. The audience then votes and renders its "verdict" for each case. Only then do I reveal the actual court decisions. I purposefully select cases that have an unusual twist somewhere along the way. As a result, the audiences that participate in my programs often find themselves in spirited debates and evenly split in deciding the verdicts.

This book is an attempt to convey the same energy of those live programs to the written page. The odds are you have never heard of any of the fifty cases in this book—at least, that's what I am hoping. I haven't selected any famous or notorious cases that you would have likely read about in the paper or heard about on the evening news. My goal is to have you start each case with a fresh slate. That is not to say that there aren't some very important constitutional issues raised and decided in these case studies.

People seem to love the tension that builds when waiting for the announcement of "the decision," whether it's one of the many television shows in which contestants vie for an ultimate title (such as *The Voice, Survivor, Dancing with the Stars, American Idol,* and *America's Got Talent*) or the numerous crime and trial dramas that populate the screen, or the myriad in-studio small claims courts populating the afternoon network airways—first introduced by the late Judge Joseph Wapner with *The People's Court.* A large part of the fun of these shows is seeing if one can predict the winner or the one "whodunit" or the party that the judge or jury says should prevail.

For each case presented in this book, I will provide the case caption (for example, *Smith v. Texas*) followed immediately by the citation (source) of the case and then a summary of the facts and law involved.[1] At that point, I turn the case over to the reader for a verdict. One may proceed alone or with a group. Once you have reached a verdict, you can then turn to the pages that follow each case summary, where I provide the reader with the ultimate decision of the court, the reasoning behind the majority decision, and sometimes the dissenting opinion(s) as well.

You do not have to be a lawyer to read and decide these cases. I have done my best to summarize the laws at issue in a manner that should allow the reader to grasp the concepts involved without a law school education.[2]

I urge the reader to avoid approaching these cases with the goal toward guessing the actual court's decision. It is more important to arrive at your own decision based on your own reasoned analysis, and only then comparing your reasoning with the court's.

Each case study is complete within itself. One can read the cases in any order as each separate case study contains all the facts and law

---

[1]   For those readers who would like to dig deeper into the cases and perhaps read the actual court decision, I explain and interpret the citation system in the Appendix.

[2]   But I will be so bold to suggest that even a lawyer might find this book to be an interesting and enlightening read.

needed for that particular case. Should you wish to read all the cases on a particular common issue (such as religious freedom or free speech), I have listed the case studies by category at the back of the book.

I hope that while working through this book the reader gains a better understanding of the complex nature of the issues the courts must address. Seldom is there a clear answer. Courts work in areas of gray, not black and white. Often one will find something raised in the dissenting opinion that completely changes the way one views a set of facts.

Educators, in particular, may find a use for this book in the classroom as a basis for discussion and debate. There are constitutional questions presented involving, among other issues, death penalty challenges, criminal prosecution disputes, and immigration rights matters. Perhaps by discussing these issues in the context of real-life cases, students can learn to analyze facts, debate them in a respectful format, and come to a better understanding of the complexity of issues that on first blush may have seemed straightforward.

In short, I could ask for nothing more than that these cases might give readers a heightened sense of *tolerance* for the views of others.

While proceeding through the pages of this book, one would do well to keep in mind the remarks of former appellate justice Alex Kozinski who, while discussing the deliberative process in an article he wrote entitled "What I Ate for Breakfast and Other Mysteries of Judicial Decision Making," noted: "But it is even more important to doubt your own leanings, to be skeptical of your instincts. It is frequently very difficult to tell the difference between how you think a case should be decided and how you hope it will come out."[3]

My ultimate goal was to write a book that—despite the serious issues addressed—readers would find to be a "fun" read. So please, have fun.

Tom Borcher

---

[3]   26 Loy.L.A.L.Rev. 993 (1993); Available at https://digitalcommons.lmu.edu//llr/vol26/iss4/5

Court is now in session.

Taylor v. United States

136 S.Ct. 2074 (2016)

The Issue:

Does robbing your neighborhood drug dealer interfere with interstate commerce?

The Constitution grants to the federal government the right to oversee interstate commerce. Using this broad power, Congress and the courts have, for example, asserted that the federal government can ban discriminatory seating based on race at lunch counters as well as regulate the trucking industry.

David Taylor was a member of a Roanoke, Virginia, gang that went by the name "Southwest Goonz." The gang received a tip that marijuana was being sold out of two local residences. The Goonz saw the opportunity to rob drug dealers as one which would result in not only the actual cash from the dealers' sales but also "pounds of weed." The word on the street was that the weed was an "exotic high-grade product." (The local police department, by the way, also understood that the two residences were drug dealing locations.)

In a "Keystone Cops" kind of scenario, members of the Goonz gang held up the residences. The occupants at both locations told the Goonz that they were not drug dealers and that they did not have any cash. The Goonz were hardly rewarded with the bundle of money and exotic weed they were expecting. All they were able to take from the first of the two residences was the occupant's girlfriend's jewelry, forty dollars from the girlfriend's purse, two cell phones, and one marijuana cigarette. From the second residence they scored one cell phone.

Taylor, who participated in the crime spree, was subsequently apprehended and charged with robbery under the federal Hobbs Act, which makes robbery a federal—versus state—crime if it interferes with interstate commerce.

The Trial:

Taylor's first trial on the charges resulted in a hung jury. Prior to his retrial, the government asked the judge to prohibit Taylor from introducing any evidence that the targeted drug dealers dealt only in locally grown marijuana. The government asserted that the mere fact that the victims were drug dealers was sufficient, in and of itself, to prove the required "interstate commerce" element of the crime with which Taylor was charged. In opposing the government's motion, Taylor asserted that:

> . . .[T]he prosecution must prove beyond a reasonable doubt either (1) that the particular drugs in question originated or were destined for sale out of State or (2) that the particular drug dealer targeted in the robbery operated an interstate business.

The trial judge granted the government's request and prohibited Taylor from introducing any evidence that the marijuana was locally grown.

Taylor was convicted of the charges. The US Court of Appeals for the Fourth Circuit affirmed the conviction. Taylor then appealed to the Supreme Court to have the charges dismissed.

The Applicable Law:

The Hobbs Act makes robbery a federal crime if the robbery delayed, obstructed, or affected interstate commerce even if it does so only to a minimal degree. In fact, the defendant under this law does not *actually* have to interfere with such commerce; the law only requires that his actions were *likely* to do so. It is the interstate commerce aspect of the robbery charge that allows the government to prosecute Taylor in the federal court.

The Commerce Clause is found in Article 1, Section 8, paragraph 3 of the United States Constitution. Section 8 sets forth the powers granted to Congress, and paragraph 3 of that section grants Congress the authority: "To regulate commerce with foreign nations, and among the several states, and with Indian tribes." That brief directive has precipitated much litigation.

As the Commerce Clause was originally understood, it gave Congress the authority to regulate the buying and selling of goods and services trafficked across state lines. However, the Supreme Court has ruled that the federal government may prohibit even commerce that moves exclusively within a state (intrastate commerce) if that commerce, nevertheless, has a "substantial relation to interstate commerce." Thus, activities within a state involving the sale of marijuana may be regulated by the federal government because of the impact the sales may have on the national market.

It is important to note that in a criminal trial, the government is usually required to establish each and every element of the crime by proof beyond a reasonable doubt. One of the disputes in this case that affects the final decision is whether "proving each and every element of the crime" means that the government must prove beyond a reasonable doubt that the two home invasion robberies at issue did or were likely to interfere with interstate commerce.

What's your verdict? Did the evidence prove beyond a reasonable doubt that the theft of the jewelry, forty dollars cash, a purse, three cell phones, a marijuana cigarette from *suspected* drug dealers sufficiently interferes with interstate commerce such that Taylor's conviction under the Hobbs Act should be affirmed? If your answer to that question is "yes," then Taylor will spend some time behind bars. If your answer is "no," then the defendant's conviction is overturned.

STOP HERE AND DECIDE THE CASE
BEFORE GOING FURTHER

The Court's Decision follows on the next page.

The Court's Decision

Held: The interstate commerce clause element of robbery under the Hobbs Act is satisfied once the government has shown that the defendant robbed a drug dealer of drugs or drug proceeds. Taylor's conviction was affirmed.

The Supreme Court held, in a 7-to-1 decision, that all the government had to do was prove the robber targeted a marijuana dealer's drugs or the dealer's illegal proceeds to meet its burden of proving beyond a reasonable doubt that commerce over which the United States has jurisdiction was affected. Since the evidence showed that the Goonz specifically selected victims they believed to be drug dealers in order to enhance their ill-gotten gains, a sufficient showing was made to prove a Hobbs Act violation.

In his dissenting opinion, Justice Clarence Thomas argued against such a broad interpretation of the Hobbs Act and the Commerce Clause. He warned that:

> . . . Congress could, under its commerce power, regulate
> *any* robbery: In the aggregate, any type of robbery could
> be deemed to substantially affect interstate commerce.
> (emphasis in the original)

Consider this hypothetical scenario in light of the Supreme Court's decision: Two professional home invasion burglars have identified a particular home as the residence of the chief executive officer (CEO) of a large national trucking company. They break into the home and steal money, jewels, and some very rare paintings. Obviously, the burglars are stealing the assets the CEO had purchased with income from his trucking business. The trucking company is a major interstate carrier. Could the burglars be convicted of robbery under the Hobbs Act?

Commonwealth of Pennsylvania v. Kirchner

Sup.Crt. Penn. No. 1873 MDA 2018 (2019)[4]

The Issue:

Can a simple hand gesture make one guilty of disorderly conduct?

Josh Klingseisen and his next-door neighbor Elaine Natore did not get along very well, to put it mildly. An alley was all that separated their two homes. Due to ongoing problems with Natore, Klingseisen had installed six security cameras around his home. Natore, on the other hand, had obtained a "no contact" order from the court against Klingseisen.

Into this feud walks Natore's friend Stephen Kirchner.

One day while mulching in his backyard, Klingseisen sees Natore and Kirchner walking down the alley between Klingseisen's and Natore's homes. Kirchner stops. He makes eye contact with Klingseisen. Kirchner extends his arm toward Klingseisen, makes a fist, and extends his index finger, raises his thumb, points this "gun" gesture at Klingseisen, and then makes a recoil motion. Based on Klingseisen's claim that he felt

---

[4] This case study is not published in a reporter. It is a Memorandum Decision from the Superior Court of Lancaster County Pennsylvania, and has no precedential authority unlike most of the other cases in this book.

extremely threatened by Kirchner's "handgun," Kirchner was issued a citation for disorderly conduct.

The Trial:

At his trial, Kirchner testified that he made the gesture only after Klingseisen had given him the middle finger of both hands.

Another neighbor of Klingseisen's, Yvonne Rodriguez, testified she saw the incident. She said she saw Kirchner "turn towards Klingseisen and 'put his finger up like he was going to shoot him.'" Seeing this caused Rodriguez to feel insecure and fearful as to what might follow. She was so upset that she called 911.

The Applicable Law:

The criminal code of Pennsylvania provides:

> [A] person is guilty of disorderly conduct, if, with intent
> to cause public inconvenience, annoyance, or alarm, or
> recklessly creating a risk thereof, [the person] . . . creates
> a hazardous or physically offensive condition by any act
> which serves no legitimate purpose of the actor.

Kirchner argued that since his hand gesture could never have been mistaken for an actual firearm, it could not reasonably create a hazardous or physically offensive condition.

The government, on the other hand, asserted that "Kirchner's act of mimicking his shooting Klingseisen created the requisite hazardous condition as it risked an altercation."

Kirchner's trial resulted in a guilty verdict. He appealed the decision.

What's your verdict? Was Kirchner's making a hand gesture in the form of a gun intentional or reckless and sufficient to have created "a hazardous or physically offensive condition"? If you answer that question "yes," then Kirchner's conviction stands. If you answer that question "no," then the trial court is reversed, and Kirchner is a free man.

STOP HERE AND DECIDE THE CASE
BEFORE GOING FURTHER

The Court's Decision

Held: The court agreed with the trial court and found Kirchner was guilty of disorderly conduct.

The superior court's decision to affirm the trial court verdict was, in large part, due to the testimony of both Josh Klingseisen and his across-the-street neighbor Yvonne Rodriguez that they felt threatened and insecure as a result of Kirchner's gesture, even leading Rodriguez to call 911.

The appellate panel said that "there was sufficient evidence that Kirchner's act of mimicking his shooting Klingseisen created a hazardous condition as it risked an altercation." The superior court cited the fact that there was bad blood between Klingseisen and his neighbor Natore, to the extent that security cameras had been installed and a no-contact order issued. These activities were evidence of heightened tensions that could easily have been dangerously escalated by Kirchner's gun gesture.

Do you think Josh Klingseisen could have been found guilty of the same charges? Remember, the evidence was that Klingseisen first gave the middle finger of both hands to Kirchner before Kirchner reacted with his own gesture. If the court felt that the fake gun gesture met the requirements for disorderly conduct in that the gesture was likely to cause an altercation, could not the same be said of Klingseisen's gesture?

Mr. Kirchner has some company. In October of 2019, a Kansas school girl was charged with "felony threatening." A fellow student had asked her if she could kill five people whom would she choose. The girl responded by directing a handgun gesture at four other students as well as herself. There was no indication that the girl had access to an actual gun. The matter never went to trial. The young girl was directed to a community diversion program as she had no prior offenses. Upon successful completion of that program, all charges will be dismissed without a finding of guilt.

Van Orden v. Perry

545 U.S. 677 (2005)

The Issue:

Can the State of Texas put a stone marker displaying the Ten Commandments on the state capitol grounds without violating the Constitution?

Religious disputes frequently divide the Supreme Court. In this case, for instance, you will find that it was decided by only five votes versus the dissenters' four votes.

There are twenty-two acres comprising the grounds of the Texas State Capitol. It is the home of about seventeen monuments and twenty-one historical markers that can be observed as one walks the paths.

The monument we will be addressing was donated in 1961 to the state by a group called the Fraternal Order of Eagles of Texas, a social, civic, and patriotic organization. In addition to donating the monument, the Eagles paid for its installation.[5]

---

[5]   Movie buffs may find it interesting to note that the famous director Cecil B. DeMille, who at the time was filming his movie classic *The Ten Commandments*, assisted the Eagles in producing the monuments that they placed at several different locations in addition to the Texas state capitol. It is unknown whether DeMille's interest in the project was more religious or commercial!

The monument sets out the text of the Ten Commandments. The first line, with portions in large print and in capital letters, reads: "I AM the LORD thy GOD." Thereafter, the following ten admonitions are literally carved in stone:

Thou shalt have no other gods before me.
Thou shalt not make to thyself any graven images.
Thou shalt not take the Name of the Lord thy God in vain.
Remember the Sabbath day, to keep it holy.
Honor they father and thy mother, that thy days may be long upon the
    land which the Lord thy God giveth thee.
Thou shalt not kill.
Thou shalt not commit adultery.
Thou shalt not steal.
Thou shalt not bear false witness against thy neighbor.
Thou shalt not covet thy neighbor's house.
Thou shalt not covet thy neighbor's wife, nor his manservant, nor his
    maidservant, nor his cattle nor anything that is thy neighbor's.

Thomas Van Orden, an attorney, frequently walked through the capitol grounds on his way to the nearby State Supreme Court building. In doing so, he would pass by the Ten Commandments monument. Van Orden brought suit against the State of Texas (by suing the state governor, Perry), seeking to have the monument removed.

Exactly how one characterizes the Ten Commandments may vary from one person to the next. Obviously, the text has a religious message. (The Ten Commandments are derived, after all, from the Bible.) But does it not also have a secular message setting forth proper standards of conduct regardless of one's religion or lack of it? (Most everyone agrees that lying, cheating, stealing, and killing are to be condemned without respect to any religion.) And the commandments may also be regarded as a historical influence on the formation of our laws. (One may find them included in displays in government buildings alongside the Magna Carta, the Declaration of Independence, and the

Constitution in recognition of these documents' influence on the laws of the United States.)

The Trial:

Van Orden testified that, in his role as an attorney, he often used the law library in the State Supreme Court building located next to the state capitol building. For six years, his visits to the library would lead to his walking by the stone marker. He argued that the marker violated the Establishment Clause of the Constitution since it was on government property. After hearing the evidence and argument of the parties, the district court determined that the marker did not violate the provisions of the First Amendment's Establishment Clause. Van Orden challenged the district court's decision in the court of appeals, which upheld the ruling of the trial court. Van Orden then appealed to the United States Supreme Court.

The Applicable Law:

The Constitution, as originally written, made no reference to religion or God. Rather, religious freedom was established by way of the First Amendment to the Constitution by the following language which is referred to as the "Establishment Clause": "Congress shall make no law respecting an establishment of religion, or prohibiting the free exercise thereof . . ."[6]

In an earlier case from Kentucky, the Supreme Court held it was unconstitutional to require the posting of the Ten Commandments in every public schoolroom. On the other hand, the Supreme Court has allowed state legislatures to open their daily sessions with a prayer by a chaplain.

---

[6] This provision was made applicable to the individual states, and not just the federal government, by way of the Fourteenth Amendment, which prohibits the states from denying any person the *equal protection* of the law.

What's your verdict? Does the Ten Commandments marker located on the Texas State Capitol grounds violate the Establishment Clause of the United States Constitution? If you answer "yes," then the monument would be removed. If you answer "no," then the monument remains in place.

STOP HERE AND DECIDE THE CASE
BEFORE GOING FURTHER

The Court's Decision follows on the next page.

The Court's Decision

Held: The Ten Commandments monument on the Texas state capitol grounds does not violate the Constitution's Establishment Clause and, therefore, may remain in place.

The 5-to-4 plurality opinion consists of only ten pages, not many compared to most cases. On the other hand, the concurring and dissenting opinions cover seventy-six pages. In fact, there is not a real *majority* opinion, only a *plurality* one (in which four of the nine justices joined). The fifth justice voting to affirm the lower court, Justice Stephen Breyer, wrote his own separate opinion stating reasons for doing so that were different from those stated in the plurality opinion. That so many of the justices felt the need to qualify, explain, or oppose the plurality opinion demonstrates the volatility of the issues involved.

A plurality of the justices distinguished the Kentucky school Ten Commandments case from this Texas dispute by noting that the Kentucky holding addressed a special location and a special audience: a classroom occupied by young, impressionable children.

The plurality found that the Texas monument was consistent with the nation's tradition of acknowledging the commandments' historical significance. It said that "simply having religious content or promoting a message consistent with a religious doctrine does not run afoul of the Establishment Clause." They agreed with the finding of the district court, which had determined in ruling in favor of Texas, that: ". . . [A] reasonable observer, mindful of the history, purpose, and context would not conclude that this passive monument conveyed the message that the State was seeking to endorse religion."

The argument is often made in support of such monuments as the one at issue here, that our country recognizes "God" in numerous ways that have been found to be constitutional. For example, our coins are inscribed with "In God we Trust." But in his dissent, Justice Stevens argued that there was a difference between those allusions to God and the Texas monument:

For many followers, the Commandments represent the literal word of God as spoken to Moses and repeated to his followers after descending from Mount Sinai. The message conveyed by the Ten Commandments thus cannot be analogized to an appendage to a common article of commerce ("In God we Trust") or an incidental part of a familiar recital ("God save the United States and this honorable Court").[7]

Justice Stevens went on to assert that if a state's endorsement of the admonition that one is to have "no other gods before me" does not run afoul of the Constitution, it would be difficult to imagine any biblical related display that would.

In both the plurality opinion and in Justice Stevens's dissent, the justices discussed the extent to which Texas may or may not have "endorsed" the contents of the monument by allowing it on state property. Does simply placing the marker on the state grounds "endorse" its message? What reasons would you assert as to why it should be perceived that way and why it should not?

---

[7] This last pronouncement is spoken by the clerk when calling a session of the United States Supreme Court to order.

Stephens v. ABC Manufacturing Co.

Anoka County District Court, Minn. (1989)

The Issue:

Were the consumer warnings on the ATV at issue sufficient to protect purchasers of the recreational vehicle from harm?

A civil lawsuit for monetary damages can arise from injuries incurred using a "product." Liability may result not only from a physical defect with the product but also from a manufacturer's and/or dealer's failure to warn purchasers of known potential risks of using the product, including known or expected risks of *misusing* the item.

This incident started out when a wife bought a Christmas gift for her husband.[8] It will make the case a little easier to follow if the cast of characters is listed at the outset:

- Plaintiff Stephens, a twelve-year-old boy
- Plaintiff's brother, a fifteen-year-old boy
- Plaintiff's aunt, the actual purchaser of the ATV involved
- Plaintiff's uncle, the one who received the ATV as a gift

---

[8] This *is* a real case, but for reasons set out in the Appendix the names of the parties have been changed.

The plaintiff's aunt purchased an ABC Manufacturing Company ATV for her husband as a Christmas gift in December of 1984. (This particular ATV was a four-wheeler without a roll bar.)

On the day of the incident at issue, the plaintiff's uncle set out with the plaintiff's fifteen-year-old brother to ride some trails. Eventually, the uncle returned home, leaving the ATV in the possession of the plaintiff's brother and the twelve-year-old plaintiff. The two of them took to the trails, with the plaintiff driving and his brother seated behind him.

As the plaintiff was steering the ATV up a slight incline, he lost control. The ATV pitched backward and then rolled over, throwing both boys off the unit. In the course of the rollover, one of the ATV's foot pegs pierced the skull of the twelve-year-old plaintiff, resulting in severe permanent brain injury. The plaintiff had not been wearing a helmet.

The plaintiff filed suit against the manufacturer of the ATV and the dealer that sold it to the aunt. (The manufacturer and dealer collectively are subsequently referred to as the "defendants.") In his products liability lawsuit, the plaintiff claimed that the defendants failed to provide adequate warnings about the vehicle's propensity to tip backward and to roll side over side. The plaintiff also asserted that magazine and TV advertising about the particular ATV model involved misrepresented the inherent dangers of the ATV by portraying the vehicles as stable and safe.

The manufacturer and dealer asserted that there are obvious hazards involved in operating a four-wheel ATV, and the owner and operator assume those risks when using one. They argued that if the product is used in a *reasonable* manner, it would not flip backward or roll side over side.

The Trial:

At the trial, the plaintiff's uncle testified that he had not read the owners' manual before the three family members used it on the day of the incident. The uncle claimed he did not see the owners' manual because it was located in a well-disguised glove box toward the rear of the vehicle, which was not pointed out by the dealer. The plaintiff alleged the dealer had been requested several times by the manufacturer to review the owners' manual and the machine with all prospective purchasers, but the dealer's salesperson did not do so during the sale of this particular ATV.

The manufacturer and dealer responded by asserting that the uncle should have located the owners' manual before using the ATV, even if he had to call the dealership after the purchase and ask where the manual was located. The defendants also claimed that the uncle's leaving the ATV with twelve- and fifteen-year-old youths without supervision was unreasonable and the primary cause of the incident. The evidence indicated that the plaintiff had violated several of the safety instructions set forth in the manual.

The Applicable Law:

This is a "products liability" case, which would be tried in a civil—versus criminal—court. This case falls under the sub-type of cases called "failure to warn." The plaintiff's claim is not that the ATV was broken or had a manufacturing defect. Rather, the plaintiff claims the manufacturer and dealer had a legal duty to warn of the hazards of using the equipment.

Here are the issues you need to address in regard to the plaintiff's claims: (1) Did the manufacturer and dealer (defendants) know there were potential risks in using the ATV that could lead to injuries when the ATV was used in a reasonable or foreseeable manner? (2) Did the defendants fail to adequately warn of those risks? (3) Would it be reasonable for the ordinary consumer not to be aware of those risks before using the ATV? (4) Was a lack of sufficient instructions or warnings a substantial cause of plaintiff being harmed?

The ATV at issue in this lawsuit was purchased by the plaintiff's aunt and given as a gift to her husband, the plaintiff's uncle. In determining whether or not the twelve-year-old plaintiff was provided adequate instructions or warnings in regard to use of the vehicle, you should weigh whether or not the *aunt or uncle* received adequate instructions or warnings, since we know the plaintiff was not involved in the sale transaction. Would better or more effective instructions or warnings have likely made a difference in the aunt's or uncle's conduct?

The plaintiff was a minor at the time of the incident. As a juror, the judge would instruct you on the standard of care for a minor:

> The plaintiff is a child who was twelve years old at the time of the incident. Children are not held to the same standards of behavior as adults. A child is required to use the amount of care that a reasonably careful child of the same age, intelligence, knowledge, and experience would use in that same situation.

The defendants asserted that the plaintiff and his aunt and uncle were negligent and were mostly responsible for the incident. As to this assertion, you must decide whether the aunt's and uncle's conduct was unreasonable and, if so, whether that conduct was a substantial factor in the plaintiff being injured.

The plaintiff must present enough evidence and argument to meet his burden of proof, which in this case is measured by a "preponderance of the evidence." The criminal burden of "beyond a reasonable doubt," a stricter standard, does not apply in civil cases. If you were to weigh the plaintiff's evidence on one side of a scale and the defendants' on another, the plaintiff must at least tip the scale slightly in his favor.

What's your verdict? Did the defendants fail to provide proper instructions or warnings regarding the potential use or misuse of the ATV such that they are *primarily* responsible for the plaintiff's injuries?

STOP HERE AND DECIDE THE CASE
BEFORE GOING FURTHER

The Court's Decision

Held: The jury found in favor of plaintiff Stephens and against both the manufacturer and the dealership. The jury did not attribute any degree of fault to the plaintiff nor to the plaintiff's aunt or uncle.

The jury awarded the plaintiff $2.9 million in damages.

State of Louisiana v. Tucker

La. State Supreme Court Case No. 2013-KA-1631 (2015)

The Issue:

Should the decision whether one is given the death sentence or life imprisonment be influenced by your race or where you live?

In September of 2008, Lamondre Tucker, a Black male eighteen years of age, shot and killed Tavia Sills, who was nearly five months pregnant and who believed Tucker was the father of her unborn child. Tucker and his friend Marcus Taylor took Sills to a secluded pond under false pretenses. There, Tucker shot her three times with a handgun he obtained from Taylor. Taylor then suggested they call the police, but instead Tucker pushed her body into the pond. The coroner could not determine if Sills died of her gunshot wounds or from drowning. The police uncovered evidence leading them to Tucker, who admitted under questioning that he had taken Sills to the pond and had shot her.

Tucker was charged with first-degree murder. Prosecutors sought the death penalty based on two separate aggravating circumstances: (1) The killing occurred during a kidnapping, and (2) Tucker knew at the time of the shooting he was killing two people, mother and unborn child. Either of these two aggravating circumstances standing alone could possibly result in a death sentence in Louisiana.

In addition to being just slightly older than the cutoff age for the death penalty, Tucker also had a low IQ. Specifically, Tucker had a full scale IQ of 74. A defense expert psychologist found Tucker was a "'pseudo adult' who lives and acts like an adult but thinks like a child." Tucker's school grades ranged from an A to an F. His final grade point average was 2.20.

Taylor, the accomplice, was charged with second-degree murder, and in a separate trial, was found guilty of manslaughter and sentenced to thirty years imprisonment at hard labor.

The Trial:

The results of DNA testing proved Tucker was not the father of the unborn child. Furthermore, experts testified that the fetus was about nineteen weeks old at the time of the crime—a stage at which the fetus would not have been viable outside the womb.

The ballistics evidence failed to demonstrate an exact match between the gun that police located and the bullets obtained from the scene. Tucker was able to show that there were discrepancies between the physical evidence and statements in Tucker's purported confession (following hours of interrogation).

In March of 2011, a jury found Tucker guilty of first-degree murder.[9] The case then proceeded to a second phase: the penalty hearing. At that point, the jury was asked to decide whether Tucker's sentence should be death or life in prison. After hearing evidence from both sides, the jury returned a verdict of death. Tucker appealed.

Even though he challenged the evidence of and denied his guilt for the crimes with which he was charged, for this case study we will accept that Lamondre Tucker did, in fact, commit the acts for which he was tried and found guilty. Upon his appeal to the Louisiana State Supreme Court, Tucker's challenges to the evidence used against him and his guilt were rejected. However, Tucker also asserted that the manner

---

[9]   Tucker was the first person convicted of first-degree murder pursuant to a Louisiana law making it a capital offense to shoot someone with the "intent to kill or harm more than one person"—in Tucker's case, his killing a pregnant woman and an unborn child.

in which his case was handled violated his equal protection and due process rights. The constitutional claims will be addressed in this case study. His equal protection and his due process claims were that race and geography improperly influenced his receiving the death penalty.

The Applicable Law:

The Fourteenth Amendment provides, in relevant part, " . . . [N]or shall any State deprive any person of life, liberty, or property, without due process of law; nor deny to any person within its jurisdiction the equal protection of the law."

Tucker also asserted that his sentence of death violated the Eighth Amendment's ban on "cruel and unusual punishment."

In a death penalty case, the potential jurors are usually questioned about their feelings regarding the death penalty. Individuals who either state their unyielding opposition to the death penalty or who refuse to consider life imprisonment instead of the death penalty may both be stricken from the potential jury pool. But it is important to note that these prospective jurors must indicate they would not consider either potential penalty under *any* conditions. For example, a very grudging statement that the potential juror has strong feelings against the death penalty *but* is nevertheless willing to consider the options the court gives the jury in its instructions may well be sufficient to preclude the potential juror from automatic disqualification.

In a parish where half the population was African American, the fourteen jurors who ultimately heard Tucker's case (twelve with two alternates) were comprised of twelve White jurors and two Blacks. Tucker alleged the manner in which his jury was chosen made race an improper factor in his sentence.

Tucker's trial took place in Caddo Parish, Louisiana. Tucker claimed that striking jury candidates who would not consider the death penalty resulted in a disproportionate number of African Americans being struck from the jury pool. One-third of the entire community was removed from the list of potential jurors in Caddo Parish due to their opposition to the death penalty.

His counsel also provided statistics that showed a disproportionate number of death sentences were imposed in the parish. Counsel noted in one of their briefs:

> Since 2005, Caddo Parish – which has only 5% of Louisiana's population and 5% of its homicides – has accounted for almost half of the death sentences in Louisiana. Caddo Parish imposes more death sentences per capita than any other parish or county in the nation.

The defense noted seventeen of the twenty-two defendants sitting on death row after trials in Caddo Parish were African American men. And, they pointed out, they could not find one single case in the entire history of Louisiana where a white person was executed for killing a black male.

Did the statistics offered by Tucker's counsel prove that sentences of death in Caddo Parish were handed out in a cruel and unusual manner?

Did those statistics provide a basis for finding that Tucker was denied due process and equal protection of the law in Caddo Parish when compared to other counties and states and compared to White males? Or did the statistics, while perhaps troubling on their face, fail to rise to a level where his sentence should have been set aside?

What's your verdict? Should Tucker's death sentence be converted to life imprisonment due to a denial of his equal protection and due process rights and/or because the sentence amounted to cruel and unusual punishment?

STOP HERE AND DECIDE THE CASE
BEFORE GOING FURTHER

The Court's Decision follows on the next page.

The Court's Decision

Held: The Louisiana State Supreme Court rejected Tucker's Eighth and Fourteenth Amendment arguments for setting aside the death penalty.[10]

In its ruling, the Louisiana Supreme Court justices relied upon prior United States Supreme Court cases holding that striking jurors who would refuse to vote for *either* death or life imprisonment did not serve to exclude any groups or communities based on race or ethnicity from jury service. Therefore, the court was not persuaded by Tucker's claim that dismissing potential jurors who refused to vote for the death sentence resulted in the rejection of a greater proportion of Blacks than Whites.

Regarding the claim that Blacks were disproportionately given the death sentence in Caddo Parish, the Court said a careful review of the actual statistics tendered by the defense—versus its summary of them—did not reveal a disparity sufficient for a constitutional challenge to Tucker's death sentence under either the Eighth or Fourteenth Amendments. The justices did not find the disparities in sentences to be of such a significant degree as to warrant a reversal.

After the Louisiana Supreme Court rejected Tucker's claims, he filed a petition with the United States Supreme Court asking it to hear his appeal. That Court denied his petition and refused to consider the case. In his dissent to the US Supreme Court's order denying the appeal, Justice Breyer wrote:

> Given these facts, Tucker may well have received the death
> penalty not because of the comparative egregiousness of
> his crimes, but because of an arbitrary feature of his

---

[10]   While Tucker did appeal the state's assertion that killing a mother and her fetus qualified as killing two people under Louisiana's first-degree murder statute, the state supreme court found the fact that the killing took place during a kidnapping (taking Sills to the pond) was sufficient in and of itself to support a first-degree murder charge. Therefore, the court did not rule on the mother/fetus aspect of Tucker's appeal.

case, namely geography. [citations omitted.] One could reasonably believe that if Tucker had committed the same crime but been tried and sentenced just across the Red River in, say, Bossier Parish, he would not now be on death row.[11]

As of January of 2022, Lamondre Tucker still sits on death row awaiting his execution.

---

[11]   *Tucker v. Louisiana*, 578 U.S. _____(2016); On Petition for Writ of Certiorari

Bernal v. Texas Secretary of State

467 U.S. 216 (1984)

The Issue:

Should a resident alien be allowed to obtain a commission as a notary public?

A notary public is one who is certified by the government to authenticate written instruments, administer oaths, and take out-of-court sworn statements. In Texas, where this case originates, notaries public are designated "public officers" by the state constitution.

Bernal, a native of Mexico, a green card holder, and a resident alien living in Texas, applied to the Texas Secretary of State to become a notary public.[12] The state does not require an applicant to pass any type of test to be appointed. Bernal's application was denied because he failed to satisfy a Texas statute that requires a notary public be a United States citizen. Bernal filed suit to challenge his denial.

---

[12]   One who wishes to immigrate to the United States on a permanent basis usually obtains a "green card" as the first step toward citizenship. If approved for the card, one becomes a lawful permanent resident. After obtaining a green card, most residents will have to wait several years (usually about five) before they can take the next step toward applying to become a US citizen.

Bernal's Appeal:

Bernal's appeal was heard in the federal district court. That court held that the citizenship requirement violated the Equal Protection Clause of the Fourteenth Amendment. In the district court's opinion, the citizenship requirement was not related to any valid state interest. The court overturned Texas's denial of Bernal's application.

Texas then appealed the district court's decision. The state argued that the statute assured that notaries public were familiar with Texas law, and that they would likely be available in the future should they have to testify about an act they performed.

The federal court of appeal reversed the district court and found in favor of Texas, thus denying Bernal his commission. The court of appeal panel of judges found there was a rational relationship between the citizenship requirement and the state's interest in the manner and legitimacy of the proper and orderly handling of legal documents important to the state. In its decision, the court of appeals argued:

> With the power to acknowledge instruments such as wills and deeds and leases and mortgages; to take out-of-court depositions; to administer oaths; and the discretion to refuse to perform any of the foregoing acts, notaries public in Texas are involved in countless matters of importance to the day-to-day functioning of state government. The Texas political community depends upon the notary public to ensure that those persons executing documents are accurately identified, to refuse to certify any identification that is false or uncertain, and to insist that oaths are properly and accurately administered. Land titles and property succession depend upon the care and integrity of the notary public, as well as the familiarity of the notary

with the community, to verify the authenticity of the execution of the documents.

Bernal appealed to the United States Supreme Court.

The Applicable Law:

A "resident alien" is a foreign person who is a permanent resident of the country in which he or she resides but does not have actual citizenship. To fall under this classification in the United States, a person needs to have either a current green card or have had one in the previous calendar year. In this case, we consider whether a resident alien should be allowed a commission as a notary public.

Bernal's opposition to the Texas statute governing notaries public is founded upon the Fourteenth Amendment to the United States Constitution. The relevant portion of that amendment commands that no state shall "deprive any person of life, liberty, or property, without due process of law; nor deny to any person within its jurisdiction the equal protection of the laws." Bernal contends that he has been denied the due process of law because there is no rational basis for Texas's requiring notaries public to be US citizens. He also argues that he is being denied the equal protection of the laws in that the Texas statute treats him differently from US citizens without any legitimate reason for doing so.

Texas Article 5949(2) provides that "'[t]o be eligible for appointment as a Notary Public, a person shall be a resident citizen of the United States and of this state . . .'"

The primary question at issue in this matter is whether the position of Texas notary public is one involving the exercise of broad discretionary power over the formulation or execution of public policies importantly affecting the citizen population. If so, then there would be a rational basis for the citizenship requirement. In addition, the Texas statute would have to advance a compelling state interest in the least restrictive means available to be valid.

What's your verdict? Should the State of Texas be able to exclude resident aliens from the position of notary public?

STOP HERE AND DECIDE THE CASE
BEFORE GOING FURTHER

The Court's Decision

Held: The Texas statute violated the Equal Protection Clause of the Fourteenth Amendment to the Constitution. Texas may not exclude resident aliens from the position of notary public.

In an 8-to-1 decision, the Supreme Court determined that the duties of a notary public are "essentially clerical and ministerial." Notaries public do not, the Court said, perform functions that go to the heart of representative government simply because they are designated public officers by the Texas Constitution, nor do they exercise broad discretionary power over the formulation or execution of public policies.

Referencing the Equal Protection Clause of the Fourteenth Amendment to the Constitution, the justices noted that its text does not distinguish between the protections it affords *citizens* and *non-citizens*. Rather, the amendment states, in part, "No State shall deny to any *person* . . . the equal protection of the laws." (emphasis added)

The justices also addressed the state's contention that the citizenship requirement would further the goal of ensuring that notaries public are familiar with Texas law. The record before the Court was void of any indication that resident aliens were in some way incapable of familiarizing themselves with the state's laws. Furthermore, the justices noted, if the state was seriously concerned about this issue "one would expect the State to give some sort of test actually measuring a person's familiarity with the law" whether an applicant was a citizen or a resident alien. But no such test exists in Texas.

Highlighting the double standard of the Texas statute, the Court noted that Texas does not even require the Texas Secretary of State to be a citizen, even though it is that very secretary of state who appoints notaries public.

The Florida Star v. B.J.F.

491 U.S. 524 (1989)

The Issue:

Can a state prohibit the publication of a rape victim's name without violating the free press guarantee of the First Amendment?

It is well-recognized that rape victims often suffer almost as much trauma from the events following the rape as from the rape itself. In an attempt to protect victims from the release of very personal and private information, many states have passed "rape shield laws" that prevent the media from releasing the names of rape victims.

In October of 1983, B.J.F. reported to the Duval County Sheriff's Department that she had been robbed and sexually assaulted by an unknown assailant. The department posted a release about the rape in its press room. Contrary to the sheriff's department's policy, the release inadvertently listed the full name of the victim instead of simply her initials.

As fate would have it, a reporter-trainee of *The Florida Star* was sent to the sheriff's department to check the news releases posted by the department. The reporter-trainee wrote down the text of the B.J.F. related release verbatim and submitted it to the *Star*. The incident then appeared in the paper's regular "Police Reports" section. Reflecting the information provided to the paper by the reporter, the column identified the victim by name—a violation of the *Star's* own standards and practices.

B.J.F. sued both the sheriff's department and *The Florida Star*, claiming damages from their violation of the Florida statute that prohibits the dissemination of a rape victim's name.

The Trial:

B.J.F. claimed that after the paper identified her, she began to receive threatening phone calls from a man who said he would rape her again. She was forced to change her phone number and residence. She sought police protection and required mental health counseling.

The *Star's* reporter conceded at trial that signs posted on the wall of the sheriff department's press room made "it clear that the names of rape victims were not matters of public record and were not to be published."

The Florida Star's defense was primarily based upon the fact that it had gotten the information from the sheriff's department's own press release, and therefore should not be responsible for the name being revealed since the information came from an official government document. It was not, the paper pointed out, obtained in any surreptitious manner. The *Star* also challenged the suit, claiming that ordering the *Star* to pay damages to B.J.F. violated the First Amendment to the United States Constitution. The trial judge denied the *Star's* First Amendment challenge.

The trial verdict was in favor of B.J.F. The *Star* was ordered to pay her $100,000 in damages. The paper took the case to the First District Court of Appeals. The appellate court affirmed the trial court's verdict. The *Star* then appealed to the United States Supreme Court.

The Applicable Law:

The relevant part of the First Amendment at issue in this case states: "Congress shall make no law . . . abridging the freedom of speech, or of the press . . ."

Florida Statute Section 794.03 states:

> No person shall print, publish, or broadcast, or cause
> or allow to be printed, published, or broadcast, in any
> instrument of mass communication the name, address,
> or other identifying fact or information of the victim of
> any sexual offense within this chapter.

The trial judge ruled that the statute at issue "was constitutional because it reflected a proper balance between the First Amendment and privacy rights, as it applied only to a narrow set of 'rather sensitive . . . criminal offenses.'"

Decisions in three prior Supreme Court cases addressed the constitutionality of laws restricting the media from releasing the names of individuals involved in the criminal justice system. In each of the three earlier cases, the laws were held to be unconstitutional. But those cases all involved information that had been obtained by the press from court records or open courtroom hearings to which the public had access. As the Supreme Court stated in one of those prior decisions, "By placing the information in the public domain on official court records, the State must be presumed to have concluded that the public interest was thereby being served."

In the case of B.J.F., her name had been obtained from a press release posted in the sheriff department's press room, a room open to the general public. At the same time, there were clearly posted signs in the press room prohibiting the publication of rape victims' names. Do these unique facts serve to distinguish this case from the holdings in the earlier cases?

What's your verdict? Should the verdict against *The Florida Star* be affirmed?

STOP HERE AND DECIDE THE CASE
BEFORE GOING FURTHER

The Court's Decision

Held: Imposing damages on *The Florida Star* for publishing B.J.F.'s name violates the First Amendment. The verdict against the *Star* was set aside.

In a 6-to-3 decision, the United States Supreme Court said that to punish the newspaper for publishing information that had been posted in a government press release (albeit inadvertently) would lead to a dangerous inhibition on the part of the press that would have grave First Amendment consequences. Reporters and their editors would have to scrutinize and question every press release to be sure that the authors of the releases had not possibly made an error in the information provided, or else face possible damages arising from simply repeating the contents of the releases.

The majority also found that the Florida statute failed constitutional muster because it did not apply in an evenhanded and rational manner. The statute only precluded mass media from disseminating the identities. The Court noted that the statute does not punish the "smalltime disseminator" even though such publication could be equally as damaging to the crime victim.

The dissenting justices argued there was no public disclosure of the victim's name by the government in light of the signs posted on the press room walls restricting publication of rape victims' names. As set forth in Justice White's dissenting opinion:

> Unfortunately, as this case illustrates, mistakes happen: even when States take measures to "avoid" disclosure, sometimes rape victims' names are found out. As I see it, it is not too much to ask the press in instances such as this, to respect simple standards of decency and refrain from publishing a victims' (sic) name, address, and/or phone number.

Elvis Presley Enterprises
v. Barry Capece

141 F.3d 188 (5th Cir. 1998)

The Issue:

How likely are the customers of a bar called The Velvet Elvis to believe it is in some way affiliated with Elvis Presley and his estate?

This case presents a fun set of facts. A word of caution however: The reader would be wise to give careful consideration to each of the facts presented in considering a verdict in this trademark infringement case.

In April 1991, defendant Barry Capece (through his partnership Beers R' Us) opened a nightclub in Houston, Texas, called The Velvet Elvis. Capece filed an application for a federal service mark for The Velvet Elvis as a restaurant and tavern with the federal trademark office. The notice of the application was published by the trademark office, and Elvis Presley Enterprises (EPE) was aware of the publication but did not take any action in response. Accordingly, the trademark office issued the service mark to Capece's partnership Beers R' Us.

You need to know a little bit about the club. The Velvet Elvis served food (appetizers to entrées) and liquor. Live music was featured regularly. A cover charge was required occasionally when bands performed. The decor included velvet paintings of celebrities (including Elvis and a bare-chested Mona Lisa). There were lava lamps, cheap ceramic sculptures, beaded curtains, and vinyl furniture. The wallpaper in the men's room consisted of *Playboy* centerfolds. The bar's menu and decor included other Elvis references such as "Love Me Blenders," a type of frozen drink. The menu bears the caption "The King of Dive Bars." Advertising for the bar included phrases like "Hunka-Hunka Happy Hour" and "Elvis has not left the building." Numerous photographs of Elvis were placed throughout the restaurant, as well as a statue of The King playing a guitar.

After being in operation for two years, Capece's nightclub closed in July of 1993. Capece began courting investors to reopen the club using the same name, The Velvet Elvis, at a different address and to be owned by a different partnership. Capece's new partnership opened The Velvet Elvis at its new location in August of 1994.

Elvis Presley Enterprises holds at least seventeen federal trademark registrations for "Elvis Presley," "Elvis," and other registrations for his likeness. EPE is the official representative of the estate of Elvis Presley from a commercial standpoint, and operates Graceland. None of the trademarks it holds, however, are for a restaurant or tavern business.

In July of 1994, one month before Capece and his partners opened the bar at its new location, EPE's attorneys sent a cease-and-desist letter to Capece, claiming the use of the name The Velvet Elvis was an infringement on EPE's trademark rights.

When Capece proceeded to open the bar at its new location, EPE filed a federal lawsuit alleging trademark infringement and trademark dilution (a claim that Capece's actions lessened the value of EPE's trademark).

The Trial:

At the trial, several witnesses told the court that they entered the bar thinking it might be affiliated with the Elvis estate and perhaps they could purchase souvenirs. But, they testified, once they had entered, they quickly concluded that it was not affiliated with Presley and left. Some, however, bought drinks before leaving.

The federal judge hearing the case ruled in favor of Capece on the grounds that there was no reasonable possibility of confusion that the nightclub was actually affiliated with EPE. The district court found that the bar symbolized the tacky, cheesy, atmosphere of faddish bars of the sixties, and was intended to parody the Las Vegas lounge scene. The district court also noted that Elvis's fans were "middle-aged white women" and the "The Velvet Elvis" customers were "young professionals, ranging in age from early twenties to late thirties."

EPE appealed the decision, and it is the appeal you will be deciding. Did the district court get it right?

The Applicable Law:

For EPE to prevail on its trademark infringement claim, it must show that the defendants' use of "The Velvet Elvis" created a likelihood of confusion between the marks at issue. Likelihood of confusion is synonymous with a *probability* of confusion, which is more than a *possibility* of confusion.

What's your verdict? Are prospective customers likely to believe that EPE and Capece's business were somehow associated? If you answer this question "yes," then your verdict will be in favor of EPE and will overturn the district court's decision. If you answer this question "no," then you will be affirming the district court, finding in favor of Capece, and The Velvet Elvis will live on.

STOP HERE AND DECIDE THE CASE
BEFORE GOING FURTHER

The Court's Decision follows on the next page.

The Court's Decision

Held: The Tenth Circuit Court of Appeal ruled that the use of "The Velvet Elvis" as the name of the bar infringed on Elvis Presley Enterprises' trademark rights and ruled against Capece and his partnership.

The heavy use of (and references to) Elvis, along with evidence of the trademark name drawing in customers with an initial interest—even though once in they concluded it was not affiliated with the Elvis estate—was strong evidence of initial confusion over a possible affiliation with the Elvis estate. The restaurant's name served to the benefit of the nightclub as it was a draw to get folks in the door, some paying a cover charge and spending money before they concluded that there was unlikely any connection between EPE and the tavern. The appellate court found The Velvet Elvis was making money off this "initial-interest confusion."

As a result of its ruling, an injunction was issued prohibiting Capece from using the name "The Velvet Elvis" for his restaurant.

The outcome of this case might have been quite different except that Capece closed the first location and formed a new partnership before opening again. EPE's failure to object to Capece's original trademark application after notice of the application had been published by the trademark office barred EPE from contesting the use of the name at the first location. However, the subsequent change of address and ownership opened the door for EPE to contest "The Velvet Elvis" as the name of the second location.

Simon & Schuster, Inc. v. New York State Crime Victims Board

502 U.S. 105 (1991)

The Issue:

Does New York's interest in seeing that criminals do not profit from their stories interfere with a publisher's First Amendment right to free speech?

New York passed the "Son of Sam" law in 1977 to keep criminals from making money from the sale of their stories. The statute required any proceeds from the sales of books written by accused or convicted criminals, as well as proceeds received by any person or entity with whom the accused or convicted criminal contracts to publish the material, to be turned over to the New York State Crime Victims Board. The board would deposit the money in a special account from which victims of crime could make claims for compensation.

The Son of Sam law was named after a murderous crime wave that occurred in the New York City area in the summer of 1976. A serial killer, David Berkowitz, who called himself the "Son of Sam," created fear throughout New York City due to the complete random nature of his assaults—mostly on young couples sitting in their cars at night. Who was "Sam," you might well ask. Sam was Berkowitz's neighbor's dog. Berkowitz claimed he killed his victims because Sam ordered him to do so. Berkowitz was ultimately apprehended. (No charges were ever brought against Sam.)

Due to the substantial publicity about the case, the state recognized the probability that Berkowitz could make a significant amount of money by writing and selling his story. As a result, the state legislature passed the "Son of Sam" law. Ironically, the law could not be applied to Berkowitz. He was determined to be mentally incompetent and therefore unable to stand trial. He never achieved the status of a convicted criminal.[13] Berkowitz and his publishers were therefore allowed to keep their profits. The case considered here, however, arose about fifteen years later, and involves Henry Hill, not David Berkowitz.

Even as a child, Henry Hill had big ambitions. "As far back as I can remember, I always wanted to be a gangster," he said. He certainly succeeded in reaching his childhood goal. Hill ultimately had a career in organized crime that spanned twenty-six years. One of his most famous heists was a six-million-dollar theft from the offices of Lufthansa Airlines. "Whenever we needed money, we'd rob the airport. To us, it was better than Citibank." But his luck eventually ran out. He was arrested but given immunity from prosecution in exchange for his testimony against his former "business partners."

After being placed in the witness protection program, Hill decided to write his memoirs with the assistance of an author, Nicholas Pileggi. The two of them hired Simon & Schuster to publish their book entitled *Wiseguy: Life in a Mafia Family.* The book was so popular (within nineteen months it sold more than a million copies) that Hollywood turned it into the blockbuster movie *Goodfellas,* in which exploits based on Hill's book played out on the big screen.

New York decided to apply the Son of Sam law provisions on Hill's literary efforts. In 1987, the state ordered Simon & Schuster to turn over to the Crime Victims Board "all money payable to Hill at the time or in the future." It also ordered Hill to turn over all monies previously

---

[13]   At the time of Berkowitz's arrest, the Son of Sam law only applied to "convicted criminals." It was subsequently amended to apply also to "accused criminals."

received from the sale of the book. Simon & Schuster filed suit against the board, arguing that the Son of Sam law violated the Constitution's First Amendment free speech guarantees.

The Trial:

The statute was upheld in the first trial. The court found that the statute did not violate the Constitution. Simon & Schuster then sought to overturn the trial court in the court of appeals. The appeals court also found in favor of the Crime Victims Board. The publisher then appealed to the United States Supreme Court.

The Applicable Law:

The portion of the New York Son of Sam law that applied to publisher Simon & Schuster provides:

> Every person, firm, corporation, partnership, association or other legal entity contracting with any person or the representative or assignee of any person, accused or convicted of a crime in this state, with respect to the reenactment of such crime, by way of a movie, book, magazine article, tape recording, phonograph record, radio or television presentation, live entertainment of any kind, or from the expression of such accused or convicted person's thoughts, feelings, opinions or emotions regarding such crime, shall submit a copy of such contract to the board and pay over to the board any moneys which would otherwise, by terms of such contract, be owing to the person so accused or convicted or his representatives.

If within five years of depositing the funds into the crime victim's account no claim is made against those funds by any victim, the monies are returned to the authors and publishers.

The free speech clause of the First Amendment states that the government shall "make no law" limiting the freedom of speech. The Supreme Court has previously ruled that the state may violate the constitutional guarantee of free speech when it places a financial burden on speakers because of the *content* of their speech.[14] There was a concern that the government, by its taxing authority, could essentially drive certain types of speech out of the marketplace.

The Crime Victims Board, however, argues that the courts have permitted such financial assessments when the "regulation is necessary to serve a compelling state interest, and is narrowly drawn to achieve that end."[15] The state argues that it does, in fact, have a compelling state interest in (1) preventing criminals from profiting from their crimes and (2) having criminals compensate the victims of crime. The state asserts that the Son of Sam law meets these two state interests in a sufficiently narrow manner, and therefore the statute passes constitutional muster.

Simon & Schuster argues that since publishers would be unwilling to distribute criminals' books if the publisher could not retain the proceeds from the books, the ultimate effect of the law is to stifle only speech about a specific subject: criminal activity. And it follows that if publishers do not publish because they cannot make money from doing so, then writers will not write.

What's your verdict? Does the "Son of Sam" law violate Henry Hill's and Simon & Schuster's free speech rights under the First Amendment?

STOP HERE AND DECIDE THE CASE
BEFORE GOING FURTHER

---

[14]   *Leathers v. Medlock*, 409 U.S. 439, 447 (1991)

[15]   *Arkansas Writers' Project v. Ragland*, 481 U.S. 221, 231 (1987)

The Court's Decision follows on the next page.

The Court's Decision

Held: The "Son of Sam" law was an unconstitutional infringement on free speech.

In a unanimous 9-to-0 decision, the Supreme Court held that the Son of Sam law "singled out speech on a particular subject for a financial penalty that was placed on no other speech and no other income." Thus, the Court found the law violated the First Amendment's free speech protections.

The Supreme Court acknowledged that the state may well have a valid interest in seeing that criminals are not able to retain the "fruits of their crime," and that crime victims are compensated. But to limit the "fruits" to monies received from writing about those crimes versus the many other potential sources (bank accounts and property holdings, for example) directly impacts the First Amendment. The Supreme Court said, "In short, the State has a compelling interest in compensating victims from the fruits of the crime, but little if any interest in limiting such compensation to the proceeds of the wrongdoer's speech."

The Court also found that the statute was overbroad. An author's earnings could be impounded even if the author had never been accused or convicted of a crime. All the author had to do was admit in his writing to having committed a crime at some point. For example, *The Autobiography of Malcolm X* would have been susceptible to its proceeds being impounded under the Son of Sam law since the civil rights leader wrote in his book about crimes he had committed before he became a public figure.

The justices noted:

> Should a prominent figure write his autobiography at the end of his career, and include in an early chapter a brief recollection of having stolen (in New York) a nearly worthless item as a youthful prank, the Board would control his entire income from the book for five

years, and would make that income available to all of
the author's creditors, despite the fact that the . . . [time
limit for the state to prosecute the author] for this minor
incident had long since run. That the Son of Sam law
can produce such an outcome indicates that the statute
is, to say the least, not narrowly tailored to achieve the
state's objective of compensating crime victims from the
profits of crime.

Consequently, Henry Hill and Simon & Schuster were able to keep
the proceeds from the publication of Henry Hill's book.

Acosta, Secretary of Labor
v. Cathedral Buffet, Inc.

No. 17-3427; U.S. Court of Appeals for the Sixth Circuit (April 2018)

The Issue:

Is it a violation of labor law for a church-run, profit-based business to use unpaid "volunteers" to do the exact same work as paid employees?

Cathedral Buffet, incorporated in 2013, was a restaurant operated by the Grace Cathedral Church in Cuyahoga Falls, Ohio. The restaurant was a for-profit business open to the public. It was staffed by both paid employees and unpaid church members. Despite its for-profit status, the restaurant had not actually generated a profit, and it was subsidized by the church. The pastor of the church, Reverend Angley, also served as president of the corporation that operated the buffet.

There were two classes of workers at the Cathedral Buffet: "employees" and "volunteers." Both performed the same basic tasks: cleaning, washing dishes, serving cake, chopping vegetables, and staffing the cash register. Employees were paid for these services while volunteers were not.

The federal Department of Labor sued the restaurant, asserting that it was in violation of the Fair Labor Standards Act (FLSA) because the restaurant's use of unpaid labor violated the minimum wage requirement of the act.

The Trial:

According to trial testimony, when staffing ran low, the restaurant manager would advise Reverend Angley, who would, just before he was to deliver the Sunday sermon, tell the congregation that more volunteers were needed. According to the court's statement of facts, Angley told parishioners who considered refusing to volunteer at the buffet:

> [T]he restaurant was "the Lord's buffet," and "[e]very time you say no, you are closing the door on God." He suggested that church members who repeatedly refused to volunteer at the restaurant were at risk of "blaspheming against the Holy Ghost," which was an unforgivable sin in the church's doctrine.

Managers were told to make sure that those who refused to work knew that Angley would be advised of that refusal. One worker who did not return a phone call asking her to come in for a shift was called directly by Angley. The worker agreed to come in as she feared "failing God."

The district court judge ruled in favor of the Department of Labor's challenge. The Cathedral Buffet appealed the district court's decision to the federal US Circuit Court of Appeals for the Sixth Circuit.

The Applicable Law:

The Fair Labor Standards Act directs that all employers must pay the minimum wage set by Congress "to each of his employees who . . . is employed in an enterprise engaged in commerce or in the production of goods for commerce." The restaurant conceded that it is covered by the provisions of the FLSA but contended that the "volunteer" workers were not "employees" covered by the act. Thus, the only question to be resolved is whether the church member volunteers are employees within the meaning of the act. If they are considered employees, then the Cathedral Buffet must pay them at least a minimum wage.

Although the "business" involved is a church-run company, this is not a "religious freedom" case. The business was not exempt from the provisions of the FLSA because of its religious affiliation since the act's requirements apply to the "'ordinary commercial activities' of religious organizations."

Prior court decisions addressing the requirement for businesses to pay the minimum wage under the FLSA were primarily decided by looking at whether the workers expected compensation. If workers received any kind of benefit such as health coverage, bonuses, or discounts, the courts have ruled those benefits were often sufficient to show an "expectation of compensation," and such businesses must pay their employees at least the minimum wage.

Cathedral Buffet argued that its volunteers did not receive any type of benefits that would have given them a reasonable expectation of compensation, and therefore, under the case law, Cathedral Buffet was not required to pay them.

The Department of Labor countered that the church was coercing its members to work as volunteers, which would negate the requirement that volunteers must expect to be paid a wage. Prior court decisions expressed a concern that the expectation of compensation requirement might lead employers to put undue pressure on workers to agree to forgo compensation. In this instance, the Department of Labor pointed to the pastor's use of religious coercion in asserting from the pulpit that if the congregants did not volunteer to work at the buffet they would, among other ramifications, be "closing the door on God."

What's your verdict? Did the Cathedral Buffet violate the Fair Labor Standards Act by not paying the volunteers working at the restaurant? If you vote "yes" to that question, then the restaurant would be required to pay those workers it had previously classified as "volunteers." If you vote "no" to that question, then the restaurant could continue using "volunteer" workers even though they were doing the same work as "paid" workers.

STOP HERE AND DECIDE THE CASE
BEFORE GOING FURTHER

The Court's Decision follows on the next page.

The Court's Decision

Held: The United States Court of Appeals for the Sixth Circuit overturned the decision of the trial judge and ruled that the Cathedral Buffet did not violate the FLSA in using unpaid labor at the restaurant.

In a 3-to-0 decision, the appeals panel affirmed the prior court holdings that for workers to come within the minimum wage protections of the Fair Labor Standards Act they must first *expect* to be paid. In this case, the circuit court ruled, it was undisputed that the volunteer workers at the restaurant had no such expectations.

As to the issue of "coercion," the court said the exercise of "spiritual" coercion (versus "economic" coercion) on congregants had never been found by any court to warrant overturning the status of a worker as a "volunteer." The justices pointed out that there are many actions taken by churchgoers to support their churches that do not result in expectations of compensation under the FLSA, such as volunteering as an usher, teaching a Bible study class, cleaning vestments, and setting up for services. The Department of Labor had argued that unlike the services rendered by volunteers at Cathedral Buffet, the types of church-related activities described by the justices were not profit-making operations. The court's opinion dismissed this argument, stating, "what matters is not the object of the enterprise, but instead the purpose of the worker."

The appeal court stated that Reverend Angley's exhortations from the pulpit did not come within the coercion exception to the "expectation of compensation" standard.

Frazier v. The State (Cupp)
394 U.S. 731 (1969)

The Issue:

At what point do the interrogation techniques used by police to obtain a confession or trial techniques used by the prosecution to obtain a conviction violate a defendant's constitutional rights?

Who would admit to a crime they did not commit? Turns out it's not all that uncommon an occurrence. Of the 365 accused individuals exonerated in recent decades by the Innocence Project, more than a quarter had confessed to their alleged crimes. In 1819, a man who confessed to having committed a murder barely missed his date with the hangman's noose when the supposedly deceased victim was subsequently found living in New Jersey.

Martin Renee Frazier and his cousin Jerry Lee Rawls were indicted jointly for the September 1964 murder of Russell Marleau.

Shortly after his arrest, Frazier was interrogated by police. He was told he could have an attorney if he wanted one, and anything he said could be used against him at trial. Seeing that Frazier was reluctant to talk, the interrogating officer told Frazier that Rawls had confessed. In reality, at that point in time, Rawls had done no such thing. (Rawls did later confess.)

Frazier then began to speak about his activities with Rawls on the night of the murder, but still showed signs that he was reluctant to talk. At one point he stated, "I think I had better get a lawyer before I talk any more. I am going to get into trouble more than I am in now." Following the officer's reply that Frazier could not be in any more trouble than he was already in, Frazier signed a written confession. The interrogation took about an hour.

The Trial:

At Frazier's October 1965 jury trial, over his objection, the written confession was admitted.

In pretrial discussions between Frazier's trial attorney and the prosecutor, Frazier's attorney told the prosecutor that if Rawls (who had pleaded guilty and was awaiting sentencing) was called to the stand, he would claim his Fifth Amendment right and refuse to testify. Defense counsel warned the prosecutor not to reference Rawls's confession in the prosecutor's opening statement. Nevertheless, in his opening statement to the jury, the prosecutor gave a brief summary of Rawls's "expected testimony" based upon the confession Rawls had eventually made.

The prosecutor claimed that he had told the jury about Rawls despite defense counsel's warning since the prosecutor received information from both a police officer, as well as some members of Rawls's family, that Rawls *would* testify in Frazier's trial. However, when prosecutors called Rawls to the stand, he claimed his privilege against self-incrimination and refused to testify. Based on the prosecutor's opening statement, Frazier moved for a mistrial. The court refused, and instead instructed the jury that the opening statements of counsel should not be considered evidence.

The jury found Frazier guilty of murder.

Frazier appealed the state court's guilty verdict to the federal district court, claiming violations of his federal constitutional rights. He asserted that his confession was involuntary since the police lied about Rawls's confession and did not allow him to retain an attorney after saying he thought he should have one. In addition, he claimed that the prosecutor's recitation to the jury about Rawls's confession, combined with Rawls refusing to testify, denied Frazier his constitutional rights to confront witnesses against him as guaranteed by the Sixth and Fourteenth Amendments. Frazier's pleadings asserted the prosecutor's statement "added substantial, perhaps even critical, weight to the government's case in a form not subject to cross-examination."

The district court granted his request to set aside the verdict, but the Ninth Circuit Court of Appeals reversed and reinstated the guilty verdict. Frazier then appealed to the United States Supreme Court.

The Applicable Law:

Applying the law to this case requires a review of two distinct legal issues involved in Frazier's constitutional challenges: (1) the confession and (2) the prosecutor's opening statement.

- ### The Confession:

One reason confessions must be carefully reviewed is that it is well known some innocent people can confess for a variety of reasons, including the desire to simply end a particularly long or trying interrogation.

Frazier's challenge to the confession was based on his claim that he was denied the right to counsel in violation of the Sixth Amendment to the Constitution. The relevant part of the amendment states: "In all criminal prosecutions, the accused shall enjoy the right . . . to have the assistance of counsel for his defense." Frazier argues that he signed the confession only after the police continued their interrogation despite Frazier stating he thought he should probably get an attorney before further questioning.

The governing case on the admissibility of confessions at the time of Frazier's confession was *Escobedo v Illinois* (1964).[16] The defendant's

---

[16]   378 U.S. 478 (1964)

confession in that case was ruled inadmissible because the Court determined the defendant had made a *clear and unequivocal demand* that he be allowed to consult with an attorney before the interrogation preceding his confession. In addition, Escobedo's attorney was present in the police station and repeatedly requested permission to speak to his client while the interrogation was in progress.[17]

Frazier also challenged the admissibility of his confession on the grounds that it was, at least in part, the result of the officer lying to Frazier about Rawls having confessed. In order for a confession to pass constitutional muster, it must be *voluntary*. Part of the test about whether or not a confession is voluntary is if the defendant had a fair opportunity to weigh the costs and benefits of a confession. One might argue that the police officer's falsely reporting that Rawls had confessed deprived Frazier of an accurate analysis of the case against him. He might have thought, for example, that Rawls's confession—even if Frazier knew it was not true—would inevitably have led to a guilty verdict for Frazier, so he confessed hoping to get a lighter sentence. On the other hand, some argue that if Frazier really did not commit the crime, he had to know either the police officer was lying or Rawls was lying. Those who agree with this argument would contend Frazier in fact *did* have all the information he needed to decide whether or not to confess voluntarily.

- **The Prosecutor's Opening Statement:**

Frazier's claim that the prosecutor's references to Rawls's confession in the absence of Rawls's testimony at trial was based on the Sixth and Fourteenth Amendments to the Constitution. The Sixth Amendment provides, in relevant part, "In all criminal prosecutions, the accused shall enjoy the right . . . to be confronted with the witnesses against him." The Fourteenth Amendment mandates that "No State shall make or enforce any law which shall . . . deprive any person of life, liberty, or property, without due process of law."

---

[17]   The case of *Miranda v. Arizona*—often cited in "right to counsel" cases—had not yet been decided at the time of Frazier's confession. 384 U.S. 436 (1966)

Frazier argued that Rawls "testified" through the prosecutor's opening statement when the prosecutor referred to Rawls's confession. However, since Rawls did not end up testifying in the case, Frazier did not get the opportunity to "confront" Rawls in the form of cross-examination as required by the Sixth Amendment. Frazier's counsel had advised the prosecutor in advance that Rawls was going to assert his Fifth Amendment right to refuse to testify, but the prosecutor mentioned Rawls's confession anyway. The judge attempted to remedy this issue by instructing the jury that the contents of counsels' opening and closing statements were *not* evidence, and that the only evidence was the testimony and exhibits admitted during the trial.

What's your verdict? If you think that Frazier's conviction should be overturned based on either or both of his claims (the confession and the prosecutor's opening statement), you should vote in favor of Frazier. If you think the verdict should stand, you should vote for the state.

STOP HERE AND DECIDE THE CASE
BEFORE GOING FURTHER

The Court's Decision

Held: Neither the confession nor the prosecutor's opening statement violated Frazier's constitutional rights. The guilty verdict was affirmed.

In a unanimous 8-to-0 decision (Justice Fortas did not take part in the case), the Supreme Court analyzed the two constitutional challenges as follows:

- **The Confession:**

Although it was possible that the interrogating officer took the petitioner's remark about seeing an attorney not as a request to cease the interrogation but as a passing comment, there was no denial of the right to counsel such as existed pre-Miranda. The Court said that Frazier's request for counsel was not as direct and unambiguous as in the *Escobedo* case. Frazier was a mature individual and of normal intelligence, and had received at least partial warnings of his constitutional rights. The Court did not err in holding that Frazier's confession was voluntary.

The justices also did not believe Frazier's confession was made any less voluntary by the interrogating officer's false statement to Frazier that Rawls had confessed. The Court had previously held that lying to a suspect during a police interrogation is, in most instances, within the bounds of fair play and due process. The Court said that the police lying to Frazier about Rawls having confessed was "while relevant, insufficient in our view to make this otherwise voluntary confession inadmissible."

- **The Opening Statement Addressing Rawls's Confession:**

Because the prosecutor reasonably expected to present Rawls's testimony when he made his opening statement because the prosecutor only briefly summarized it, and because Rawls's confession was not subsequently touted as crucial to the prosecution's case, the trial court's limiting instruction to the jury was sufficient to protect Frazier's constitutional rights.

The justices also refused to find "bad faith" conduct on the part of the prosecutor in making the references to Rawls's statement. Although "warned" by Frazier's counsel not to make such references, the prosecutor had also received information that could have reasonably led him to believe that Rawls would testify at trial. Not everything an attorney promises in an opening statement is ultimately submitted to the jury. In this case, the Court found that the prosecutor's allusion to Rawls's confession was not significantly prejudicial to Frazier's due process rights.

Kennedy v. JLCT, Inc.

Los Angeles County Superior Court (2002)

The Issue:

Who was primarily responsible for the plaintiffs' son's fall from the top of an office building where he had been hired to wash windows?

Everything seemed to be going so well for thirty-eight-year-old Rob Kennedy of Huntington Beach, California.[18] In July of 2000, he and his fiancée were looking forward to their upcoming nuptials. He had purchased a new home for them, and the commercial window-washing business he owned was going well. He was also contemplating a new career as a stuntman for TV and movies.

But all that ended abruptly when, while preparing to wash the windows on a ten-story high-rise in downtown Los Angeles, he lost his footing, fell seventy feet to the ground below, and died instantly.

For approximately fourteen years, Kennedy had been washing the windows of the building where the accident occurred. At the top of the building was an ornamental overhang, a soffit, which extended out from the face of the building. It was constructed with a box-like frame composed of one-inch thick iron rods on which were mounted multiple large colored fiberglass panels. The soffit's flooring consisted

---

[18]   This *is* a real case, but for reasons set out in the Appendix the names of the parties have been changed.

of the same non-weight-bearing fiberglass panels mounted onto the iron frame. The soffit was large enough that a person could stand erect inside it, and it extended across the entire front of the building. The high-rise had been remodeled in the late 1960s, and the purely cosmetic soffit was added to the top at that time.

Kennedy's parents (the plaintiffs) brought a lawsuit seeking damages for the wrongful death of their son. They sued the building owner JLCT Inc., alleging the company was negligent in the construction and maintenance of the building.

The Trial:

Evidence presented at the trial of the case revealed that when washing the windows of this building, Kennedy would clip his safety harness to an overhead iron bar that ran the entire length of the soffit. However, because of interfering cross bars preventing the safety harness clips from freely sliding along the iron bar, Kennedy had to walk approximately eight feet into the soffit on one-inch thick iron rods before he could clip the harness at a point where it could slide along the bar for the remaining length of the soffit. Kennedy would remove the bottom fiberglass panels, then drop down the front of the building on a wooden seat, washing the windows from top to bottom. Afterward, he would go back up to the top, enter the soffit from the roof, move his apparatus down the soffit to the next vertical row of windows, and repeat the process.

The building owner, defendant JLCT Inc., knew that the window washers had to drop down from the iron soffit frame to access and clean the windows on the ten-story building. They provided Kennedy with access to the inside of the soffit by way of a rooftop door.

Apparently, on the day of Kennedy's fall, at some point during his walking over the initial eight-foot length of frame, his foot slipped off the iron bars before he was able to hook up his safety harness, causing him to lose his balance and fall through the fiberglass panels.

The parents alleged the way the soffit was built, such that window washers could not hook up a safety harness until they were eight feet into the framed area, was an unreasonably dangerous condition.

JLCT's attorneys asserted its employees had never had a reason to go into the soffit since they purchased the building in 1978. They argued Kennedy was the "expert" who should have brought the harness hook-up issue to their attention. They asserted Kennedy knowingly accepted the risk of entering the soffit during the fourteen years he serviced the building.

The Applicable Law:

The judge would provide a jury instruction on the "burden of proof" that each side must meet. In a civil case like this, a party must meet its burden by a "preponderance of the evidence" as opposed to the more difficult criminal standard of "beyond a reasonable doubt."

To hold the property owner liable for the death of plaintiffs' son, the plaintiffs must prove that the owner, JLCT Inc., was negligent in the maintenance of the property, and that its negligence was the primary factor in causing the death of the plaintiffs' son. A person who owns or controls property must use reasonable care to discover any unsafe conditions and to repair, replace, or give adequate warning of anything that could be reasonably expected to harm others. Factors to consider in regard to JLCT's conduct include the likelihood that someone would come on to the property in the same manner as the plaintiffs' son did, as well as the degree to which the owner could have reasonably protected against the alleged dangerous condition(s).

Since JLCT asserted the plaintiffs' son was at fault for the incident, the judge would also instruct the jury that JLCT must prove by a preponderance of the evidence that Rob Kennedy was negligent and that *his* conduct was the primary factor in causing his death.

What's your verdict? Who was *primarily* responsible for Rob Kennedy's fall: Kennedy himself or JLCT, the building owner?

STOP HERE AND DECIDE THE CASE
BEFORE GOING FURTHER

The Court's Decision

Held: The jury found the defendant, JLCT, primarily at fault and awarded damages to the plaintiffs.

Although the jury found the negligence of the defendant in the maintenance and operation of its building to be the primary cause of Kennedy's death, it also found Kennedy himself was partially at fault. Based on its finding that negligence on Kennedy's part played a role in his fall, the jury's award to the plaintiffs in the amount of $4,042,117 was reduced to $2,220,964.

Florida v. Riley

488 U.S. 445 (1989)

The Issue:

Does warrantless police surveillance by flying over one's private property violate the landowner's reasonable expectation of privacy?

This case brings to mind a passage from George Orwell's book *Nineteen Eighty-Four*: "In the far distance, a helicopter skimmed down between roofs, hovered for an instant like a [hummingbird], and darted away again with a curving flight. It was the Police Patrol, snooping into people's windows."

Michael Riley lived in a mobile home situated on five acres of rural land in Florida. He maintained a greenhouse behind his home. From the ground, the contents of Riley's greenhouse were shielded from view by walls and trees on his property. Two of the greenhouse's roof panels had been removed for repair. The two panels comprised about 10 percent of the roof. Riley's property, including his mobile home and the greenhouse, was surrounded by a wire fence posted with a "Do Not Enter" sign. Despite the missing panels, there is no dispute that Riley intended and expected that his greenhouse would not be open to public inspection, and that he had taken affirmative precautions to protect against ground-level observation.

The Pasco County Sheriff's Office received an anonymous tip that Riley was growing marijuana on his property. The investigating officer tried to see into the greenhouse from the ground but could not. He then secured a helicopter and circled about four hundred feet above the greenhouse. The altitude from which the officer viewed the greenhouse was within the permissible air space for helicopters. From that vantage point, he could see with his naked eye through the open roof panels what he believed to be marijuana growing inside. Using this information to demonstrate probable cause that a crime was being committed, the investigating officer obtained a search warrant for Riley's property. In a search of the greenhouse, officers found numerous marijuana plants. Riley was charged with possession of marijuana.

Riley's Motion to Suppress:

Prior to the start of his trial, Riley requested that the court throw out the evidence discovered as a result of the helicopter surveillance. (Such a request is known as a "Motion to Suppress.") The trial court granted his motion and held that viewing his property from the helicopter violated Riley's reasonable expectation of privacy. The District Court of Appeal of Florida reversed the trial court and denied Riley's motion to dismiss the evidence. The Supreme Court of Florida reinstated the trial court's order to suppress the evidence, holding that the initial helicopter surveillance constituted a search for which a warrant was required under the Fourth Amendment. Therefore, the unconstitutional viewing from the helicopter could not be used as the basis for the subsequent search warrant. Under the "exclusionary rule" the evidence garnered from the search of the greenhouse was thrown out.

The government appealed the evidentiary ruling to the US Supreme Court.

The Applicable Law:

The Fourth Amendment:

> The right of the people to be secure in their persons, houses, papers, and effects, against unreasonable searches and seizures, shall not be violated, and no Warrants shall issue, but upon probable cause, supported by Oath or affirmation, and particularly describing the place to be searched, and the persons or things to be seized.

The purpose of this amendment is to safeguard the privacy and security of individuals against arbitrary invasions. Generally, where an owner of property has a reasonable expectation of privacy in that property, law enforcement must secure a warrant based on probable cause *prior* to conducting a search of the grounds. Usually, an anonymous tip, without more to corroborate it, is not sufficient for a warrant's "probable cause" requirement.

What's your verdict? Does surveillance of the interior of a partially covered greenhouse in a residential backyard from the vantage point of a helicopter located four hundred feet above the greenhouse constitute a "search" for which a warrant is required under the Fourth Amendment? If you vote "yes," then the evidence the government wanted to use against Riley is tossed out. If you vote "no," then the government can use the evidence gleaned from the two searches of Riley's property.

STOP HERE AND DECIDE THE CASE
BEFORE GOING FURTHER

The Court's Decision follows on the next page.

The Court's Decision

Held: The Supreme Court held that Riley had no reasonable expectation of privacy regarding the exposed marijuana plants because anyone could view Riley's property from a helicopter flying in navigable airspace and determine what was inside the greenhouse.

In its 5-to-4 decision, the United States Supreme Court based its finding that Riley did not have a reasonable expectation of privacy in the greenhouse's contents on the fact that the police officer did not enter Riley's land or interfere with it in any way, and the fact that the four-hundred-foot distance from ground to helicopter was not prohibited by FAA regulations. The majority said the helicopter surveillance was not a *search* as that term is used in the Fourth Amendment, and therefore a warrant was not required for the officer to have flown over and observed the greenhouse. "What a person knowingly exposes to the public, even in his own home or office, is not a subject of Fourth Amendment protection."

The majority stated that there was nothing in the record to suggest that helicopters flying at four hundred feet were sufficiently rare that Riley could have *reasonably* anticipated that his greenhouse would not be observed from that altitude.

The dissenters, however, pointed out that there was no evidence in the record either way about whether such flights were or were not frequent. The extent to which it was or was not commonplace for helicopters to be flying over Riley's property was never established by the evidence in the case. Thus, the state had not proven that Riley's expectation of privacy was *unreasonable.* "The question before us must be not whether the police were where they had a right to be, but whether public observation of Riley's [residential property] was so commonplace that Riley's expectation of privacy in his backyard could not be considered reasonable."

The dissenters noted that even individuals who have taken effective precautions to ensure against ground-level observations cannot block off all conceivable aerial views of their outdoor patios and yards without entirely giving up their enjoyment of those areas. To require individuals to completely cover and enclose their property is to demand more than the "precautions customarily taken by those seeking privacy."

The minority suggested that the majority decision was driven by a distaste for the activity in which Riley was engaged. In that regard, the minority opinion quoted Justice Frankfurter, who noted that "[i]t is a fair summary of history to say that the safeguards of liberty have frequently been forged in controversies involving not very nice people."

Brian J. Karem v. President Donald J. Trump and White House Press Secretary Stephanie A. Grisham

United States Court of Appeals for the District of Columbia Circuit
No. 19-5255 (June 2020)

The Issue:

How much authority does the White House press secretary have to revoke a reporter's White House press pass?

There has always been a playful tension between the White House press corps and the president's staff. Sarcastic and sometimes crude comments are frequently bantered back and forth. However, in this Rose Garden event, the White House press secretary determined that one reporter went too far.

The White House is unique in so many ways. Within the building's West Wing are press facilities where members of the media can prepare and send reports to their respective employers. These members of the White House press corps are credentialed and given special access passes to the White House grounds.

In July of 2019, President Donald Trump held a social media summit at the White House. Those in attendance included various internet influencers and personalities. Also on the invitation list was Sebastian

Gorka, a former presidential advisor. The event was brought to a close by President Trump's addressing the attendees in the Rose Garden. As with any White House event, there was a press contingent also in attendance. One of the reporters was Brian J. Karem, a credentialed member of the White House press corps, a correspondent for *Playboy* magazine and a CNN contributor. He stood with other reporters in a roped-off area surrounding the rows of chairs provided for the invited guests.

At the conclusion of his remarks, President Trump turned and walked back toward the Oval Office. Karem shouted a question at the president. Although the president didn't respond, some of the guests did. Several verbally taunted Karem. One shouted: "He talked to us, the real news." Karem responded by gesturing toward the assembled group and declaring, "This is a group eager for demonic possession." Several attendees laughed.

Sebastian Gorka, however, did not. He turned and yelled at Karem, "And you're a 'journalist,' right?" Karem shouted back, "Hey, come on over here and talk to me, brother, or we can go outside and have a long conversation." Gorka advanced on Karem, shouting, "Are you threatening me now in the White House? In the Rose Garden? You are threatening me in the Rose Garden?" With the two men standing face to face, Karem lowered his voice and asserted, "I said I'd be happy to talk to you." Gorka yelled back, "You are a punk! You're not a journalist! You're a punk!" Gorka then turned and began to walk away. Karem shouted, "Go home." And, "Hey, Gorka, get a job!"

Three weeks later, Karem was notified that Press Secretary Stephanie Grisham had decided to suspend his White House press credentials for thirty days. She said Karem's "demonic possession" comment was "inappropriate and unprofessional," and denigrated the mental state of the Rose Garden guests even if it was meant as "nothing more than a good-natured exchange." She also stated that the "go outside" remark could have been reasonably interpreted as an invitation to a physical confrontation. The suspension of his press pass was an appropriate response, she said, in order to ensure such conduct would not happen again.

Prior to the Trump administration, the White House had never issued a specific set of formal, written guidelines addressing proper conduct on the part of the press pass holders. In fact, until President Trump took office, there had never been an instance of a press pass being revoked because of misconduct during a press conference or other White House event.

Karem filed suit to have his credentials immediately restored.

The Trial:

Karem argued he had not been given any prior notice that conduct such as he participated in at the Rose Garden event might lead to some type of sanction. He asserted that he was entitled to such notice.

The White House argued it had previously provided reporters with notice of a reasonable framework for conduct, and it would be unreasonable for the press office to have to anticipate each and every type of misbehavior that might need to be addressed by some form of discipline. Without the ability to address inappropriate conduct, the press secretary argued, reporters could, for example, moon the president with impunity.

The Applicable Law:

Due to the unique relationship between the press and the White House, the courts have held that "the protection afforded news gathering under the first amendment . . . requires that this access not be denied arbitrarily or for less than compelling reasons." Furthermore, it is established case law that:

> "[T]he interest of a bona fide Washington correspondent in obtaining a White House press pass" is not only "protected by the first amendment" but also "undoubtedly qualifies as [a] liberty [interest] which

may not be denied without due process of law under
the fifth amendment."[19]

Prior to the suspension of Karem's pass, the Trump press office had
attempted to revoke the pass of a reporter, Jim Acosta, who (in a regular
press conference) had refused to yield the microphone until President
Trump responded to his questions. Acosta challenged the revocation
in the courts, asserting he had not been provided any prior notice as to
what actions might lead to a suspension of a press pass. The court found
that the lack of any set standards or specified penalties was fatal to the
White House attempt at punishing the reporter. The court ordered
Acosta's credentials be restored to him.

Instead of appealing the court's *Acosta* decision, the White House
Press Office issued a letter (the "Acosta Letter") setting out "understood
practices" and norms governing "White House press conferences." The
letter went on to state that a more elaborate set of rules might be devised
for conduct of the press in "open (non-press room) areas of the White
House." But instead of doing so, the press secretary's office said that for
the time being it would rely on "the hope that professional journalistic
norms will suffice to regulate conduct in those places."

The conduct giving rise to Karem's press credentials being revoked
for thirty days occurred during one of those open (non-press room)
events.

The legal question at issue, therefore, is whether or not Karem
had been given adequate notice that the alleged misconduct for which
he was sanctioned could result in his press pass being revoked. Was
the conduct of a nature that he should reasonably have known might
lead to some form of sanction—such as revocation of his pass—based
on the press office's earlier "Acosta Letter" and that letter's reference
to "professional journalistic norms." In short, was Karem afforded
appropriate due process?

---

[19] The relevant portion of the Fifth Amendment mandates that a person shall not
be deprived of life, liberty, or property without due process of law.

What's your verdict? Did the White House press secretary have the authority to pull Karem's credentials for thirty days as a form of punishment for Karem's Rose Garden behavior?

STOP HERE AND DECIDE THE CASE
BEFORE GOING FURTHER

The Court's Decision follows on the next page.

The Court's Decision

Held: The Court of Appeals ruled that Karem was likely to prevail on his claims against the White House, and granted the injunction he requested.

As a result of the court's unanimous decision, the White House press secretary was ordered to restore Karem's pass immediately."[20]

The court of appeals determined Karem had not been given adequate notice of the type of conduct that might lead to a revocation of his press pass. The letter sent out after the Acosta incident was insufficient and too vague, the judges said. The letter only addressed possible sanctions for conduct during a "press conference" and not an "open" event.

Regarding the potential "mooning" of the president, the court stated:

> Finally, raising the specter of the absurd, the White House argues that it cannot be the case that "the Press Secretary would be powerless to take action even were a reporter to 'moon' the President, shout racial epithets at a foreign dignitary, or sexually harass another member of the press corps." . . . [T]he White House cannot defend the thirty-day suspension here on the ground that some other, egregious conduct might justify the same sanction. And even if the White House could impose that sanction for such egregious conduct consistent with due process, Karem's behavior as reflected in the preliminary injunction record fell below that threshold. Notions of professionalism are, after all, context-dependent. . . .

---

[20] The judges also ruled that President Trump was an improper party to the action—a determination that Karem had not opposed—and therefore the order applied only to Press Secretary Grisham.

In any event, the White House can rest assured that principles of due process do not limit its authority to maintain order and decorum at White House events by, for example, ordering the immediate removal of rogue, mooning journalists.

Postscript: Since the original sanction (revocation of Karem's press pass) was for thirty days, by the time the court of appeals ruled in the case, there were only eighteen days left to be restored.

Halter v. Nebraska

205 U.S. 34 (1907)

The Issue:

Can a state prohibit the US flag to be used in an advertisement?

Burning the United States flag is a frequent form of protest against government actions. Flag desecration cases have led to several important constitutional decisions by the United States Supreme Court. But in this case, we look at a more mundane use of the flag: advertising.

It's not the first time that a bottle of beer has gotten someone in trouble. But in the case of the accused in this dispute, Nicholas Halter, it was the outside of the bottle, not the inside, that was the source of his run-in with the law. The bottles of beer that he possessed, advertised, and sold to the public, a beer he called Stars and Stripes, prominently displayed an American flag on the bottles.

He was arrested and charged with violation of Nebraska's Act to Prevent and Punish the Desecration of the Flag of the United States. The penalty for violating this state statute was a maximum fine of $100 or imprisonment for a maximum of thirty days, or both, at the discretion of the court. The anti-desecration statute provided an exception for the flag to be displayed in newspapers, periodicals, and books so long as the flag was not affiliated with any advertisement.

The Trial:

Halter pleaded not guilty. He asserted that the Nebraska statute was null and void under the Fourteenth Amendment of the Constitution, as the statute deprived him of the right to exercise his constitutional rights. He argued that the statute infringed upon his personal right in how he chose to use the flag. He also claimed that he was deprived of the equal protection of the laws since an exception was made for depictions of the flag by publishers, newspapers, books, and periodicals; thus, discriminating in favor of one class over another.[21]

The State of Nebraska defended its statute by asserting that using the flag on advertising disrespected the flag, a cherished symbol of our nation. Disruptions and even violence were likely to be committed by those who were offended when the flag was dishonored. Thus, the state statute preserved the peace and well-being of its citizens.

Halter was found guilty. He then appealed the verdict. The conviction was upheld by the Nebraska Supreme Court. Halter then appealed to the United States Supreme Court.

The Applicable Law:

Nebraska's Act to Prevent and Punish the Desecration of the Flag of the United States

> . . . makes it a misdemeanor, punishable by fine or imprisonment, or both, for anyone to sell, expose for sale, or have in possession for sale, any article of merchandise upon which shall have been printed or placed, for purposes of advertisement, a representation of the flag of the United States.

---

[21] Halter did not assert a "free speech" claim under the First Amendment. In 1907 when this case was decided, the first ten amendments, unlike the Fourteenth Amendment, had not yet been held to apply to the states, only to the federal government.

The relevant part of the Fourteenth Amendment upon which Halter based his defense states:

> ... No state shall make or enforce any law which shall abridge the privileges or immunities of citizens of the United States; nor shall any State deprive any person of life, liberty, or property, without due process of law; nor deny to any person within its jurisdiction the equal protection of the laws.

What's your verdict? Was the Nebraska statute constitutional in making it illegal to use the American flag in any form of advertising?

STOP HERE AND DECIDE THE CASE
BEFORE GOING FURTHER

The Court's Decision follows on the next page.

The Court's Decision

Held: The United States Supreme Court found that the Nebraska statute was constitutional, deciding that there was no right or privilege to use the American flag in an advertisement. The Court upheld Halter's conviction.

In an 8-to-1 decision, the Supreme Court said that since the federal government had not, as of the date of this case (1907), passed a law regarding the treatment of the American flag that would have preempted state action, Nebraska was free to legislate protections for the emblem of national sovereignty.[22]

The Court's analysis began with the acknowledgment that a state statute may only be considered unconstitutional if it has been found to be *manifestly* so.

Next, the justices acknowledged that states were free to pass legislation that provides "not only for the health, morals, and safety of its people, but for the common good, as involved in the well-being, peace, happiness, and prosperity of the people." A state may, by statute, "exert its power to strengthen the bonds of the Union, and therefore, to that end, may encourage patriotism and love of country among its people." And by extending that principle, the Court noted that encouraging love of country is likely to lead to love of the state as well.

From that vantage point, the justices wrote that the flag is a cherished symbol of our nation held in great reverence by anyone who enjoys the privileges of American citizenship.

> Hence, it has often occurred that insults to a flag have been the cause of war, and indignities put upon it, in the presence of those who revere it, have often been resented and sometimes punished on the spot.

---

[22]   At the time of Halter's arrest, the only *federal* flag statute precluded registering the flag or other national emblems as trademarks with the US Patent Office.

Thus, the Court's logic led it to conclude that antiflag desecration statutes such as Nebraska's were consistent with a state's legislative power to promote and protect the "well-being, peace, happiness, and prosperity" of its citizens in part by discouraging possible discord generated by insults to the flag. Allowing the flag to be used in advertising cheapens its place of honor and could well be considered an insult by many.

Halter also claimed that the statute discriminated against him since it allows other media to use the flag imprint—newspapers, periodicals, books, and pamphlets. The Court said the differences in the application of a law among those to whom it is applied is permissible if based "upon some reasonable ground – some difference which bears a just and proper relation to the attempted classification, and is not a mere arbitrary selection." The Court rejected Halter's equal protection claim by holding:

> [Nebraska] chose not to forbid the use of the flag
> for the exceptional purposes specified in the statute,
> prescribing the fundamental condition that its use for
> any of those purposes should be "disconnected from
> any advertisement." All are alike forbidden to use the
> flag as an advertisement. It is easy to be seen how a
> representation of the flag may be wholly disconnected
> from an advertisement, and be used upon a newspaper,
> periodical, book, etc., in such way as not to arouse a
> feeling of indignation nor offend the sentiments and
> feelings of those who revere it.

Subsequent flag desecration cases have focused on the flag's use in political protests rather than in advertising. The decision of the United States Supreme Court in this *Halter* case is still good law. It has not been overturned despite subsequent flag desecration decisions. This may well be the result of Nebraska's having not charged anyone else with violating the advertising portion of its desecration law. If Nebraska has not subsequently arrested anyone else for violating the flag advertising prohibition, then there can be no actionable dispute that would afford the courts an opportunity to reconsider the matter.

Heien v. North Carolina

574 U.S. 54 (2014)

The Issue:

"Ignorance of the law is no excuse." Or is it?

In April of 2010, Maynor Vasquez was driving on I-77 in North Carolina. Lying under a blanket in the back seat was Nicholas Heien. The car they occupied had a broken brake light.

Sergeant Darisse of the Surry County Sheriff's Department was following behind the car when the officer noted that only one of the car's two brake lights was working, which he believed was a violation of the law. He activated his lights and siren, and pulled Vasquez over. Darisse spoke to Vasquez and Heien. The officer felt that there were some troubling inconsistencies in the two men's stories. He was also concerned that Heien remained lying on the back seat. Darisse then asked if he could search the vehicle, and received both Vasquez's and Heien's consent to do so. The officer found fifty-four and two-tenths grams of cocaine in the car (a little over a tenth of a pound).

There was, however, a problem with the stop and search. In North Carolina, it is only a violation of the law if *both* brake lights are malfunctioning. Since only one of the two brake lights was out, the condition of Heien's vehicle was not in any *apparent* violation of the law. Thus, there was no legal basis for the officer to have stopped the car. (The officer's confusion may have arisen because the same law that requires only *one* operating brake light requires all *other* lamps on *both* sides of the rear of the vehicle to be functioning.) If the *stopping* of the vehicle violated the Fourth Amendment rights of the occupants, any evidence discovered in the subsequent search would be inadmissible, even if the occupants had consented to the search after being stopped.

Heien, the owner of the vehicle, was charged with two counts of trafficking cocaine. (Vasquez was dealt with in a separate case.)

The Trial:

Heien requested that the court throw out the evidence discovered during the course of the vehicle search. (Such a request is known as a "Motion to Suppress.") The trial court denied the motion. Heien then entered a plea of guilty, but reserved his right to appeal the denial of his suppression motion.

The case was subsequently presented to the North Carolina Court of Appeals, where the trial court's denial of the suppression motion was reversed. The appellate court held that the traffic stop was not valid because driving with one functioning brake light did not violate North Carolina law.

But on the state's appeal to the North Carolina Supreme Court, the justices reversed the court of appeals and said that when an officer's mistake of law was reasonable, it may give rise to the "reasonable suspicion" required for a traffic stop under the Fourth Amendment. Eventually, the case made it to the United States Supreme Court to determine the legality of admitting the evidence obtained as a result of Deputy Darisse's stopping the vehicle.

The Applicable Law:

The Fourth Amendment to the Constitution prohibits unreasonable searches and seizures. The stopping of a vehicle by law enforcement based on a suspected violation of the law is considered a seizure of the occupants, and thus gives rise to Fourth Amendment review. Based upon this *reasonableness* test, searches that were commenced by an officer based on a good faith mistake of *fact* have often been found to be reasonable, and the evidence admitted against the defendant. But in the case of Heien, the officer's stop and search was based upon a mistake of *law*.

Perhaps two examples would be useful to demonstrate the difference between the two types of mistakes.

A police officer is parked in front of a convenience store. He notices a man rush in the store, and very shortly thereafter run back out the door and jump into a car. The officer interprets this behavior as being consistent with someone who had just shoplifted an item. The officer then stops the man's vehicle and detains him. It turns out that the man is a diabetic and was having a bad insulin reaction. He had run into the store to purchase some orange juice but once inside he saw that there was a long line at the checkout stand and so ran out of the store. The officer was certainly correct on the *law* as theft is a criminal act. However, the officer's stopping the vehicle was based upon a mistake of *fact*: the detained individual had not shoplifted anything from the store.

The second example takes place in a public park in which vehicles are prohibited. An officer stationed in the park sees someone zooming by on a Segway. He stops the Segway user and issues a ticket for violation of the "no vehicles" ordinance. Under the laws of that jurisdiction, Segways are not considered vehicles. There was no legal basis for the stop. The officer was correct on his *facts*: the detained person *was* riding a Segway. However, the officer's stopping the Segway was based upon a mistake of *law*: Segways were not covered by the law prohibiting vehicles in the park.

Heien argued there was an important distinction between errors of fact and law on the part of an arresting officer. He contended the reasons that the Fourth Amendment allows for some errors of fact in an officer's stopping a vehicle do not apply to errors of law. Officers in the field must make factual assessments on the fly, and often are required to interpret events being viewed. Therefore, they deserve a margin of error in determining "reasonableness." But, Heien argued, no such margin is appropriate for questions of law. The statute here requires either one working brake light or two, and the question of law does not turn on anything "an officer might suddenly confront in the field."

What's your verdict? Can a "reasonable suspicion" for a traffic stop rest on a mistaken understanding of the law on the part of the officer? If your answer to this question is "yes," then the evidence of cocaine possession Sergeant Darisse discovered is admissible and Heien's guilty plea stands. If your answer to the question is "no," then the evidence is not admissible and Heien's guilty plea is set aside.

STOP HERE AND DECIDE THE CASE
BEFORE GOING FURTHER

The Court's Decision

Held: The officer's mistake about the brake light law was reasonable, and the stopping of the vehicle was lawful under the Fourth Amendment.

In an 8-to-1 decision, the United States Supreme Court held that there was no reason under the Fourth Amendment to treat a mistake of law differently from a mistake of fact. (As noted earlier in this case study, prior Supreme Court cases had held that a reasonable mistake of *fact* could provide the basis for a reasonable suspicion in stop-and-search challenges.)

Addressing Heien's argument that a mistake of fact must be evaluated differently from a mistake of law, the Supreme Court stated that similar snap decisions must often be made by an officer about the law and the facts. The justices used the Segway example that was discussed previously in this case study in their discussion of mistakes of law. The officer's mistake of law in the Segway incident, the majority said, should be afforded the same margin of error as mistakes of fact.

Doesn't the Court's decision discourage officers from learning the law? The Court (no surprise) said it did not. "The Fourth Amendment tolerates only *reasonable* mistakes, and those mistakes – whether of fact or of law – must be *objectively* reasonable." (emphasis in original)

And finally, the majority addressed the maxim we considered at the start of this case. "Ignorance of the law is no excuse."

> If the law required two working brake-lights [sic], Heien could not escape a ticket by claiming he reasonably thought he needed only one; if the law required only one, Sergeant Darisse could not issue a valid ticket by claiming he reasonably thought drivers needed two. But just because mistakes of law cannot justify either the imposition or the avoidance of criminal liability, it does not follow that they cannot justify an investigatory stop. And Heien is not appealing a brake-light [sic] ticket;

he is appealing a cocaine-trafficking conviction as to which there is no asserted mistake of fact or law.

In her dissenting opinion, Justice Sotomayor insisted that there was a difference in an officer's mistake of fact and mistake of law, and that the latter should not be a basis for a "reasonable suspicion" to stop and search under the Fourth Amendment. She noted, "'[T]he notion that the law is definite and knowable' sits at the foundation of our legal system."

Evans v. Muncy, Warden

498 U.S. 927 (1990)

The Issue:

How important is "procedural finality" in our system of justice?

"We are not final because we are infallible, but we are infallible only because we are final." This statement by Justice Robert H. Jackson from a 1952 Supreme Court concurring opinion seems applicable to the issues raised in this death penalty case that you are about to decide.[23]

Wilbert Lee Evans was convicted in Virginia of capital murder and sentenced to death. He received the death penalty rather than life without parole *based on one aggravating circumstance*: if allowed to live, Evans would pose a serious threat of future danger. Without this finding, Evans could not have been sentenced to death. In his subsequent appeal, Evans asserted that his conduct while in prison was proof the jury's finding that he posed a "serious threat of future danger" (the sole aggravating circumstance) was wrong.

In January of 1981, while Evans was being led back to jail after a hearing in an adjacent courthouse, he grabbed police officer William Truesdale's service gun and shot and killed the officer. While fleeing from this shooting, he was confronted by another officer. Evans pointed

---

23   Jackson quote from Brown v. Allen, 344 U.S. 443, 540 (1952)

Truesdale's gun at that officer and pulled the trigger, but the gun jammed and Evans was immediately apprehended.

The Trial:

Evans was convicted of officer Truesdale's murder. The jury then had to determine whether Evans's penalty would be life in prison without parole or death. The state argued that based on past conduct, Evans would pose a continuing threat of future danger if he was allowed to live. The state put into evidence that Evans had seven prior convictions. The jury determined that Evans should receive the death penalty based upon the special circumstance of his being a future threat to safety and security.

Subsequently, the state's prosecutor admitted he knew at the time he presented evidence of the seven past arrests that two of them were not actual convictions. Evans appealed his death sentence, citing the state's admission that it had submitted evidence to the jury that the state knew to be false.

Evans's appeal was granted. As a result, his case was sent back for a rehearing on the appropriate penalty.

In his second penalty hearing, the jury again reached a sentence of death. Evans appealed this sentence. This time he argued that the one basis for his receiving the death penalty—future dangerousness—was no longer applicable, as demonstrated in certain events that occurred while he was on death row.

On May 31, 1984, six inmates on death row at the prison where Evans was being held engineered an escape. Armed with makeshift knives, the inmates took twelve prison guards and two female nurses hostage. The hostages were stripped of their clothes, bound, and blindfolded.

According to undisputed testimony by the hostages, both guards and nurses, Evans took decisive steps to calm the riot, saving the lives of several hostages and preventing the rape of one of the nurses. One guard that was held hostage testified in a subsequent hearing: "Based upon what I saw and heard it is my firm opinion that if any of the escaping inmates had tried to harm us, Evans would have come to our aid. It is

my belief that had it not been for Evans, I might not be here today."
Other guards taken hostage verified that Evans protected them and the
other hostages from danger.

Furthermore, the testimony was that Evans's conduct during the
May 1984 uprising was consistent with his exemplary behavior during
his close to ten years on death row.

The State of Virginia's opposition to Evans's application to stay
the execution barely contests either Evans's depiction of the relevant
events or the conclusion that these events reveal the clear error of the
jury's prediction that Evans posed a continuing threat. Indeed, the
state concedes that the sole basis for Evans's death sentence—he posed
a continuing serious threat to society—in fact does not exist.

The only ground asserted by the state for permitting Evans's
execution to go forward is its interest in *procedural finality*. According
to the state, permitting a death row inmate to challenge a finding of
future dangerousness by reference to facts occurring *after* a sentence has
been imposed will unleash an endless stream of litigation.

Evans's petition to the district court resulted in the court staying
his execution and ordering a full hearing on the issue presented in the
petition. However, upon the state's appealing that order, the court of
appeals reversed the district court and vacated the stay of execution.
Evans then appealed to the United States Supreme Court.

The Applicable Law:

The United States Supreme Court has held that to reach a verdict
of death, the jury must be required to find and specifically identify at
least one designated "special circumstance" or "aggravating" factor as
to the crime charged and/or the defendant's character. One such factor
set out in Virginia's statutes is the defendant's propensity to commit
violent acts in the future:

> Upon a finding that the defendant is guilty of an offense
> which may be punishable by death, a proceeding shall

be held which shall be limited to a determination as to whether the defendant shall be sentenced to death or life imprisonment . . . In case of a trial by jury, where a sentence of death is not recommended, the defendant shall be sentenced to imprisonment for life . . .

The penalty of death shall not be imposed unless the Commonwealth shall prove beyond a reasonable doubt that there is a probability based upon evidence of the prior history of the defendant or of the circumstances surrounding the commission of the offense of which he is accused *that he would commit criminal acts of violence that would constitute a continuing serious threat to society* . . .[24] [emphasis added]

What's your verdict? In light of the state's conceding that the one aggravating circumstance which made Evans eligible for the death penalty—"future dangerousness"—no longer applied, should Evans be granted a stay of execution, or should the state's interest in "procedural finality" allow for his execution?

STOP HERE AND DECIDE THE CASE
BEFORE GOING FURTHER

---

[24] Va. Code 19.2-264.4(A and (C)

The Court's Decision

Held: The United States Supreme Court denied Evans's request for a stay of execution.

The majority of justices agreed with the State of Virginia that to grant the stay would lead to circumstances wherein any death sentence based on future dangerousness could be contested repeatedly each time a prisoner's behavior could be characterized as meritorious.[25]

Justice Thurgood Marshal dissented. He asserted that

> Just as the jury occasionally "gets it wrong" about whether a defendant charged with murder is innocent or guilty, so, too, can the jury "get it wrong" about whether a defendant convicted of murder is deserving of death . . .

> [I]f it is impossible to construct a system capable of accommodating all evidence relevant to a man's entitlement to be spared death – no matter when that evidence is disclosed – then it is the system, not the life of the man sentenced to death, that should be dispatched . . .

> A death sentence that is dead wrong is no less so simply because its deficiency is not uncovered until the eleventh hour.

Wilbert Evans was executed in the electric chair shortly after 11:00 p.m. on October 17, 1990, the very same day that the Supreme Court issued its order denying a stay of execution.

---

[25]   Because this was simply a petition for an order staying the execution and was summarily denied by the Court, the "vote count" of the justices is not known. The only member of the Court who wrote an opinion was Justice Marshall.

County of Allegheny v. ACLU, Greater Pittsburgh Chapter

492 U.S. 573 (1989)

The Issue:

At what point does a holiday display on public property become an improper endorsement of religion?

On June 8, 1789, James Madison of Virginia proposed to the First Congress an amendment to the Constitution. His proffered amendment stated: "The civil rights of none shall be abridged on account of religious belief or worship, nor shall any national religion be established, nor shall the full and equal rights of conscience be in any manner, or on any pretext, infringed." The religious concerns of our forefathers stemmed from their experiences with England's taxation to support a favored church. After being debated and amended, Madison's proposal found its way into the First Amendment in the Bill of Rights. The meaning and parameters of that amendment's Establishment Clause and Free Exercise Clause have been the subject of debate ever since.

In 1982, Pittsburgh, Pennsylvania, celebrated the December holidays with a nativity scene, a crèche, placed on the Grand Staircase inside the Allegheny Courthouse. In addition, a forty-five-foot tall Christmas tree and an eighteen-foot Chanukah menorah were displayed outside the City-County Building. All three displays were installed by private entities.

The crèche, located inside the courthouse, was consistent with manger scenes displayed in homes, churches, and businesses throughout the world. It included figures of Jesus, Mary, Joseph, farm animals, sheep and shepherds, and wise men. At the top of the manger was an angel bearing a banner proclaiming "*Gloria in Excelsis Deo*" (meaning "Glory to God in the Highest"). A sign posted by the display read "This Display Donated by the Holy Name Society." The county had placed the crèche at the Grand Staircase during the holiday season for many years. Other than some ornamental plants, there were no other holiday-related items displayed with the crèche.

The menorah at issue was placed outside the City-County Building, located about a block away from the courthouse. For several years, the city had placed a large Christmas tree under an arch at one entrance to the building. Eventually, the city added the eighteen-foot menorah nearby in order to include a symbolic recognition of Chanukah, the Jewish celebration that falls closest in time to the December holiday period.

According to Jewish tradition, in 165 BC the Maccabees, a group of Jewish rebel warriors, recaptured the Temple of Jerusalem from the Greeks during a political rebellion. Within the temple was a seven-branch menorah that was to be kept burning continuously. But when the Maccabees took back the temple, there was only enough oil to burn for one more day. Miraculously, the oil burned for eight days until additional oil was finally procured. The menorah honors this miracle of the inextinguishable flame.

The city placed a sign near the two outdoor displays that read "During this holiday season, the city of Pittsburgh salutes liberty. Let these festive lights remind us that we are the keepers of the flame of liberty and our legacy of freedom."

Asserting that the crèche *and* menorah violated the Establishment Clause, the Greater Pittsburgh Chapter of the American Civil Liberties Union and seven local residents filed a lawsuit seeking to permanently enjoin the city and county from placing the nativity scene and the menorah on public property.

The Trial:

The district court ruled in favor of the county and city. However, the court of appeals overturned the district court. The appeals court determined both the menorah and the crèche amounted to an impermissible government endorsement of Christianity and Judaism. The county and city appealed to the United States Supreme Court.

The Applicable Law:

The First Congress debated and amended James Madison's proposed religious liberty clause. Ultimately, this was the agreed upon language included in the First Amendment: "Congress shall make no law respecting an establishment of religion, or prohibiting the free exercise thereof . . ."

Over the years, courts have held "the prohibition against governmental endorsement of religion 'preclude[s] government from conveying or attempting to convey a message that religion or a particular religious belief is favored or preferred.'" The Establishment Clause has been interpreted to mean the government should not make adherence to a religion "relevant in any way to a person's standing in the political community." The government should not take any action that indicates that religion or a particular religion is favored or preferred.

In a prior case involving a city's placement of a nativity scene, the Supreme Court found the crèche was permissible because it was placed in a city's shopping district and was accompanied by a Santa Claus house, a Christmas tree, and a banner reading "Seasons Greetings."[26] In that particular setting, the Court said no reasonable observer would think the city was endorsing any one particular religion. The Supreme Court

---

[26]   *Lynch v. Donnelly* 465 U.S. 668 (1984)

said government *recognition* of religion in the form of the crèche was not the equivalent of government *endorsement* of religion. It explained the degree to which a display was a "recognition" versus an "endorsement" was highly dependent on the specific facts of any given case.

For example, if a large wooden cross were placed year-round on the roof of city hall, it would be reasonable for a spectator to believe the city was endorsing some form of Christianity. If a carving of Moses holding the Ten Commandments was hung on the wall of a courtroom, the reasonable observer may see that as an endorsement of religion generally or Judaism in particular. But if the carving of Moses was accompanied by secular figures like Caesar Augustus, William Blackstone, Napoleon Bonaparte, and John Marshall, the more likely interpretation would be a tribute to lawgivers rather than religion.[27] Nor would there be an Establishment Clause problem if a public art museum displayed a historical religious painting since its primary purpose is to feature the art and not necessarily the religious message.

Prior Supreme Court decisions have also held that starting a session of Congress with a prayer or placing "In God We Trust" on our currency does not involve government in religion to the extent that a First Amendment violation is involved.

The First Amendment analysis must include a review of the context in which the display with religious association is presented.

What's your verdict? You have two separate decisions to make in this case: (1) Was the nativity scene placed inside the county courthouse an impermissible endorsement of religion on the part of the government? (2) Was the menorah placed outside the City-County Building next to a Christmas tree an impermissible endorsement of religion on the part of the government?

STOP HERE AND DECIDE THE CASE
BEFORE GOING FURTHER

---

[27]   Indeed, all these leaders appear in friezes on the walls of the courtroom of the Supreme Court.

The Court's Decision

Held: (1) The courthouse lobby nativity scene violated the Establishment Clause and was an impermissible endorsement of religion. (2) The menorah did not violate the Establishment Clause and could remain in place.

The difficult analysis and decisions required of the Supreme Court in this case are evidenced by the arguments presented in several concurring and dissenting opinions and the vote of the justices regarding the two displays. The decision that the crèche violated the First Amendment was arrived at by a 5-to-4 vote, while the decision that the menorah did not violate the First Amendment was arrived at by a 6-to-3 vote. The justices found that applying First Amendment analysis to each of the two displays resulted in a different result for each. Three justices believed that *both* displays violated the First Amendment, while four justices believed that *neither* of the displays violated the amendment.

The primary basis for the differing judgments was the placement of the particular displays. The crèche (found to violate the First Amendment) was placed in a very prominent place in the county building, right at the Grand Staircase. It stood alone. It also was significant to the majority opinion that the angel at the very center of the display held a banner that had a religious message: "*Gloria in Excelsis Deo.*"

The majority wrote:

> Celebrating Christmas as a religious, as opposed to secular, holiday necessarily entails professing, proclaiming, or believing that Jesus of Nazareth, born in a manger in Bethlehem, is the Christ, the Messiah. If the government celebrates Christmas as a religious holiday (for example, by issuing an official proclamation saying, "We rejoice in the glory of Christ's birth!"), it means that the government really is declaring Jesus to be the Messiah, a specifically Christian belief. In

contrast, confining the government's own celebration of Christmas to the holiday's secular aspects does not favor the religious beliefs of non-Christians over those of Christians.

On the other hand, the menorah (found not to violate the First Amendment) was placed outside and next to a Christmas tree. The majority found its close proximity to the secular Christmas tree along with the sign extolling liberty made the menorah more of a secular symbol of the holidays than a religious display, even though the menorah, unlike the Christmas tree, is a religious symbol. Had the menorah stood alone inside a city or county building, it is likely the Court would have found it violated the Establishment Clause.

In disagreeing with the majority's opinion that the crèche violated the First Amendment, the dissenting justices argued the nativity scene was a recognition of the country's religious background and the holiday season, and nothing more. They criticized the test they claimed the majority was advocating: the religious or secular nature of a display depended upon what other decorations were close by. To the dissenting justices, counting how many candy canes or poinsettias were in close proximity to a nativity scene was a poor determinant of an Establishment Clause dispute.

Justice Brennan wrote a dissenting opinion regarding the menorah. He argued its proximity to the Christmas tree did not diminish its religious meaning:

> Even though the tree alone may be deemed predominantly secular, it can hardly be so characterized when placed next to such a forthrightly religious symbol [referring to the menorah]. Consider a poster featuring a star of David, a statue of Buddha, a Christmas tree, a mosque, and a drawing of Krishna. There can be no doubt that, when found in such company, the tree serves as an unabashedly religious symbol.

Board of Education of Independent School District No. 92 of Pottawatomie County v. Earls

536 U.S. 822 (2002)

The Issue:

Is it reasonable for a school district to subject all students wishing to participate in any form of extracurricular activity to random drug testing?

Random drug testing of employees in some professions associated with special dangers or particular drug predilections is allowed in order to protect the public. Railway employees and customs agents, for example, may be subjected to random and warrantless drug testing. But what about requiring random drug testing simply because one wants to join the high school chess club?

Independent School District No. 92 in Tecumseh, Oklahoma, established the Student Activities Drug Testing Policy, which requires all middle and high school students to consent to urinalysis testing for drugs in order to participate in *any extracurricular activity*. Activities included within the policy parameters include the Academic Team, Future Farmers of America, Future Homemakers of America, band, choir, cheerleading, and athletics. The urinalysis tests are only used to detect illegal drugs, including amphetamines, marijuana, cocaine, opiates, and barbiturates but not medical conditions or authorized prescription medications.

The superintendent of Independent School District No. 92 stated that although the district did not consider drug use by students to be a significant problem presently on the campuses, drug testing was a way to ensure a healthy environment at the school, and to protect against drug use on campus *before* it became a significant problem.

The policy does not require any showing of probable cause or reasonable suspicion of drug use before testing can proceed against any individual student. The only penalty for having found evidence of drug use is that the student is not allowed to participate in extracurricular activities, not criminal prosecution or any academic penalty. Indeed, the policy prohibits the school from turning over any record of the drug testing to law enforcement. Likewise, the only penalty for refusing to take a random drug test when requested by the school is the loss of the objecting student's option to participate in extracurricular activities.

Lindsay Earls filed suit against the school district when she was required to submit to drug testing in order to participate in the high school band, choir, Academic Team, and the National Honor Society.

The Trial:

Earls, and the others who filed the action, assert that the school district should have to make a showing of some *individualized suspicion* before testing a student. The students and their parents alleged that the policy violated the students' Fourth Amendment rights.

The trial court ruled in favor of the school district. On appeal to the Tenth Circuit Court of Appeals, the trial court decision was reversed. The appeals court held that the state must first have some suspicion of drug use or an identifiable drug use problem among the groups of students subject to the policy before imposing the random tests in order to comply with the Fourth Amendment to the United States Constitution.

The Applicable Law:

The relevant portion of the Fourth Amendment states: "The right of the people to be secure in their persons, houses, papers, and effects, against unreasonable searches and seizures, shall not be violated . . ." Drug testing implicates Fourth Amendment interests.

The school district's policy must be reviewed in a context of "reasonableness." A search in the school context may be reasonable if it is based upon the "special needs" of the education program. The Supreme Court has held that "A search unsupported by probable cause nevertheless may be consistent with the Fourth Amendment 'when special needs, beyond the normal need for law enforcement, make the warrant and probable cause requirement impracticable.'"

In a prior Supreme Court case, *Vernonia School District vs. Acton*, the Court ruled that suspicionless drug testing of student *athletes* was not prohibited under the Fourth Amendment.[28] The *Vernonia* case involved a school where the evidence showed there was a serious drug problem of epidemic proportions in the general student population and especially among athletes. In that case, the Court found that "special needs" existed that gave rise to an exception to the Fourth Amendment search protections: (1) the testing would address a specific student drug problem that existed and act as a deterrent to such use; (2) the policy was consistent with the swift and informal disciplinary procedures needed in a public school context; and (3) evidence was presented as to the serious health risks of drug use specifically by those participating in strenuous exercise and sporting events.

School District 92 took the *Vernonia* decision one step further and required drug testing of all students who wish to participate in any extracurricular activities. Thus, those who wish to join the Future Farmers of America, the Chess Club, the French Club, and the Future Homemakers of America, as well as football and baseball players and track and field athletes must undergo drug testing before they may

---

[28]   515 U.S. 646 (1995)

participate in those activities. The students must also agree to submit to random testing at any time *after* joining the extracurricular activity.

What's your verdict? Should the drug testing policy be allowed based on the "special needs" exception to the Fourth Amendment? If so, your verdict will be in favor of the school board. Or does the policy violate the protections of the Fourth Amendment? If so, your verdict will be in favor of Earls.

STOP HERE AND DECIDE THE CASE
BEFORE GOING FURTHER

The Court's Decision

Held: The Supreme Court ruled that the drug testing policy qualified as a "special needs" exception to the Fourth Amendment and ruled in favor of the school district.

In its 5-to-4 decision, the majority believed that the deterrence effect on student drug use was sufficient to override the need for individualized suspicion. The Court held that participating in extracurricular activities gives rise to a more limited expectation of privacy among those students than the overall student population. For example, the students would expect to be closely monitored during travel for an organization's off-campus event. The majority stated:

> A student's privacy interest is limited in a public school environment where the State is responsible for maintaining discipline, health, and safety. Schoolchildren are routinely required to submit to physical examinations and vaccinations against disease.

The "special needs" requirement for the policy's suspicionless testing was met, the Court wrote, as "the nationwide drug epidemic makes the war against drugs a pressing concern in every school."

The dissent, noting the lack of an actual drug problem in the district, argued the school district failed to justify the exposure of the students to the invasion of their privacy necessarily incurred by the testing procedures. The dissenting justices argued that the policy targeted those students who were least likely to be at risk for illicit drug use such as Future Homemakers, Future Farmers, and band members. The dissent stated:

> Notwithstanding nightmarish images of out-of-control flatware, livestock run amok, and colliding tubas

disturbing the peace and quiet of Tecumseh, the great majority of students the School District seeks to test in truth are engaged in activities that are not safety sensitive to an unusual degree.

Bearden v. Georgia

461 U.S. 660 (1983)

The Issue:

Can a court revoke a defendant's probation for failure to pay a court-ordered fine and restitution without first determining if the defendant was somehow responsible for the failure, or that alternative forms of punishment were inadequate?

At sentencing, a criminal defendant may be ordered to pay a fine, either in addition to or instead of being incarcerated. Some states have provisions that allow for defendants who do not pay the fine under terms set by the court to be summarily ordered to jail for breaking the terms of their parole. This case considers the constitutionality of that incarceration.

Bearden pled guilty in a Georgia state court to felony charges of burglary and theft by receiving stolen property. The trial court sentenced Bearden to five years in prison, but then suspended the prison term and placed Bearden on probation for the five years. As a condition of his probation, Bearden was ordered to pay $750 in fines as well as restitution to the victims. If he violated the probation terms, he would be sentenced to prison for the remainder of the five-year period.

Many state and local courts have become increasingly reliant on funding provided by fees charged to people convicted of crimes, including fees for public defenders, prosecutors, court administration, jail operation, and probation supervision. Paying for the costs of the court system with these fees is more attractive to politicians than raising taxes on everyone.

The Trial:

The state asserts three arguments why incarceration for unpaid fines is constitutional: (1) it will encourage probationers to make sincere attempts to pay their fines and restitution to the victims; (2) the state has an interest in removing convicted persons from the temptation of committing other crimes; and (3) the state must be able to revoke probation for failure to pay a fine or restitution in order to punish the lawbreaker and deter others from criminal behavior by demonstrating there are consequences to not paying a fine.

In opposition to Georgia's arguments, Bearden contended: (1) the state has other options to enforce fines for those who do not have the ability to pay, such as extending the time for making payments or ordering the probationer to perform some form of public service in lieu of the fine; (2) the state's interest in deterring the nonpayment of fines would be realized by incarcerating only those delinquent probationers who have the ability to pay but refuse to do so; and (3) the state's sole justification for incarceration is nonpayment of the fine without regard as to exactly how sincerely the probationer tried to find work. In many cases involving a probationer like Bearden, the initial trial court did not find the probationer deserved incarceration in the first place.

Based on the fact that Bearden had fallen behind on his payments, the trial court summarily ordered Bearden's parole revoked and ordered his immediate incarceration. Bearden challenged the parole revocation order. The Georgia Court of Appeals affirmed the trial court's decision. Because the appeals courts in different states had ruled in a conflicting manner regarding incarceration for failure to pay a fine, the United States Supreme Court decided to hear Bearden's case to resolve the issue.

The Applicable Law:

Automatically converting an unpaid fine to a prison sentence is subject to review under the Fourteenth Amendment to the US Constitution, which reads in relevant part:

> No State shall make or enforce any law which shall abridge the privileges or immunities of citizens of the United States; nor shall any State deprive any person of life, liberty, or property, without the due process of law; nor deny to any person within its jurisdiction the equal protection of the laws.

As late as the mid-nineteenth century, debtors' prisons were a common punishment to deal with unpaid debts. Often, people who were unable to pay a court-ordered judgment would be incarcerated until they worked off their debt through forced labor. Debtors' prisons were used in early colonial America and up until the mid-1800s, when new federal laws prohibited them. In fact, two of the signers of the Declaration of Independence served time in such prisons. One, James Wilson, did so while he was sitting as an associate justice of the US Supreme Court.

Incarcerating a person over a debt is still allowed in many states. For example, several jurisdictions permit the jailing of persons who are delinquent in paying child support. The proponents argue that the incarceration is not for the *debt*, but rather for not obeying a court order to *pay* the debt.

What's your verdict? Does the Fourteenth Amendment prohibit a State from automatically revoking an indigent defendant's probation for failure to pay a fine?

STOP HERE AND DECIDE THE CASE
BEFORE GOING FURTHER

The Court's Decision follows on the next page.

The Court's Decision

Held: Indigent defendants' Fourteenth Amendment rights are violated when parole is revoked because of the inability to pay a fine without the court first determining that the petitioners had not made a sufficient bona fide effort to pay or that adequate alternative forms of punishment did not exist.

In a unanimous 9-to-0 decision, the Supreme Court ruled that the trial court erred when it ordered Bearden incarcerated (revoked his parole) for nonpayment of the assessed fine without first looking into the circumstances surrounding the nonpayment. Had Bearden made sincere efforts to pay the fine but just did not have the funds? Or did Bearden have some means of paying but just arbitrarily stopped paying? Was an alternative such as community service available for Bearden instead of incarceration? These were all questions that the trial court did not examine but should have examined before ordering Bearden incarcerated if the court were to act consistently with the Fourteenth Amendment. The majority stated:

> By sentencing petitioner to imprisonment simply because he could not pay the fine, without considering the reasons for the inability to pay or the propriety of reducing the fine or extending the time for payment or making alternative orders the court automatically turned a fine into a prison sentence.

The justices did not make a blanket rule that a defendant could never be sent to jail should the defendant stop paying an assessed fine. They acknowledged that there would be no constitutional abridgment in revoking parole and sending a defendant to jail who had simply chosen not to make the payments when he had the capacity to do so, or who made no attempt at trying to obtain the funds to pay the fine. After all, the justices noted: "The State, of course, has a fundamental interest in appropriately punishing persons – rich and poor – who violate its criminal laws. A defendant's poverty in no way immunizes him from punishment."

It was not much of a victory for Mr. Bearden. The Supreme Court ordered the matter returned to the trial court for a new hearing on the probation revocation, at which time the trial court had to conduct a review of Bearden's circumstances consistent with the Supreme Court's ruling. However, by the time the matter made its way back to the Georgia courts, Mr. Bearden—who had been incarcerated pursuant to the parole revocation while his case wound its way through the appellate courts—had just about completed the full term of his five-year sentence. In an agreement between Bearden and prosecutors, he was released from prison and no further action was taken against him.

Reynolds v. Vitoni and Clark
San Mateo County Superior Court (2018)

The Issue:

If you voluntarily insert yourself in a conflict, can you hold the other involved parties responsible for the injuries you sustain as a result of your involvement?

"No good deed goes unpunished." This case requires you to determine if anyone could be held responsible for punishing a "good-deed-doer." This is a civil case in which the plaintiff is seeking monetary damages.

Meet Greg Reynolds. Reynolds was a former major and minor league baseball player who had pitched his first major league game in May of 2008. Later, he went on to pitch for the Texas Rangers and the Cincinnati Reds. In 2013, he was sent to the minor leagues. He played professional ball in Japan in 2014. At the time of the incident involved in this case, January of 2015, he was thirty-two years old and a free agent not affiliated with any team but attempting to work his way back into the major leagues.

Meet Jerry Vitoni.[29] In January of 2015, Vitoni threw a party at his home in San Mateo County, California. According to testimony at the trial of this case, during his party, Vitoni passed around (or at least made accessible) LSD, a hallucinogenic.

---

[29] I have changed the names of the two defendants in this case for reasons set out in the Appendix.

Meet Alexander Clark. In January of 2015, he attended the party hosted by Jerry Vitoni. Testimony at the trial of this case also indicated that Clark partook of the LSD at the party.

The Trial:

Here is the story that unfolded during the trial of the case:

From his house nearby, Greg Reynolds noticed a man out in the street who was naked, cursing at passersby, and trying to knock over a mailbox. The man was Alexander Clark, who had left Vitoni's party. Reynolds walked out to the street to see if he could render aid to the obviously distressed man. Clark then attacked Reynolds, allegedly punching Reynolds several times. Reynolds quickly returned to his home, went inside, and shut the door.

Clark, on the other hand, was apparently not finished with Reynolds. Clark went up to Reynolds's door and began banging on it and throwing his weight against it as if to break it down.

Reynolds opened the door, stepped out, and punched Clark one time in the face, knocking him into the bushes. Clark walked away and was soon restrained by police using a stun gun.

However, as a result of the punch that put Clark in the bushes, Reynolds fractured the knuckles in his right hand, his pitching hand. He contended that the injury put a halt to his baseball career. (The San Diego Padres signed Reynolds to a minor league contract shortly after the incident but released him after only three months.)

The Applicable Law:

This is a "negligence" case, which would be tried in a civil—as opposed to a criminal—court. The plaintiff must prove each element of his case by a "preponderance of the evidence." In other words, the evidence must lead you to find that in weighing the evidence the scales must tip in plaintiff's favor, if only by a slight degree. If you were sitting on the jury in this case, you would be given instructions on the law by the judge, which would include the following legal principles.[30]

Plaintiff Gregory Reynolds would need to prove that Jerry Vitoni and Alexander Clark had acted negligently under the circumstances and that their negligence was the cause of Reynolds's injuries. The judge might give the following instruction defining "negligence":

> Negligence is the failure to use reasonable care to prevent harm to oneself or to others. A person can be negligent by acting or by failing to act. A person is negligent if he or she does something that a reasonably careful person would not do in the same situation or fails to do something that a reasonably careful person would do in the same situation. You must decide how a reasonably careful person would have acted in Clark's and/or Vitoni's situation.

There are two "defendants" in this case: Clark and Vitoni. In reaching a verdict, you may find (1) neither of them was negligent, (2) both were negligent, or (3) one but not the other was negligent.

In addition, you must also consider whether or not Reynolds may have been negligent, and if so, whether and to what extent his own negligence may have contributed to his having sustained injuries.

What's your verdict? Who was primarily at fault for Gregory Reynolds's injuries? Alexander Clark? Jerry Vitoni? Gregory Reynolds? You may find any one of them at fault, or you may find more than one of them at fault, or you may decide no one is at fault.

STOP HERE AND DECIDE THE CASE
BEFORE GOING FURTHER

---

[30]   Each state has its own set of jury instructions, as do the federal courts. In negligence cases, the basic content of the jury instructions does not change much substantively from state to state.

The Court's Decision follows on the next page.

The Court's Decision

Held: The jury found Alexander Clark and Jerry Vitoni primarily liable for Reynolds's injuries. The jury also found that Reynolds was partially at fault for his own injuries.

After a day and a half of deliberations, the jury returned a verdict in favor of Reynolds and awarded him $2,229,000. His primary monetary claim was that the injury he sustained to his hand cut short his baseball career. "The biggest problem was that I broke my index finger knuckle, the most important finger for throwing the ball," Reynolds said. He subsequently earned a degree in economics and now works in finance.

In regard to the apportionment of fault for Reynolds's injuries, the jury found as follows:

Clark	55 percent fault
Vitoni	40 percent fault
Reynolds	5 percent fault

As a result of this apportionment, Reynolds's monetary award was reduced by 5 percent.

One of the more interesting aspects of this case is Reynolds's decision to come back out of the house after retreating there into relative safety. On the one hand, Clark was banging against the door. On the other hand, Reynolds could have called the police and let them take care of the wild man at his door and likely not have sustained the injury that ruined his baseball career. How did you deal with this issue in your deliberations?

Jacobson v. United States

503 U.S. 540 (1992)

The Issue:

Where is the line between the government's agents inducing a person to commit a crime versus the individual subject's own independent inclinations to commit the crime?

This case involves a sensitive issue: child pornography. It also provides a valuable introduction to the subject of *government entrapment*. It examines just how far the government can go to test tendencies of someone to commit a crime. Even the Supreme Court justices who ultimately heard the case had a difficult time answering these questions, indicated by their deciding the matter in a 5-to-4 vote. Because the case can be presented without graphic descriptions, as well as my assumption that readers will have the maturity to deal with the difficult type of subject matter involved, the case is submitted for your consideration.

Keith Jacobson had an obvious interest in portrayals of young boys having sex. At one point, the fifty-six-year-old veteran-turned-farmer ordered and received two magazines containing photographs of nude preteen and teenage boys. When he ordered the magazines, he enclosed a note stating "If I like your product, I will order more later." At the time he received these magazines (before 1984), no existing law made the receipt of such materials illegal.

However, in 1984, Congress passed the Child Protection Act, which for the first time made it a federal offense to receive sexually explicit depictions of children through the mail.

Government agents gained access to the records of the bookstore from which Jacobson had previously obtained the two magazines. As a result of their review of the bookstore's records, they came across Jacobson's name and address.

During a two and one-half year period, various government agencies sent Jacobson solicitations from fictitious organizations and created a bogus pen pal to explore his willingness to purchase child pornography through the mail. Some of these mailings took the form of catalog solicitations, and others were supposed "surveys" inquiring about Jacobson's sexual preferences. None of the mailings actually described or offered depictions of children participating in sexual acts, and Jacobson never gave any response to the surveys indicating that he was interested in purchasing materials depicting child pornography. Rather, the mailings often claimed an interest in promoting sexual freedom and freedom of choice.

The first mailing sent from the American Hedonist Society (a fictitious organization created by the government) included a membership application. The mailing included a statement of the society's doctrine "that members had the 'right to share our philosophy, and finally that we have the right to seek pleasure without restrictions being placed on us by outdated puritan morality.'" Jacobson enrolled in the organization.

This mailing included a survey, which Jacobson also returned. In it, respondents were asked to rank their level of interest in sexual materials on a scale of one to four, with one being "really enjoy," to four, meaning "do not enjoy." To the question about the respondent's enjoyment of "[p]re-teen sex," Jacobson gave a rating of "two," but added that he was opposed to pedophilia.

During the ensuing twenty-six-month period, more surveys and catalog offers made their way to Jacobson's mailbox, all sent by the government. In one of those subsequent surveys, Jacobson indicated that his interest in "[p]reteen sex – homosexual" material was above average but not high.

After numerous such solicitations, Jacobson received a catalog from which he ordered a magazine, the content of which was described as: "11-year-old and 14-year-old boys get it on in every way possible." A note Jacobson included with his order stated "Will order other items later. I want to be discreet in order to protect you and me."

He was arrested when the magazine was delivered to his residence. A search of his house revealed no other materials other than items the government agencies had sent him and the two magazines he had legally bought before the law had changed.

The Trial:

At trial, Jacobson asserted the defense of government entrapment. He testified he had been curious about what would be depicted in the two magazines he had ordered legally (before 1984) and was surprised to find they contained nude photos of underage boys. He said he had thought the magazines would depict "young men 18 years or older." The boys depicted in the photos in the pre-1984 magazines were not posed in a sexual way. Rather, Jacobson stated, it looked to him like a nudist magazine since the photos were taken in a rural outdoor setting.

Likewise, he testified that while he knew the magazine he had ordered after 1984 and resulting in his arrest would contain young subjects, he had not expected it to contain photos of minors.

Nevertheless, he was convicted. He appealed the conviction, but the court of appeals affirmed the jury verdict.

The Applicable Law:

The Child Protection Act of 1984 "criminalizes the knowing receipt through the mails of a 'visual depiction [that] involves the use of a minor engaging in sexually explicit conduct'"[31]

---

[31]   18. U.S.C. Sec. 2252(a)(2)(A)

When a defendant asserts the defense of entrapment, the government has the burden of proving beyond a reasonable doubt that the petitioner was predisposed to break the law and was not entrapped. The jury in this case was given the following instruction on the issue of entrapment:

> If the defendant before contact with law-enforcement officers or their agents did not have any intent or disposition to commit the crime charged and was induced or persuaded by law-enforcement officers o[r] their agents to commit that crime, then he was entrapped. On the other hand, if the defendant before contact with law-enforcement officers or their agents did have an intent or disposition to commit the crime charged, then he was not entrapped even though law-enforcement officers or their agents provided a favorable opportunity to commit the crime or made committing the crime easier or even participated in acts essential to the crime.

What's your verdict? Was Jacobson improperly entrapped into committing an illegal act by the government's agents? Or before the government mailings, did Jacobson display a sufficiently independent leaning toward the purchase of materials depicting minor boys having sex such that a jury could reasonably find that he was not entrapped?

STOP HERE AND DECIDE THE CASE
BEFORE GOING FURTHER

The Court's Decision follows on the next page.

The Court's Decision

Held: The Supreme Court held the prosecution had failed to prove Jacobson had a proclivity toward purchasing child pornography independent of the government's acts; thus, finding the government had not overcome Jacobson's entrapment defense.

The Court's 5-to-4 decision overturned the jury's verdict. The Court said that in the government's agents' zeal to enforce the law, they may not originate a criminal design, implant in a person's mind the disposition to commit a criminal act, and then induce commission of a criminal act so that the government can prosecute. In this case, the Court noted, Jacobson was targeted for twenty-six months with repeated government mailings and communications. Thus, the government could not carry its burden to prove a predisposition on Jacobson's part absent the government's actions.

The majority opinion stated:

> Therefore, although he had become predisposed to break the law by May 1987 [when he purchased the magazine that resulted in his arrest], it is our view that the Government did not prove that this predisposition was independent and not the product of the attention that the Government had directed at petitioner since January 1985.

The justices voting with the minority pointed out that on both occasions when Jacobson ordered magazines, "he asked for opportunities to buy more . . . a reasonable jury could permissibly infer beyond a reasonable doubt that he was predisposed to commit the crime."

Katz v. United States

389 U.S. 347 (1967)

The Issue:

How much "privacy" should one expect when using a public phone booth?

"Please deposit twenty-five cents for the first three minutes." Remember the telephone booth? The caller would step into the small cubicle on the street corner, close the door, pick up the handset, drop some money in the coin slots, and place a call. But what happens when the government thinks someone is using the booth for criminal purposes? How "private" is your conversation in a public telephone booth? Even though telephone booths are rare these days, the privacy questions addressed in this case are still the subject of debate. The reasonableness of one's expectation of privacy plays a major role in the case you are about to decide.

Federal agents received information that Katz was illegally transmitting gambling information over the phone to clients in other states. Based on their surveillance of Katz, the FBI determined he would likely use a particular booth for a few minutes at the same time each morning to make the suspected gambling connections. Without first obtaining a warrant, agents attached an electronic listening and recording device to the *outside* of the phone booth Katz used.

The Trial:

Based on the recordings of only his end of the conversations, Katz was arrested and subsequently convicted under an eight-count indictment for the illegal transmission of wagering information.

Katz appealed his conviction, arguing the failure of the agents to first obtain a warrant from a neutral magistrate violated his Fourth Amendment right to be free from unreasonable searches and seizures. Therefore, he argued, the recordings could not be used as evidence against him. The court of appeals ruled that because there was not an actual physical intrusion into the booth itself—the police attached the listening device to the *outside* of the public phone booth—there was no Fourth Amendment violation.

Katz appealed to the United States Supreme Court.

The Applicable Law:

The Fourth Amendment to the Constitution states:

> The right of the people to be secure in their persons, houses, papers, and effects, against unreasonable searches and seizures, shall not be violated, and no Warrants shall issue, but upon probable cause, supported by Oath or affirmation, and particularly describing the place to be searched and the persons or things to be seized.

One of the first things to consider in deciding this case is whether or not the public phone booth would fall within the criteria of "persons, houses, papers, and effects" set out in the amendment. Katz would be on fairly solid ground in challenging the evidence if, for example, the FBI had acquired it by secretly placing a wiretap in his home without a warrant.

Or would he?

Is eavesdropping even subject to the Fourth Amendment regardless of how it is done? It is interesting to note that even though the drafters of the Constitution did not yet enjoy the benefits of the telephone, they still would have been aware of incursions into one's privacy by eavesdropping. Indeed, when the Constitution was drafted, eavesdropping was already considered an "ancient practice" historically condemned as a nuisance. Therefore, one might argue the drafters knowingly chose not to include it in the list of prohibited invasions set out in the Fourth Amendment.

Another issue for consideration in this case is whether or not Katz was entitled to a reasonable expectation of privacy in using a public phone booth. If he was not entitled to such an expectation, there would not likely be an illegal violation of his person in attaching the listening device without a warrant.

What's your verdict? Does the Fourth Amendment protection against unreasonable searches and seizures require the police to obtain a search warrant in order to place a wiretap on the outside of a public pay phone? If you decide it does, then you would rule in Katz's favor and toss out the evidence against him. If you decide it does not require a warrant before attaching the device, you would rule against Katz and his conviction would stand.

STOP HERE AND DECIDE THE CASE
BEFORE GOING FURTHER

The Court's Decision follows on the next page.

The Court's Decision

Held: The United States Supreme Court ruled the placing of a listening and recording device on the public phone booth without first obtaining a warrant violated Katz's Fourth Amendment rights. The evidence gained by the device was ruled inadmissible and his conviction was overturned.

In a 7-to-1 decision, the majority asserted that once Katz closed the doors to the phone booth, he displayed an indisputable expectation of privacy in the phone calls he placed. The justices found no import in the argument that the listening device was placed on the outside of the phone booth, and therefore did not physically invade Katz's private space.

The Court said,

> . . . [T]he Fourth Amendment protects people, not places. What a person knowingly exposes to the public, even in his own home or office, is not a subject of Fourth Amendment protection . . . But what he seeks to preserve as private, even in an area accessible to the public, may be constitutionally protected.

The fact that *words* were "seized" rather than *property* or *person* was not really an issue for the majority. They asserted a "seizure" could apply equally to one's words as to one's property.

The justices also noted that since the police had determined from their prior investigation that Katz was likely to use the phone booth on the date and time that he did, they could have first obtained a warrant for the placing of the wiretap. The majority was not moved by the government's argument that the agents had sufficient evidence in their possession to have obtained a warrant had they applied for one, so no harm, no foul. The majority dismissed this argument, noting the importance of obtaining an actual warrant:

Searches conducted without warrants have been held unlawful "notwithstanding facts unquestionably showing probable cause" . . . for the Constitution requires "that the deliberate, impartial judgment of a judicial officer . . . be interposed between the citizen and the police . . ."

Justice Hugo Black dissented. He asserted that the majority had rewritten the Fourth Amendment to improperly include "eavesdropping." He noted that the amendment only refers to searches and seizures of "persons, houses, papers, and effects."

Justice Black also argued that it is an improper interpretation of the Fourth Amendment to say it provides any kind of general right to privacy. Therefore, Justice Black asserted, Katz's expectation of privacy in using the phone booth should be of no import. "I will not distort the words of the Amendment in order to 'keep the Constitution up to date' or 'to bring it into harmony with the times,'" he said.

Postscript: The debate over the existence and extent of a right to privacy is as heated today as it was when the Court decided Katz's fate. In a 2018 Supreme Court case applying the right to privacy to the law of search and seizure, Justice Thomas, a conservative justice, referring to the 1967 phone booth case, wrote in his dissent:

> Jurists and commentators tasked with deciphering our jurisprudence have described the *Katz* regime as "an unpredictable jumble," "a mass of contradictions and obscurities," "all over the map," "riddled with inconsistency and incoherence," "a series of inconsistent and bizarre results that [the Court] has left entirely undefended," "unstable," "chameleon-like," "notoriously unhelpful," "a conclusion rather than a starting point for analysis," "distressingly unmanageable," "a dismal

failure," flawed to the core," "unadorned fiat," and "inspired by the kind of logic that produced Rube Goldberg's bizarre contraptions."[32]

Clearly, the fact that the *Katz* decision is still settled law is an irritant to Justice Thomas.

---

[32] *Carpenter vs. United States,* 138 S.Ct. 2206 (2018), the case from which Justice Thomas's remarks are drawn, is one of the cases included in this book.

Ohio Secretary of State (Husted) v. A. Philip Randolph Institute

138 S.Ct.1833 (2018)

The Issue:

To what extent is a state required to provide notice to a citizen that he or she is being dropped from the list of eligible voters?

This case arises from a challenge to Ohio's "use-it-or-lose-it" voting registration law.

In order to vote in the State of Ohio, one must be a resident of the state for the thirty days before an election as well as a resident of the county and precinct in which one intends to vote. To keep its voter registration records up to date, Ohio instituted a process for purging the state voter rolls of individuals it suspects have relocated. The process works like this:

1. Voters who have not voted for two years—whether in general, primary, special, federal, state, or local elections—are sent notices to confirm their registration.
2. If the state receives no response *and* the recipients of the notice do not vote at some time over the next four years, they are removed from the state rolls.

The plaintiffs, a voter who had been purged from the Ohio rolls and a pair of civil rights organizations (including the A. Philip Randolph Institute), filed suit against the Ohio Secretary of State, Jon Husted (the defendant), challenging the state's voter-roll maintenance procedure. The plaintiffs contend that the procedure unlawfully relies on a person's failure to vote as a "trigger" for commencing the process of clearing its voter rolls of allegedly stale information.

Larry Harmon, the individual plaintiff, usually voted only in presidential elections. But he was not happy with either of the 2012 presidential candidates, Obama or Romney, so he did not vote that year. A few years later, he went to vote on a marijuana legalization measure but was informed he had been removed from voter rolls because he had not voted in the past four-year period and had not returned the notice that was sent to him requesting he confirm his address.

The Trial:

Harmon said he did not remember ever receiving a notice from the state even though he had lived at the same address for over sixteen years. He asserted there were multiple actions that the state could have taken to verify his residence, such as checking property records, tax forms, and driver's license records. As quoted in an article written by Nina Totenberg for the NPR Online Newsletter (June 11, 2018), Harmon, a navy veteran said, "I earned the right to vote. Whether I use it or not is up to my personal discretion. They don't take away my right to buy a gun if I don't buy a gun."

While the district court held in favor of the state, the US Court of Appeals for the Sixth Circuit ruled in favor of Harmon and the civil rights groups, having determined that Ohio's rules were in violation of federal law. Ohio appealed that decision to the US Supreme Court.

The Applicable Law:

The federal government decided to involve itself in voter registration issues in 1993 when it enacted the National Voter Registration Act (NVRA). Congress' two main objectives in passing the act were (1) increasing voter registration and (2) removing ineligible persons from the voter rolls. Prior to the NVRA, there were states that removed voters from the rolls without providing the voter any notice. The NVRA sought to preclude this practice by prohibiting the removal of a voter's name from the registration rolls unless either:

(A) the registrant confirms in writing that he or she has moved or

(B) the registrant fails to return a preaddressed, postage-paid "return card" containing statutorily prescribed content.[33]

If the voter fails to return the card (step B above), the voter's name will be kept on the rolls for at least two general elections for federal office (usually about four years). If the voter does not either return the card or vote during that period, the states may then remove the voter from the rolls.

The act does not specifically set out the factors a state may or may not consider in sending out the return card, although it does make some suggestions. For example, a state may send out the cards to someone who has submitted a change of address notice to the post office. Some states send out a card to *every* registered voter at specified intervals.

The NVRA specifically provides that a state procedure "shall not result in the removal of the name of any person . . . by reason of the person's failure to vote." And another section of the act states "no registrant may be removed *solely* by reason of a failure to vote." (emphasis added)

Ohio argues that its procedure is in keeping with the law because it asserts that removal from the rolls primarily results from not responding to the return card rather than a failure to vote.

---

[33]   For purposes of deciding this case, you may assume that the card that Ohio sends out to voters meets the statutory content requirements.

However, the plaintiffs point out that Ohio's procedure for purging the voter rolls relies on a voter's failure to vote not once but twice—first as a "trigger" for initially sending out the return card, and again four years later (if the voter did not return the card) and the voter still has not voted.

In summary, the dispute over Ohio's voter registration maintenance system arises because it uses a voter's failure to vote as a trigger for sending the original return card. The plaintiffs' interpretation of the law at issue is that non-voting can be used as a basis for removing a voter from the rolls if the voter fails to return the card, but not as a basis for sending the card in the first place. Ohio, on the other hand, argues that its two-step process does not rely solely on a period of non-voting.

What's your verdict? Does Ohio's procedure for updating its voter rolls violate the National Voter Registration Act by using a failure to vote as the catalyst for sending out the "return card"?

STOP HERE AND DECIDE THE CASE
BEFORE GOING FURTHER

The Court's Decision follows on the next page.

The Court's Decision

Held: Ohio's voter list maintenance program does not violate the law.

The Supreme Court ruled in a 5-to-4 decision that the applicable laws only prohibit a procedure in which a failure to vote is the *sole reason* for purging voters from the registration lists. The justices said that there is no violation since Ohio's process requires *both* a period of non-voting *and* a failure to return the confirmation notice.

The plaintiffs noted a significant fault in the system. Their brief to the Supreme Court included statistics that demonstrate a high rate of non-returned cards by voters who have not moved. Many registered voters simply discarded the return card notifications, some believing them to be junk mail. Thus, the plaintiffs assert, the cards are, in reality, useless in determining if someone has moved. Their counsel had argued, "a notice that doesn't get returned" tells the state "absolutely nothing about whether the person has moved." The state's procedure, the plaintiffs contend, functionally removes people solely for non-voting. In that regard, Justice Breyer wrote in his dissenting opinion, "the purpose of our election process is not to test the fortitude and determination of the voter, but to discern the will of the majority."

Binyam Mohamed et al. v. Jeppesen Dataplan, Inc. and the United States of America

614 F.3d 1070 (9th Cir. 2010)

The Issue:

To what extent may the government, pursuant to a claim of "national security," refuse to produce relevant documents in a case?

Rendition: to transmit to another[34]

National security and principles of liberty, justice, and accountability come into conflict in this 2010 case involving the United States' *Extraordinary Rendition Program*. The suit was filed by several men who alleged they had been kidnapped and at least some of them tortured by the government in the course of our war on terror.

Binyam Mohamed, Abou Elkassim Britel, Ahmed Agiza, Mohamed Farag Ahmad Bashmilah, and Bisher At-Rawi (plaintiffs) all asserted that they were the subjects of a CIA-led program to apprehend foreign nationals and send them to various countries for detention and interrogation by United States and foreign officials. These actions were

---

[34] Merriam-Webster (2009). Rendition. In *Collegiate Dictionary*, 11th Edition, p. 1054

taken without any opportunity for a hearing before a neutral party or any opportunity to consult with legal counsel.

The plaintiffs asserted that this program was instituted in part as a method for the governments involved to subject the plaintiffs to torture and interrogation techniques that would not otherwise be allowed under the laws of the countries participating in the rendition activities. And, they pointed out, the Extraordinary Rendition Program was not itself a state secret as the program had been publicly acknowledged by the government, including by the president of the United States.

The Trial:

Plaintiffs contended that hundreds of pages of *publicly available information* supported their claim that defendant Jeppesen Dataplan Inc., a US corporation, provided planning and logistical support services for flights that transported the plaintiffs to the various detention facilities involved.

The plaintiffs asserted that Jeppesen Dataplan provided the assistance with actual or constructive knowledge of the purpose of the flights and the rendition program. It was alleged that Jeppesen representatives knew the plaintiffs "'would be subjected to forced disappearance, detention, and torture' by U.S. and foreign government officials."

The plaintiffs were prepared to show that at least one Jeppesen employee had admitted to having actual knowledge that the company was conducting extraordinary rendition flights for the government. They also produced a sworn statement by a former Jeppesen employee who said that the flights were sometimes referred to as "the torture flights" or the "spook flights." The plaintiffs sought damages against Jeppesen for aiding and abetting the US government.

The United States responded to the lawsuit by filing a motion to dismiss the complaint. CIA then director Gen. Michael Hayden submitted sworn statements in opposition to the lawsuit, asserting that "because highly classified information is central to the allegations and issues in this case, the risk is great that further litigation will lead to disclosures harmful to U.S. national security, and, accordingly, this case should be dismissed."

The district court granted the government's motion to dismiss, holding that the plaintiffs' claims clearly involved state secrets. On an appeal filed by the plaintiffs, a three-judge panel of the Ninth Circuit Court of Appeals overturned the district court's dismissal order. The justices said that the government had not provided a sufficient basis for dismissal under the state secrets doctrine, although they allowed for the possibility that the government might be able to do so in the future and then the motion to dismiss could be refiled.

The government requested the three-judge panel's decision be revisited by an eleven-judge panel of the Ninth Circuit (called an *en banc* hearing). The circuit court agreed to an *en banc* review, and that is the status of the case as it is put before you for your verdict.[35]

The Applicable Law:

In the early 1950s, a US military aircraft testing secret electronic equipment crashed. The widows of several civilian observers who had been on the flight sued the United States and requested production of the accident investigation report and copies of any statements provided by surviving crew members. In opposing the widows' request for documents, the Secretary of the Air Force filed a claim of privilege asserting that the documents involved a "highly secret mission." Another pleading filed by the government seeking to block the documents from being produced said it could not give up the materials "without hampering national security."

In denying the widows their requested documents, the Supreme Court set out what was to become the *Reynolds Privilege*: documents involving state secrets could, if the government objected, be withheld from the litigating parties. However, the Court said, it must then be decided whether or not the lawsuit could go forward absent the state

---

[35] An *en banc* review is a reconsideration of the three-judge panel's decision by the full panel of circuit court judges (in this case, eleven judges).

secret documents. The Supreme Court sent the *Reynolds* case back to the trial court to determine if the parties could still litigate the case involving the plane crash without any reference to the secret spy equipment the plane carried.

There are three issues that must be examined in *this* case in keeping with the *Reynolds* decision:

1. The government must assert a claim of privilege, which the government has done in this case. This first issue is not in dispute.
2. Do the documents that the government contends must be withheld involve state secrets and to what extent?
3. And if they are state secrets, can the action be litigated without relying on evidence that would necessarily reveal those secrets or press so closely upon them as to create an unjustifiable risk that they would be revealed? One must consider whether the plaintiffs would be able to prove all necessary elements of their claim *and* if the defendants can present a full defense without revealing state secrets.

The plaintiffs claimed that they could proceed because they could put on their case using publicly available information. The defendants contended that even though there is public information about Jeppesen's involvement in the rendition program, their defense would be impaired without the ability to respond to the allegations with evidence that would be considered state secrets.

What's your verdict? Should the plaintiffs' case be *dismissed* without further proceedings in the interest of national security?

STOP HERE AND DECIDE THE CASE
BEFORE GOING FURTHER

The Court's Decision follows on the next page.

The Court's Decision

Held: The eleven-judge panel of the Ninth Circuit Court of Appeals ordered the case dismissed.

In a 6-to-5 decision, the court said dismissal was "required under *Reynolds* because there is no feasible way to litigate Jeppesen's alleged liability *without creating an unjustifiable risk of divulging state secrets.*" (emphasis in original)

The majority recognized that the plaintiffs asserted they could prove their case with documents in the public domain and that the government was not contending that those public materials were state secrets. However, the court stated:

> . . . [W]e conclude that even assuming plaintiffs could establish their entire case *solely* through nonprivileged evidence – unlikely as that may be – any effort by Jeppesen to defend would unjustifiably risk disclosure of state secrets.

Further, the court noted that even if some of the materials had already been divulged by *non-government* sources, those materials could still be considered state secrets.

The dissenting justices expressed a concern for the state secret doctrine, generally: "The state secrets doctrine is a judicial construct without foundation in the Constitution, yet its application often trumps what we ordinarily consider to be due process of law."

The dissenters also pointed to instances of past abuse where documents had been stamped "Classified," not to protect state secrets but to protect the government from embarrassing disclosures. Therefore, any attempt to preclude the courts from hearing disputes in which state secrets *might* be involved should be the subject of careful consideration and a review of a more substantial and complete record than the justices presently had before them.

Therefore, the dissenting justices said, it was premature to dismiss the action in its present status. Rather, they argued, the proper thing to do was to send the matter back to the district court. In that forum, the court could better review whether the plaintiffs could have proceeded, and the defendants could have defended, *only* with evidence that would not harm national security interests.

Caetano v. Massachusetts

136 S.Ct. 1027 (2016)

The Issue:

Does the right to bear arms under the Second Amendment apply equally to electric stun guns as it does to other types of firearms?

What would a collection of constitutional disputes be without at least one Second Amendment "right to bear arms" case? Interpreting the Second Amendment to the United States Constitution has been divisive, not only for the general citizenry but also for the United States Supreme Court itself. The question presented here involves a citizen's right to bear a gun, specifically a "stun gun."

Jaime Caetano, a Massachusetts resident, believed she was being stalked by an abusive former boyfriend. Fearing a public confrontation and possible physical attack, she purchased a stun gun to carry in her purse. Massachusetts state law, however, banned the possession of an "electrical weapon." Here is how one court described a stun gun:

> . . . a black electronic device with two metal prongs and a switch. Once the switch was thrown, an electrical current appeared between the prongs. Stun guns are designed to stun a person with an electrical current after

the prongs are placed in direct contact with the person
and the switch is thrown.

On September 29, 2011, the manager of an Ashland, Massachusetts,
grocery store contacted police, asserting that there had been a possible
shoplifting incident at the store. The manager had detained one person
and told the police, upon their arrival, that a man and woman out in
the parking lot might have been involved as well. The manager pointed
to a man standing beside a car with a female occupant (Caetano).

While questioning the couple, the officers asked if they could search
Caetano's purse. She consented to the search, which led the officers to
discover the stun gun she carried. Caetano told the officers she carried
it for protection from her ex-boyfriend. She was, nevertheless, charged
with a violation of the Massachusetts law prohibiting possession of an
"electric weapon."

The Trial:

At trial, Caetano waived her right to have a jury decide the case.

She testified that she was homeless and living in a hotel. On at least
one prior occasion, she said, she had had to defend herself from the
ex-boyfriend during a confrontation by pointing the stun gun at him.

The judge found her guilty of the charge of possession of a stun gun.

Caetano appealed the guilty verdict. She argued that a citizen's
Second Amendment right to bear arms included the right to possess a
stun gun. The Massachusetts Supreme Judicial Court ruled against her
and affirmed her conviction.[36] It compared the stun gun to the kinds of
weapons the United States Supreme Court had previously held deserved
Second Amendment protection. The Massachusetts court determined
that the stun gun was not a military-related firearm and was not,
therefore, one entitled to protection under the Second Amendment's
"right to bear arms."

---

[36]   470 Mass. 774 (2014-2015)

Caetano applied for a hearing before the United States Supreme Court, requesting that the justices overturn the decision of the Massachusetts Supreme Judicial Court.

The Applicable Law:

The Massachusetts statute at issue:

> General Laws c. 140, Sec. 131J, forbids the private possession of a "portable device or weapon from which an electrical current, impulse, wave or beam may be directed, which current, impulse, wave or beam is designed to incapacitate temporarily, injure or kill" . . . Violation of this section is punishable "by a fine of not less than $500 nor more than $1,000 or by imprisonment in the house of correction for not less than [six] months nor more than [two and one-half] years, or by both such fine and imprisonment."

The Second Amendment states: "A well-regulated militia, being necessary to the security of a free State, the right of the people to keep and bear arms, shall not be infringed."

Two criteria for Second Amendment protection were particularly significant in the Massachusetts court's analysis: (1) stun guns were not in common use at the time of the enactment of the Second Amendment, and therefore the colonial framers could not have possibly considered stun guns protected firearms when the amendment was drafted,[37] and (2) the legislature could rationally ban use of stun guns in the interest of public health, safety, and welfare.

Two important United States Supreme Court cases interpreting the Second Amendment had an impact on Caetano's case: *United States v.*

---

[37] This is hardly an astonishing conclusion since a stun gun requires an electrical charge to function for its intended purpose.

Miller decided in 1939[38] and *District of Columbia v. Heller* decided in 2008.[39]

In the first of the two cases, *United States v. Miller,* Jack Miller and Frank Layton were arrested and charged with violation of the National Firearms Act of 1934 when they transported a sawed-off double-barrel twelve-gauge shotgun across state lines. Miller and Layton argued the arrests violated their Second Amendment rights. In upholding the guilty verdicts of the two men, the Supreme Court focused on the "well-regulated Militia" preface to the Second Amendment. The justices noted that there was no evidence that a sawed-off shotgun had "some reasonable relationship to the preservation or efficiency of a well-regulated militia." Thus, they held there was no Second Amendment protection afforded such a weapon.

Decided sixty-nine years after *Miller,* the *Heller* case involved a gun owner who challenged a Washington, DC, ordinance that outlawed possession of a pistol in one's home unless the gun was disabled by a trigger lock or by being disassembled. Heller challenged the city's ordinance on Second Amendment grounds.

In considering the prefacing phrase of the Second Amendment, the *Heller* Court reviewed what would have constituted a "militia" at the time of the drafting of the Constitution. It noted that many of the delegates were afraid to give the federal government the sole authority to raise an army. The colonial framers felt that there needed to be protections for the state militias as a counterweight to the federal authorities. In order to protect the existence of the militias, the drafters created the Second Amendment to preclude the federal government from disarming the state's citizen soldiers—the people who comprised the militias.

But the majority of justices in *Heller* ultimately determined that—in direct contrast to the earlier *Miller* decision—the amendment's protection of the right to bear arms was unconnected with service in a militia.

---

[38]   307 U.S. 174 (1939)

[39]   554 U.S. 570 (2008)

The *Heller* Court also ruled that the types of weapons eligible for Second Amendment protection are not confined to the types of weapons that were in existence at the time the amendment was ratified. The justices, however, noted that "Like most rights, the Second Amendment right is not unlimited . . . the right was not a right to keep and carry any weapon whatsoever in any manner whatsoever and for whatever purpose."

What's your verdict? Was Caetano's right to possess the stun gun protected by the Second Amendment to the United States Constitution?

STOP HERE AND DECIDE THE CASE
BEFORE GOING FURTHER

The Court's Decision follows on the next page.

The Court's Decision

Held: A citizen's right to "bear" a stun gun is guaranteed under the Second Amendment.

In a strong showing of support for the importance of precedent in our justice system, the Supreme Court issued a two-page (unsigned) order summarily setting aside the holding of the Massachusetts Supreme Judicial Court. Acknowledging that *Heller* was the governing case on the issue, the justices granted Caetano's request to consider her case, and then, without further proceedings, said, "the judgment of the Supreme Judicial Court of Massachusetts is vacated, and the case is remanded for further proceedings not inconsistent with this opinion."

In ruling in favor of Caetano, the Supreme Court, citing *Heller*, strongly disagreed with the Massachusetts court's reliance on the fact that stun guns were not in use at the time the Second Amendment was enacted and that stun guns were not readily adaptable by the military. The justices said that the first assertion was "inconsistent with *Heller's* clear statement that the Second Amendment 'extends . . . to arms . . . that were not in existence at the time of the founding,'" and *Heller* had likewise rejected the claim that Second Amendment protections applied only to weapons useful in warfare.

When the case returned to the Massachusetts court, Caetano was found not guilty of the charge against her.

Immigration and Naturalization Service v. Elias-Zacarias

502 U.S. 478 (1992)

The Issue:

In seeking asylum in the United States, did an eighteen-year-old Guatemalan provide sufficient evidence that he would be prosecuted because of his political opinions if deported to his native country?

Elias-Zacarias was a native of Guatemala. In July of 1987, he was apprehended attempting to enter the United States without proper documentation. He requested asylum.

When Elias-Zacarias was eighteen and living in Guatemala, armed and uniformed guerrillas came to his home and asked him and his parents to join with them, but all three refused. The guerillas told the family they should think it over. The family was advised that the rebels would return.

Elias-Zacarias did not want to join the guerrillas because the guerrillas were against the government, and he was afraid the government would retaliate against him and his family if he joined the guerrillas. Instead, he left Guatemala, fearing the guerrillas would return and kill him. Indeed, after his departure from the country, his family reported the guerrillas had twice returned in further efforts to recruit him.

The Hearing:

In his asylum petition, Elias-Zacarias argued the acts of the guerrillas constituted persecution on account of his political opinions. The Board of Immigration Appeals denied his request for asylum.

However, when Elias-Zacarias appealed that decision, the court of appeals reversed the INS Board, holding that Elias-Zacarias was entitled to asylum. The appellate justices ruled a guerrilla organization's forced conscription constituted persecution on account of one's political opinion and Elias-Zacarias's fear of persecution if he had to return to Guatemala was a valid one. In the opinion of the appeals court:

. . . [A] guerrilla organization's attempt to conscript a person into its military forces necessarily constitutes "persecution on account of . . . political opinion," because "the person resisting forced recruitment is expressing a political opinion hostile to the persecutor and because the persecutors' motive in carrying out the kidnapping is political."

The INS argued Elias-Zacarias failed to show a political motive for his unwillingness to return to Guatemala. It argued his real claim was that the government would retaliate against him and his family if he joined the guerrillas. The INS asserted Elias-Zacarias failed to show that the guerrillas believed that his refusal was *politically* based.

The INS appealed to the United States Supreme Court.

The Applicable Law:

The issue in this case is whether a guerrilla organization's attempt to coerce a person into performing military service necessarily constitutes "persecution on account of . . . political opinion." Section 208(a) of the Immigration and Nationality Act[40] authorizes the Attorney General to grant asylum to an alien who is unable or unwilling to return to his home country because of persecution or a well-founded fear of

---

[40]   8 U.S.C. Section 1158(a)

persecution on account of race, religion, nationality, membership in a particular social group, or political opinion.

What's your verdict? For the INS, consequently Elias-Zacarias would be deported back to Guatemala? Or for Elias-Zacarias, in which case he would be granted asylum and allowed to stay in the United States?

STOP HERE AND DECIDE THE CASE
BEFORE GOING FURTHER

The Court's Decision

Held: A guerrilla organization's attempt to coerce a person into
performing military service does not constitute "persecution on account
of . . . political opinion" under the Immigration and Nationality Act.

In a 6-to-3 decision, the Supreme Court agreed with the INS that
Elias-Zacarias should be deported to Guatemala.

Persecution on account of political opinion is not established by
the fact that the coercing guerrillas had "political" motives. Even a
person who supported the guerrilla's movement might resist military
combat. To satisfy the political opinion-based asylum requirements,
the persecution must be on account of the *victim's* political opinion,
not the persecutors'. The Court stated that the mere existence of a
generalized political motive underlying the guerrillas' forced recruitment
was inadequate to establish the proposition that Elias-Zacarias feared
persecution on account of *his* political opinions, rather than simply his
refusal to fight with the guerillas.

The Supreme Court noted there may be many reasons a person does
not join a guerilla organization, "fear of combat, a desire to remain with
one's family and friends, a desire to earn a better living in civilian life,
to mention only a few."

The majority wrote:

> The record in the present case not only failed to show
> a political motive on Elias-Zacarias' part; it showed
> the opposite. He testified that he refused to join the
> guerrillas because he was afraid that the government
> would retaliate against him and his family if he did
> so. Nor is there any indication (assuming, *arguendo*, it
> would suffice)[41] that the guerrillas erroneously *believed*
> that Elias-Zacarias' refusal was politically based.
> (emphasis in original)

---

[41]   *arguendo*: for the sake of argument

The dissenting justices believed Elias-Zacarias had proved his claim by credible evidence that he feared for his life if he was returned to Guatemala. As to the issue of whether this fear was based on political opinion, the dissenters stated:

> A political opinion can be expressed negatively as well as affirmatively. A refusal to support a cause—by staying home on election day, by refusing to take an oath of allegiance, or by refusing to step forward at an induction center – can express a political opinion as effectively as an affirmative statement or affirmative conduct. Even if the refusal is motivated by nothing more than a simple desire to continue living an ordinary life with one's family, it is the kind of political expression that the asylum provisions of the statute were intended to protect.

Payne v. Tennessee

501 U.S. 808 (1991)

The Issue:

Does the introduction of evidence as to the impact of a murder on the surviving victims violate the Eighth Amendment's guarantee of due process?

This case arises from an Eighth Amendment challenge to evidence the prosecution presented during a capital murder sentencing hearing.[42] It serves as a good primer on the concept of *stare decisis*—the important policy of deciding cases consistent with established precedent—and when it might be proper to overturn prior decisions rather than follow them.

A butcher knife was used to brutally bludgeon Charisse Christopher and her two-year-old daughter, Lacie, to death in their own apartment. Charisse's three-year-old son, Nicholas, was also attacked but survived. The Christophers lived across the hallway from Pervis Tyrone Payne's girlfriend. The prosecution asserted that Payne had spent the earlier part of the day injecting cocaine and drinking beer. It was alleged that Payne had entered Charisse's apartment and began making sexual advances,

---

[42]   A "capital" offense is one in which the sentencing options include the death penalty.

which Charisse had rebuffed. Although professing his innocence, Payne was ultimately arrested, tried, and convicted for the murders and attempted murder. Because there were multiple victims, the state sought the death penalty during the sentencing hearing that followed the trial.

The Sentencing Hearing:

During the hearing to determine whether Payne should be sentenced to death or life imprisonment, Payne produced three witnesses that testified as to his good character in an effort to demonstrate that the death penalty would be inappropriate: his mother and father, and a friend from Payne's church, Bobbie Thomas (Payne's girlfriend). He also put on the stand a clinical psychologist, Dr. John T. Hutson. Dr. Hutson testified that Payne had a low IQ test score and that he was "mentally handicapped."

During the penalty phase, the state elicited testimony from the decedent's mother:

> [Nicholas] cries for his mom. He doesn't seem to understand why she doesn't come home. And he cries for his sister Lacie. He comes to me many times during the week and asks me, Grandmama, do you miss my Lacie. And I tell him yes. He says, I'm worried about my Lacie.

During closing argument, the prosecutor asserted:

> . . . No one will ever know about Lacie Jo because she never had the chance to grow up. Her life was taken from her at the age of two years old. So, no there won't be a high school principal to talk about Lacie Jo Christopher and there won't be anybody to take her to her high school prom. And there won't be anybody there – there won't be her mother there or Nicholas'

mother there to kiss him at night. His mother will never kiss him good night or pat him as he goes off to bed, or hold him and sing him a lullaby.

The jury voted for, and the judge imposed, the death penalty on Payne. He appealed his case. The Tennessee State Supreme Court affirmed the sentencing judge's decision and let the penalty of death stand. The state supreme court concluded that "any violation of Payne's rights under [the prior Supreme Court decisions] 'was harmless beyond a reasonable doubt.'" Payne appealed to the United States Supreme Court.

The Applicable Law:

Payne's attorneys were quick to point out that prior well-established Supreme Court decisions had ruled that testimony and argument about the impact of the crime on the *victims* violated a defendant's Eighth Amendment rights in a capital sentencing hearing, and was therefore not admissible.[43]

The Eighth Amendment to the United States Constitution prohibits the imposition of "cruel and unusual punishments." This prohibition is at issue in this case because the dispute involves evidence presented in a *sentencing* hearing, the hearing that determines a defendant's *punishment.*

Established precedent mandates that in a capital sentencing hearing, the *defendant* must be allowed to offer evidence as to mitigating circumstances (such as a violent upbringing) that might lead a jury to vote for life imprisonment rather than the death penalty.

---

[43]   This case only involves the constitutionality of victim impact evidence presented during a capital offense sentencing hearing, a hearing to determine if the defendant (already found guilty) will receive a life sentence or the death penalty. Victim impact evidence in other types of criminal cases when the death penalty is not at issue was not challenged nor at issue in this case.

In *Booth v. Maryland*[44] the defendant had robbed and murdered an elderly couple. The state had a victim impact statement prepared, which was submitted to the jury during the sentencing hearing. The jury imposed the death penalty.

The Supreme Court ruled in a 5-to-4 decision that placing such evidence before a sentencing jury violated Booth's Eighth Amendment rights, and the Court overturned his death penalty. The Court observed that in a capital sentencing case (due to the finality of the death penalty), each defendant must be considered as a "uniquely individual human being." The factors the jury should be looking at are the "character of the individual and the circumstances of the crime." The *Booth* Court held that:

> To the extent that victim impact evidence presents "factors about which the defendant was unaware, and that were irrelevant to the decision to kill," the Court concluded, it has nothing to do with the "blameworthiness of a particular defendant."

Finally, the *Booth* Court asserted that victim impact evidence in a capital sentencing hearing allows for the possibility that juries would impose harsher sentences (death) when the *victims* are "assets to their community" than would be imposed when the *victims* might be considered "less worthy."

The second prior Supreme Court decision related to the question at hand, *South Carolina v. Gathers*,[45] took the *Booth* decision one step further and clarified that the prosecution may not refer to victim impact issues during the closing argument (as opposed to the evidentiary stage which *Booth* addressed) for the same reasons as set forth in *Booth*.

In arguing to the Court that Payne's death sentence should be affirmed, Tennessee asserted that *Booth* and *Gathers* were wrongly decided, and therefore the Supreme Court ought to overturn those

---

[44]   482 U.S. 496 (1987)

[45]   490 U.S. 805 (1989)

rulings. The state argued that victim impact evidence in a capital murder sentencing hearing was fair game in order to provide a counterbalance to the evidence the defense is allowed to present on mitigating factors in the defendant's life put forth to avoid the death penalty. Tennessee pointed out that both *Booth* and *Gathers* were decided by a bare one-vote margin, and that there were strong dissents issued in both cases contesting the basis for the decisions.

Our judicial system, on both the state and federal level, values the principle known as *stare decisis*. To provide order to the system of justice and to best ensure that all citizens (especially judges) know what the law is when considering their actions, the courts rely heavily upon precedent in deciding cases. *Booth* and *Gathers,* for example, were "precedents" in the area of Eighth Amendment law and the admissibility of evidence in a penalty phase hearing. The United States Supreme Court has said this about the principle of *stare decisis*:

> *Stare decisis* is the preferred course because it promotes the evenhanded, predictable, and consistent development of legal principles, fosters reliance on judicial decisions, and contributes to the actual and perceived integrity of the judicial process. [citations omitted] Adhering to precedent "is usually the wise policy, because in most matters it is more important that the applicable rule of law be settled than it be settled right."

However, there is nothing that prohibits the Supreme Court from changing its mind and overturning a prior decision. The Supreme Court has also said, "*Stare decisis* is not an [unchallengeable] command . . ." If a subsequent sitting court believes that prior precedent is wrong, it has the right to correct that perceived wrong.

A good example is the 1896 case of *Plessy v. Ferguson*.[46] At issue in the *Plessy* case was a Louisiana law entitled the Separate Car Act. It *required* separate railway cars for blacks and whites. By a 7-to-1 vote,

---

[46]   163 U.S. 537 (1896)

the United States Supreme Court found the act to be constitutional, holding that separate treatment did not necessarily mean unequal treatment – noting that there was not a significant difference between the white and black railway cars. *Plessy* remained the law of the land for fifty-eight years. It was not until the school desegregation case of *Brown v. Board of Education*,[47] decided in 1954, that the Supreme Court overturned the *Plessy* decision when it held that separate was not, in fact, equal, and that *Plessy* was wrongly decided.

Returning to the case at hand, the issue is not just whether one believes that *Booth* and *Gathers* were wrongly decided, but rather whether they were so inconsistent with the Constitution that even though a majority of justices believed them to be correct decisions at the time, they should be reversed and victim impact evidence should be permitted in a capital sentencing hearing. In the case now before you, Payne will succeed in his appeal (due to precedent) unless you decide to overturn the previous cases.

What's your verdict? Should *Booth* and *Gathers* be overturned and the victim impact evidence admitted? Or were Payne's Eighth Amendment rights violated by the introduction of evidence about the impact of the murders on the victims?

STOP HERE AND DECIDE THE CASE
BEFORE GOING FURTHER

---

[47]   347 U.S. 483 (1954)

The Court's Decision

Held: Allowing evidence of the impact of the murders on the victims does not violate Payne's Eighth Amendment rights, notwithstanding prior cases to the contrary.

In its 6-to-3 decision, the Supreme Court took the unusual step of overruling both *Booth* and *Gathers*. In defense of their stepping away from the principle of *stare decisis* and rejecting precedent, the majority noted that both *Booth* and *Gathers* were decided by only a one-vote margin (i.e., 5-to-4), and that the dissenters in both those cases had presented strong arguments in opposition to the ultimate holdings. In addition, the majority noted that several subsequent state and federal decisions had challenged the efficacy of both *Booth* and *Gathers*. In short, the majority believed that the two prior cases had been wrongly decided.

In his dissenting opinion (with whom Justice Blackmun joined), Justice Stevens wrote:

> Our cases provide no support whatsoever for the majority's conclusion that the prosecutor may introduce evidence that sheds no light on the defendant's guilt or moral culpability, and thus serves no purpose other than to encourage jurors to decide in favor of death rather than life on the basis of their emotions rather than their reason.

Postscript: In August of 2021, thirty years after the Supreme Court decided his case, Payne was still an occupant of Tennessee's death row and still maintaining his innocence. His advocates now assert that Payne has an intellectual disability. This new assertion is important because of a subsequent change in Tennessee law.

In May of 2021, the governor had signed a bill that *retroactively* prohibits the execution of an intellectually disabled person. A petition was then filed on Payne's behalf, claiming that he should not be executed because of his mental disability. (Payne had not previously filed such a claim within the existing deadline for doing so under the prior law. But under the new retroactive law, missing that earlier deadline no longer prohibits Payne from asserting the mental disability claim.)

A hearing on Payne's new petition was argued before the Shelby County Court in June of 2021. The judge ruled that Payne was to be examined by a mental health expert to determine if he does, in fact, suffer from an intellectual disability. In November of 2021, the Shelby County district attorney conceded that Payne has an intellectual disability, and therefore cannot be executed. The county court ordered Payne's death sentence set aside. A resentencing hearing will be set.

Timbs v. Indiana

139 S.Ct. 682 (2019)

Grant County Superior Court Cause No. 27D01-1308-MI-92 (2020)

The Issue:

Is it a violation of the Eighth Amendment's prohibition against "excessive fines" for the police to confiscate the Land Rover of an alleged drug dealer when it is undisputed that no funds related to the drug dealing were used to purchase the SUV?

Tyson Timbs, who had no prior criminal record, was arrested for dealing in a controlled substance and conspiracy to commit theft. Timbs became addicted to opioids after his podiatrist prescribed him hydrocodone for persistent foot pain in 2007. Eventually, his dependency led him to use a far more dangerous opiate: heroin. Despite making several attempts at overcoming his addiction, he was arrested in 2013 after arranging to sell heroin on three occasions to undercover police officers. There is no evidence that he ever attempted to sell drugs to any third parties *other than* the undercover officers.

At the time of Timbs's arrest, the police seized a Land Rover LR2 SUV Timbs had purchased in October of 2013 for $42,000 with money he received from a life insurance policy when his father died. Over a four-month period, Timbs made multiple trips within Indiana in the SUV, transporting the heroin he was using and selling. Unfortunately for Timbs, his "customers" were undercover police officers conducting a sting operation.

Indiana sought civil forfeiture of Timbs's vehicle on the grounds that the SUV had been used to transport the illicit heroin. The Land Rover had about 15,000 more miles on it at that time of Timbs's arrest than it had when Timbs purchased it, and was the only asset to his name.

Timbs ultimately pled guilty to felony dealing and conspiracy to commit theft. He was sentenced to one year of home confinement, five years of probation, required to attend a court-supervised addiction-treatment program, and to pay approximately $1,200 in fees and costs. He received about the lightest sentence one could receive for the Class B felony he committed. The charges could have led to a maximum $10,000 fine and up to twenty years in prison.

The Civil Forfeiture Proceedings:

In a separate civil proceeding, Timbs challenged the vehicle forfeiture. He argued that the value of the vehicle was more than four times the amount of the statutory fine for the charges levied against him, and was therefore disproportionate to the gravity of his offense. Taking the vehicle under these circumstances amounted to a violation of the Eighth Amendment's prohibition of "excessive fines," he contended. Timbs also noted that the police could have arrested him for possession of heroin, but instead chose to set up the drug sales resulting in the more serious charges.

The state argued that the forfeiture penalty was not so disproportional as to violate the Eighth Amendment, and that impounding the vehicle was not really a *fine* since it involved *property* rather than money.[48] The

---

[48]   Indiana also argued that the Eighth Amendment did not apply to the states but only to the federal government. That limited issue went to the United States Supreme Court, which ruled that the Eighth Amendment *was* applicable to the states. The Court traced the long history of prohibiting excessive fines dating back to 1215 and the Magna Carta. The Court held the Eighth Amendment's

state produced evidence that the value of the Land Rover at the time of Timbs's arrest was about $35,000, and that Timbs spent about $30,000 in expenses related to his drug use and the sales to the undercover officers. Thus, the state opined, the forfeiture of the $35,000 Land Rover was not *grossly* disproportional to the offense involved.

The two sides debated the weight to be given to the fact that the sales were only to law enforcement agents. On the one hand, Timbs did not know that they were officers; he believed he was selling to other addicts. On the other hand, would Timbs have sold drugs to anyone if the police had not initiated the transactions in the first place?

The Applicable Law:

The Eighth Amendment to the United States Constitution provides in relevant part: "excessive bail shall not be required, nor excessive fines imposed, nor cruel and unusual punishments inflicted."

Indiana State Statute 34-24-1 provides in relevant part:

> The following may be seized: (1) All vehicles . . . if they are used or are intended for use by the person, or persons in possession of them to transport or in any manner to facilitate the transportation of the following: (A) A controlled substance for the purpose of committing, attempting to commit, or conspiring to commit any of the following: . . . (i) Dealing in or manufacturing cocaine or a narcotic drug.

Primarily, there are two kinds of disputes that courts address: criminal and civil. Criminal cases involve people charged with breaking the law, and can result in fines and/or imprisonment. Whereas civil

---

"excessive fines" clause set out a fundamental right, making it applicable to the states. Having ruled the Eighth Amendment applied to the states, the Supreme Court ordered the matter returned to the lower courts to determine whether the forfeiture of the SUV violated the Eighth Amendment.

cases involve disputes over such things as contracts, money, property, or injuries. A person charged in a criminal case must be provided with counsel if the person cannot afford one. A person does not have the right to a court-appointed attorney in a civil case.

Various states have enacted "civil forfeiture" laws (such as Indiana's 34-24-1 above). These laws, it is argued, are meant to prevent criminals from keeping property that was in some form or fashion involved in their crimes. For example, the coast guard might impound a boat that was used for drug smuggling. Sometimes an accused's bank account is impounded as the state argues that it represents the monetary reward for criminal activity. Many civil seizures take place without any formal criminal charges being filed against the property owners. In some states, a person does not have to be arrested nor tried nor convicted to have property seized. There must merely be some indication of illegal activity taking place. Since these laws are considered "civil" in nature, the many protections provided an accused in a criminal proceeding do not apply in a civil forfeiture action.

For the state to prevail on its assertion that the forfeiture of Timbs's vehicle does not violate the Excessive Fines Clause it must meet two requirements: (1) the Timbs's property must be the actual means by which the offense was committed, and (2) the harshness of the forfeiture penalty must not be grossly disproportional to the gravity of the offense and the claimant's culpability for the property's misuse. (The first of the two requirements is not in dispute: Timbs admitted that he used the SUV for transporting the drugs.)

In this case, the only issue you will have to consider is the second of those two requirements: Was the taking of the SUV grossly disproportional to the offense committed?

What's your verdict? Was the forfeiture of Tyson Timbs's vehicle a constitutionally excessive fine?

STOP HERE AND DECIDE THE CASE
BEFORE GOING FURTHER

The Court's Decision follows on the next page.

The Court's Decision

Held: The Grant County Superior Court judge ruled in Timbs's favor, holding that compelled forfeiture of the $35,000 Land Rover violated the Eighth Amendment.

In its April 2020 ruling, the court noted not only the significance of the disproportionate value of the vehicle compared to the $10,000 maximum fine for the charges brought against Timbs, but also that the source of the funds for purchasing the SUV was not Timbs's drug trafficking but rather the life insurance policy that paid out at the time of his father's death. Thus, the truck was not some sort of "ill-gotten gain." Finally, the court was also guided by the fact that the only people to whom Timbs ever attempted to sell drugs were the officers involved in the sting operation. There were no other "victims." Of course, there is a negative impact on society in selling illicit drugs, the court acknowledged, but Timbs's transgression was relatively minor since he sold only to law enforcement agents in which the agents initiated the transaction. His attorneys suggest that the catalyst for this whole episode was the police initially seeing someone they believed to be an addict driving an upscale Land Rover, and thereby jumping to the conclusion that Timbs was a drug dealer.

The court held that the "seizure of the Land Rover was excessively punitive and unduly harsh," and ordered the vehicle be turned over to Timbs immediately—seven years after it was taken by the authorities.

Many civil libertarians argue that civil forfeiture laws are overused, in part, because the governmental agencies have found the sale of forfeited items to be a significant source of revenue. Law enforcement agencies may have an incentive to proceed with forfeiture procedures to maximize profits rather than to address public safety. Government entities have found that raising funds through civil forfeiture proceedings is a better "political" option than raising taxes.[49]

---

[49]   A brief filed in the *Timbs* case by, among other groups, the ACLU, references an incident in which a small vice squad in Bal Harbor, Florida—a town of 3,300

There is also opposition to civil forfeiture laws on the grounds that most permit impounding the property upon arrest rather than after the charges have been proven and the owner convicted of the charges. Often a court hearing to allow the confiscation is only held if the accused files a challenge to the impoundment. Since these are technically *civil* matters rather than *criminal*, and owners who want their property back are not entitled to a court-appointed lawyer, it may well be impractical to hire a lawyer to challenge the forfeiture as the lawyer's fees may exceed the value of the property.

Postscript: Timbs, who is now employed, drug-free, and gives anti-drug talks to students and legislative committees, stated in a press release from the Institute for Justice:

> To me, the State's refusal to give back my car has never made sense; if they're trying to rehabilitate me and help me help myself, why do you want to make things harder by taking away the vehicle I need to meet with my parole officer or go to a drug recovery program or go to work? Forfeiture only makes it more challenging for people in my position to clean up and be contributing members of society.

---

residences—earned nearly $50 million through civil forfeitures over a three-year period. That money ended up being used for such things as luxury car rentals, first-class plane tickets, and a $20,000 drug-prevention beach party, according to the brief.

Randy White (Warden) v. Roger Wheeler

136 S.Ct. 456 (2015)

The Issue:

What constitutes an "impartial jury" in a death penalty case?

In cases where the defendant faces a possible sentence of death, potential jurors who, because of their moral beliefs, state they could never vote for the death penalty may be removed from the panel of potential jurors. The issue, however, is not often that simple, as the case you are about to decide demonstrates.

In October of 1997, Nigel Malone and Nairobi Warfield were both found dead inside their apartment in Louisville, Kentucky. Malone had been stabbed nine times. Warfield had been beaten and strangled to death. A pair of scissors protruded from her neck. Roger Wheeler was arrested and went on trial for the double murder.

During jury selection in his case, the judge excused a juror after concluding that the juror could not give "sufficient assurance of neutrality or impartiality in considering whether the death penalty should be imposed." Was the judge's ruling as to this juror correct, or were defendant Wheeler's rights violated by the judge's ruling?

It would be helpful to look at the applicable law in this case before you read the specific questions and answers that gave rise to the juror being excused.

The Applicable Law:

The Sixth Amendment to the US Constitution guarantees to a defendant an impartial jury.

This case is an appeal to the federal courts from a decision of the Kentucky State Supreme Court. Under federal law, relief from an order from a state court is authorized only when a prisoner can show that "the state court's ruling on the claim being presented in federal court was so lacking in justification that there was an error well understood and comprehended in existing law beyond any possibility for fairminded disagreement."

Voir dire is the process by which the lawyers and the court question and decide who among all the potential jurors on a panel will ultimately sit on the actual jury hearing the case. During *voir dire,* the judge and the attorneys are given an opportunity to ask each potential juror questions related to the juror's opinions on a variety of matters to determine if the juror can be "fair and impartial." (Actually, the lawyers are trying to determine which jurors would most favorably view their particular client's position. An attorney would be fine with a juror who was not "fair and impartial" if the juror's responses indicated he or she would favor that attorney's client.) When a juror's answers *clearly* indicate to the judge that the juror could not fairly weigh the evidence and appropriately apply it to the law at issue, the juror may be removed from the potential jury panel for "cause" upon motion by one of the parties.

In addition, each side gets a specific and limited number of peremptory strikes in which, unlike strikes for cause, the parties may request potential jurors be excused without having to give a reason. For strategic purposes, attorneys want jurors whom they would prefer not to sit on the jury removed from the panel of potential jurors by the judge for cause as those types of strikes do not count against their limited number of peremptory strikes. On the other hand, an attorney wants the *opposing side* to have to use up one of their limited peremptory strikes to excuse a potential juror.

The matter you will be deciding involves a juror who was removed for cause at the request of the prosecution over the objection of the defendant. The defense argued that the prosecution should have had to use one of their limited peremptory challenges rather than have the potential juror excused by the judge for cause.

The next principle of law to consider is the standard for reviewing a potential juror's views on the death penalty as expressed during *voir dire*. In that respect, a jury should be composed of individuals who are neither "uncommonly willing to condemn a man to die" nor "substantially impaired in his or her ability to impose the death penalty."

The court is permitted a degree of interpretation in reviewing a jury candidate's responses. Potential jurors may be inhibited for one reason or another from making a direct and unequivocal expression of their beliefs regarding the death penalty. However, where true ambiguity exists, the trial court "is entitled to resolve [the ambiguity] in favor of the State" and remove the juror for cause.

Within that framework, at issue are the questions and answers of the lawyers and the potential juror in this case related to the juror's opinion about the death penalty.

Questions & Answers During Jury Selection:

In response to the judge asking the juror involved in this matter about his personal beliefs on the death penalty, the juror responded: "I'm not sure that I have formed an opinion one way or the other. I believe there are arguments on both sides of . . . it."

When asked by the prosecutor about his ability to consider "all available penalties," the juror stated that he had "never been confronted with that situation in a . . . real-life sense of having to make that kind of determination. . . . So it's difficult for me to judge how I would I guess act, uh." Seeking to clarify that response, the prosecutor asked if the juror was saying that he was not sure he could consider the death penalty as an option. The juror stated in response, "I think that would be the most accurate way I could answer your question."

During defense counsel's questioning, the juror said he saw himself as "a bit more contemplative on the issue of taking a life and, uh, whether or not we have the right to take that life." He subsequently said that he could consider all the penalty options.

The prosecution moved to strike the juror for cause based on his responses related to the death penalty. The defense opposed the motion, citing the juror's statement that he could consider all the penalty options.

The judge took the motion under review. Her handwritten notes of the exchange included comments that the juror "could consider [the] entire range" of penalties, that she did not "see him as problematic," and that she did not "hear him say that he couldn't realistically consider the death penalty."

The next day the judge granted the prosecution's motion to strike the juror for cause. She said that when she went back and actually read the testimony at issue, she was persuaded to grant the motion to strike largely as a result of the exchange between the prosecutor and the juror when the prosecutor had asked if the juror was saying that he was not sure he could consider the death penalty as an option and the juror had responded, "I think that would be the most accurate way I could answer your question."

In the ensuing trial, Wheeler was convicted of both murders and sentenced to death.

His defense team appealed the judge's decision to strike the juror for cause. Wheeler filed a petition asking the court to issue an order to Randy White, the prison warden, to set Wheeler free based on the error Wheeler asserted took place during trial. The Kentucky State Supreme Court held in favor of the state and found the judge's dismissal of the juror did not violate Wheeler's rights.

Wheeler appealed to the Sixth Circuit Federal Court of Appeals. He argued that when looking at the totality of the juror's comments, the potential juror may have sounded conflicted at times, but ultimately he had said he could consider the death penalty. The court of appeals held that the exclusion of the juror was an unreasonable application of the law, and reversed the trial court.

The warden then appealed the case to the United States Supreme Court.

What's your verdict? Was the dismissal of the potential juror for cause a violation of Wheeler's Sixth Amendment right to an impartial jury? If you answer this question "yes," Wheeler's sentence is overturned. If you answer this question "no," then Wheeler's death sentence is affirmed.

STOP HERE AND DECIDE THE CASE
BEFORE GOING FURTHER

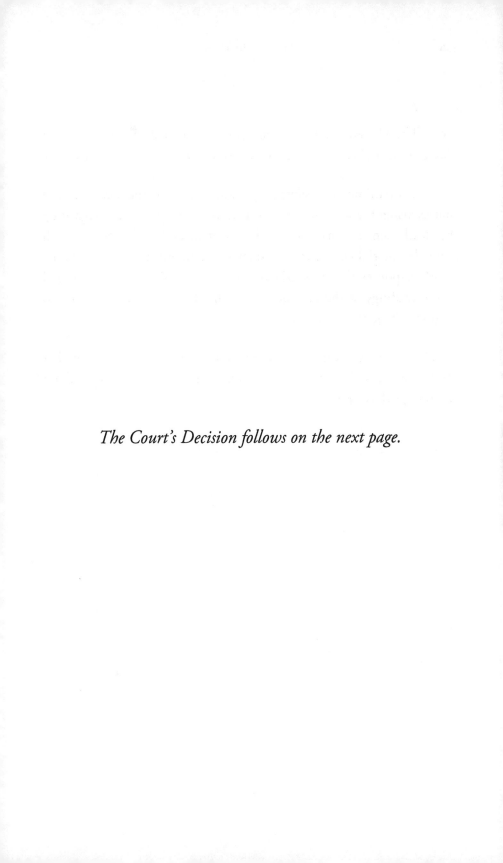

The Court's Decision follows on the next page.

The Court's Decision

Held: The United States Supreme Court overruled the Federal Sixth Circuit Court of Appeals and denied Wheeler's petition for relief.

In a unanimous unsigned decision, the Supreme Court found that excusing the juror for cause due to the answers he gave regarding the death penalty was not a violation of defendant Wheeler's Sixth Amendment rights. There was sufficient ambiguity in the potential juror's responses that the federal appeals court should have deferred to the findings of the Kentucky Supreme Court, which had upheld excusing the juror for cause.

Postscript: According to a recent internet search, as of December 2021—six years after the Supreme Court ruling—Wheeler was still on Kentucky's death row.

Beverly Martin v. Kingsford Homeowners Association

Los Angeles County Superior Court (2017)

The Issue:

Who bears primary responsibility for a fall through a roof-top skylight?

This is a civil case for personal injury damages. The case presents to you a common evidentiary issue in such cases: a battle between the experts.

Beverly Martin went up on the roof of her condominium complex on July 4, 2012, to watch the fireworks displays around the city. The door to the roof was not locked. Martin owned a unit in the complex. Kingsford Homeowners Association (subsequently referred to as the HOA) owned and operated the building. The roof had an elevated skylight on which Martin sat to view the celebratory displays. While watching the fireworks, she fell through the skylight and down three stories, hitting the concrete below.[50]

The plaintiff suffered extensive and severe injuries as a result of her three-story fall, including a laceration to the back of the head, torn diaphragm, fractured ribs, spinal cord fracture, numbness from

---

[50]   This *is* a real case, but for reasons set out in the Appendix, the names of the parties have been changed.

waist to feet, spleen laceration, fractured pelvis, left shoulder fracture, memory loss, depression, neurogenic bladder and bowel problems, and traumatic brain injury. She underwent numerous surgeries, and now has permanent urinary incontinence and must use a catheter for the rest of her life. She will not be able to return to her employment as a neonatal intensive care unit nurse. Future surgeries are anticipated.

Martin sued the HOA, seeking monetary damages for the injuries she sustained. As the plaintiff, she contended that the HOA (the defendant) was negligent in its maintenance of the skylight, and that the HOA failed to properly secure the rooftop where the skylight was located to prevent access to that area.

The Trial:

The plaintiff claimed that the door leading to the roof should have had an alarm, and it should have been locked at all times. She asserted that the skylight should have been protected by a screen and guardrails. The plaintiff asserted that it was not unusual for residents to use the rooftop for recreational purposes. Members of the board of directors of the HOA and other HOA members who had access keys used the roof for various social gatherings from time to time.

The HOA contended that the plaintiff knew the rooftop was prohibited to residents yet knowingly and willingly exposed herself by accessing the rooftop. The HOA denied that it was negligent in the management of its property.

As with many personal injury cases, each side in the conflict retained "experts" to testify on its behalf regarding the condition of the rooftop location. Usually, lay persons are not allowed to express their opinions in testifying at trial. However, when a witness is shown to have a special expertise in a particular area (due to the person's education and experience) the judge may allow that person to provide opinions relevant to the case.

During the trial on this matter, the following opinions were rendered by witnesses that the judge deemed to be experts.[51]

The plaintiff's civil engineer expert: He testified that the skylight should have been capable of withstanding a human weight load or it should have had guardrails or a protective screen around it to preclude access. He also said that the door to the roof should have been locked at all times and equipped with an alarm.

The plaintiff's human factors expert:[52] His testimony was that the plaintiff's conduct in accessing the roof and sitting on the skylight was reasonably foreseeable human behavior.

The plaintiff's property management expert: He stated that the access door should have had an alarm and should have been locked, given the fact that there was a skylight on the roof.

The defendant's general contractor expert: He pointed out that the standards in the building industry do not mandate screens or guardrails being placed on or around a skylight nor is that the "industry" custom and practice.

The defendant's property management expert: He testified that the HOA met a property owner's reasonable standard of care in its ownership, management, and maintenance of the skylight.

The defendant's combined mechanical engineer expert/human factors expert: He said that the rooftop was not intended for recreational purposes. The defendant had provided adequate warnings that residents

---

[51]   The jury hears not only the opinions of the experts but is also presented with the experts' credentials. In addition, counsel can cross-examine the experts of the opposing side to challenge or at least try to diminish the "quality" of the experts in the eyes of the jury. Finally, the demeanor of an expert may affect the weight a juror places on any one expert's opinion. Unfortunately, in the context of this book, the reader does not get the benefit of hearing and seeing the witnesses. Therefore, in deciding this case, you should assume that all the experts had similar training and experience, and that their demeanor did not differ significantly one expert from the other.

[52]   A "human factors expert" studies the reactions of human beings to certain situations. Manufacturers often retain them to examine products to determine if there would be a danger present that is not obvious to the casual observer when a product is used in an expected or even unexpected way by a consumer.

and other unauthorized persons were prohibited from accessing the roof. The skylight complied with existing building codes and was not designed to support a person's body weight.

The Applicable Law:

The jury instructions given by the court to the jurors would state that plaintiff Martin must prove by a preponderance of the evidence (a lesser burden than the "beyond a reasonable doubt" requirement in criminal cases) that the HOA was negligent in the maintenance of the property, and specifically the skylight and the area around it. In addition, the jury would be told that the plaintiff must prove that the HOA's negligence was the primary factor in causing the plaintiff's injuries.

The jury in a case like this one would also likely be instructed about the property owner/manager's basic duty of care:

> A person who owns/controls property is negligent if that person fails to use reasonable care to keep the property in a reasonably safe condition. A person who owns/ controls property must use reasonable care to discover any unsafe conditions and to repair, replace, or give adequate warning of anything that could be reasonably expected to harm others. In deciding whether the HOA used reasonable care, you may consider, among other factors, the following:
>
> 1. the location of the incident
> 2. the likelihood that someone would come on to the property in the same manner as the plaintiff did
> 3. the likelihood of harm
> 4. the probable seriousness of such harm
> 5. whether the HOA knew or should have known about the condition that created the risk of harm, and

6. the difficulty of protecting against the risk of such harm

On the issue of "customs and practices," an instruction might contain the following:

> You may consider customs or practices in the community in deciding whether the plaintiff and/or the HOA acted reasonably. Customs and practices do not necessarily determine what a reasonable person would have done in a similar situation. They are only factors for you to consider. Following a custom or practice does not excuse conduct that is unreasonable. You should consider whether the custom or practice itself is reasonable.

What's your verdict? Was the homeowners' association negligent in the operation of its property and the primary cause of plaintiff's injuries?

STOP HERE AND DECIDE THE CASE
BEFORE GOING FURTHER

The Court's Decision

Held: The jury found that the homeowners' association was not responsible for the plaintiff's injuries.

Just prior to trial, the plaintiff demanded $9 million to settle the case. Most of the demand amount represented compensatory damages—actual medical expenses and loss of income—versus general pain and suffering damages. While the jury deliberated, the plaintiff increased the demand to $50 million. Kingsford HOA offered the plaintiff $350,000 to settle prior to trial, but the plaintiff declined the offer.

Madison v. Alabama

139 S.Ct. 718 (2019)

The Issue:

Is there any purpose in carrying out a sentence of death if due to multiple strokes that occurred *after* his trial and sentencing, the prisoner is unable to remember ever committing the crime?

In 1985, Vernon Madison shot and killed a police officer who had responded to a domestic dispute. He was tried three times. The guilty verdict in his first trial was thrown out on appeal due to the prosecution's racially biased jury selection. The second trial resulted in a conviction but was also overturned because prosecutors relied on improper expert testimony. In his third trial, after finding him guilty of capital murder, the jury recommended a life sentence, but the judge overruled the jury and sentenced Madison to death.

In 2015 and 2016, after being incarcerated and while awaiting his execution, Madison suffered several strokes that resulted in a multitude of symptoms: slurred speech, blindness, inability to walk independently, urinary incontinence, disorientation, confusion, cognitive impairment, and memory loss. Madison was diagnosed with vascular dementia.

Dementia itself is not a specific disease. It is basically a collection of symptoms caused by several types of disorders that affect the brain. Someone who has displayed the symptoms of dementia usually shows significant impairment of intellectual functioning that interferes with normal activities of daily living, including memory loss. Vascular dementia is caused by a series of strokes that interfere with the person's brain receiving an adequate supply of blood. This form of dementia is the second most common cause for dementia after Alzheimer's disease in people over sixty-five.

The Hearing:

Madison sought a court order staying his execution, contending that he was mentally incompetent since he could not recollect committing the murder that resulted in his death sentence. Madison argues that executing him for a crime he does not remember committing has no retributive value, and therefore society should not allow it and the Eighth Amendment prohibits it. In deciding this case, you should assume: (1) that because of his vascular dementia, Madison cannot, in fact, remember committing the crime for which he was convicted, and (2) that if the courts rule that he may not be executed he will still spend the rest of his life in prison.

The State of Alabama contended that carrying out the execution is the appropriate punishment for the crime Madison committed without regard to whether he remembers committing the crime or not. He is not being punished for *remembering* the crime, the state asserts, but rather for *committing* the crime.

The court ruled that Madison's inability to recall committing the crime was insufficient grounds for staying his execution. Madison appealed the lower court's ruling to the United States Supreme Court.

The Applicable Law:

The Eighth Amendment prohibits executing a prisoner if his mental state is such that mental illness precludes him from having a rational understanding of the state's reason for executing him. But this case raises a subtle variant to that holding.

Does the Eighth Amendment preclude an execution on the sole basis that the prisoner, because of dementia, cannot remember committing the crime that put him on death row in the first place? The relevant provision of the Eighth Amendment prohibits cruel and unusual punishment from being inflicted.

What's your verdict? Is it a violation of Madison's Eighth Amendment rights to be executed for a crime that, because of his dementia, he cannot remember committing?

STOP HERE AND DECIDE THE CASE
BEFORE GOING FURTHER

The Court's Decision

Held: The United States Supreme Court ruled that it was not a violation of Madison's Eighth Amendment rights to proceed with the execution even though, because of his dementia, he does not remember committing the crime that led to his death sentence.

In a 5-to-3 decision (Justice Kavanaugh did not participate in the case), the Supreme Court said that the fact that a prisoner does not remember committing the crime at issue is not sufficient grounds to halt an execution. However, their decision did not end with that particular finding.

The justices also ruled that the trial court had not conducted a sufficient hearing on the issue of Madison's overall mental condition. The state's right to execute Madison depended on the outcome of two alternative possibilities: (1) because of mental illness, a prisoner may suffer dementia and not remember committing the offense which led to his trial and conviction, but nevertheless, when told and/or shown evidence of his crime, trial, and conviction, may comprehend why the state seeks to execute him. Or (2) because of mental illness, a prisoner may suffer dementia and not remember committing the offense that led to his trial and conviction, but (even after he is told and/or shown evidence of his crime, trial, and conviction) does not have the mental capacity to form a rational understanding of why the state seeks to execute him. In other words, there is more extensive mental incapacity involved than simple dementia.

The Court ordered Madison's case sent back to the trial court for further proceedings to determine which of the two scenarios listed above applied to Madison. The Court said that Madison's execution *would not* violate his Eighth Amendment rights if, despite Madison's inability to remember committing the murder, he nevertheless had the ability to understand that he was tried and found guilty of a murder for which the state sought to execute him (option 1 above). On the other hand, Madison's execution *would* violate his Eighth Amendment rights if the testimony led the trial court to find that not only did Madison not remember committing the crime, but even after he was told and/ or shown evidence of his crime, trial, and conviction, he was unable to comprehend why the state sought his execution (option 2 above).

Postscript: Madison never received the new hearing that the Supreme Court had ordered. Before the competency hearing could be held, Madison died in prison at the age of sixty-nine in February of 2020, thirty-five years after he shot the police officer.

Gamble v. United States
139 S.Ct. 1960 (2019)

The Issue:

Does the Fifth Amendment to the United States Constitution prohibit a person from being tried once in state court and again in federal court for the exact same crime?

In November 2015, a Mobile, Alabama police officer pulled Terance Gamble over after noting a damaged headlight. Smelling marijuana, the officer searched the vehicle and found a loaded nine-millimeter handgun. Since Gamble had previously been convicted of robbery, his possession of the firearm violated an Alabama law providing that no one convicted of a "crime of violence" shall own a firearm or have one in his or her possession.

The Trial:

Gamble pleaded guilty to the state charge and was sentenced to one year in prison.

Following his state court conviction, the federal government, apparently displeased with the one-year sentence, charged Gamble with the federal offense of being a felon in possession of a firearm based upon the same identical facts as the state conviction. Gamble moved to dismiss the federal charges under the Fifth Amendment "double jeopardy clause," but the court denied his motion. Gamble then pleaded guilty to the federal charge, reserving his right to appeal. The federal court sentenced Gamble to forty-six months in prison.

Citing the "dual-sovereignty doctrine," the Eleventh Circuit Court of Appeals denied Gamble's challenge to the federal conviction. Gamble then appealed to the United States Supreme Court.

The Applicable Law:

The Fifth Amendment states:

> No person shall be held to answer for a capital, or otherwise infamous crime, unless [by] a presentment or indictment [by] a Grand Jury . . .; *nor shall any person be subject for the same offence to be twice put in jeopardy of life or limb*; . . . nor be deprived of life, liberty, or property, without due process of law . . . (emphasis added)

The concept that a person should not be tried twice for the same offense goes back to ancient Greece. By the time our Constitution was drafted, the double jeopardy standard was well-established in the American colonies and in England. Embedded in our system of justice is the principle that:

> the State with all its resources and power should not be allowed to make repeated attempts to convict an individual for an alleged offense, thereby subjecting him to embarrassment, expense and ordeal and compelling him to live in a continuing state of anxiety and insecurity, as well as enhancing the possibility that even though innocent, he may be found guilty.[53]

---

[53] *Green v. United States*, 355 U.S.184, 187-188 (1957)

There has been a long-standing difference of opinion between legal scholars about exactly what the framers of the Constitution considered the governing "sovereign." The Constitution rests on the principle that the *people* are sovereign. But did the Constitution's drafters then "split the atom of sovereignty" by creating both federal and state authorities as representatives of the people?

The framers of the Bill of Rights rejected a proposed amendment that would have specifically *permitted* the federal government to prosecute a defendant a second time who was initially tried by a state. But was the proposed amendment permitting dual prosecution rejected because its opponents believed it to be unnecessary since they believed the terms of the Fifth Amendment did not prohibit dual prosecution? Or was the language permitting a second prosecution by the federal government rejected because its opponents believed the Fifth Amendment was drafted, in part, specifically to prohibit dual prosecutions by state and federal authorities?

Those who promote the "dual-sovereignty" line of reasoning assert that because the state and federal governments are separate sovereigns, trying a person for the same crime in state and federal court is permissible. Two different entities are asserting their own laws; thus, no "double jeopardy." The proponents assert: "an 'offense' is defined by law, and, each law is defined by a sovereign. So, where there are two sovereigns, there are two laws, and two 'offenses.'"

Those who oppose the "dual-sovereignty" concept argue that the state and federal governments are simply two different representatives of the people, but the *people* are the "sovereign." They contrast the relationship between the states and federal government with the separate sovereigns of two different countries. England and Portugal, for instance, would qualify as separate sovereigns. But not Rhode Island and the US federal government. Therefore, they assert, when the elements of the state and federal crime are the same, the Fifth Amendment bars trying the same person twice for the same offense.

In Gamble's case, although charged with violation of a state law and a separate federal law, the facts that had to be proved to convict Gamble were identical in both the state and federal court. Were not the crimes Gamble was charged with, therefore, the same offense?

What's your verdict? A vote in favor of Gamble would overturn only his federal conviction, holding that his dual convictions violated his Fifth Amendment right against double jeopardy. A vote in favor of the United States would affirm Gamble's federal conviction (in addition to his state conviction), holding that the "dual-sovereignty" exception should be applied to the Fifth Amendment's double jeopardy clause.

STOP HERE AND DECIDE THE CASE
BEFORE GOING FURTHER

The Court's Decision

Held: The Supreme Court ruled that an individual can be tried in state and federal court for the same crime.

In a 7-to-2 decision, the Supreme Court affirmed the dual-sovereignty doctrine and upheld the federal conviction. The majority held an "offence" is determined by law and laws of two sovereigns create two offenses. The Fifth Amendment's prohibition against a person being "subject for the same offence to be twice put in jeopardy" did not prohibit both a state and federal prosecution under similar criminal statutes.

The two dissenters, Justice Ginsburg and Justice Gorsuch, said that the dual-sovereignty exception should be discarded. They argued that the Founding Fathers described the sovereign as the *people*, not the state or federal government, so there can be no *dual* sovereignty.

In his dissent, Justice Gorsuch stated: "[a] free society does not allow its government to try the same individual for the same crime until it's happy with the result." He pointed out that in the nation's early days, there were few federal criminal statutes. Criminal laws were primarily the subject of state laws. But now the federal criminal code consists of more than 4,500 criminal statutes, giving rise to a greater opportunity for duplicate prosecutions by state and federal authorities.

State of Illinois v. Anthony McKinney

Cook County Circuit Court; #78 C 5267

The Issue:

Are college journalism students' sources and research protected by press "shield laws"?

Many states have enacted "shield laws" to protect journalists' work product (notes, interview tapes, transcripts, drafts, etc.) from compelled disclosure in a court proceeding. The purpose is, among other things, to give members of the press the ability to gather information without the threat that they will have to reveal their sources, especially those who have been interviewed based on an agreement promising confidentiality. In weighing the costs and benefits of such shield laws, states such as Illinois have apparently found the benefits of the laws—in providing for a free and unencumbered press—outweigh the need for disclosure of the information at issue. But should those laws apply to journalism *students*?

The dispute here stems from the 1981 trial of Anthony McKinney. The jury found him guilty of murder. He was sentenced to life in prison. The state claimed that McKinney (eighteen at the time) had placed a shotgun to the face of Donald Lundahl and fired at close range. Several witnesses identified McKinney as the shooter, although there was no physical evidence linking McKinney to the crime. He had signed a confession but later claimed that it had been coerced through physical beatings conducted during his police interrogation.

In 2008, McKinney filed a post-conviction petition for relief from the jury verdict, and sought his release on the grounds he was innocent of the Lundahl murder. A convicted person may have his or her conviction reviewed if the person can present newly discovered evidence of actual innocence that is material, not simply additional evidence of an already established fact, that could not have been found earlier with due diligence, and would probably change the result if the defendant were retried.

McKinney's petition was based substantially on the work of students taking an investigative journalism class at Northwestern University under the guidance of the Innocence Project at Medill School of Journalism (the Innocence Project). The students in the class learned the techniques of investigating crimes and gathering evidence. There were no tests or term papers. The students had to produce some kind of actual product as a result of their investigations to receive a passing grade in the class.

Over the years, the work of the students has been published in conjunction with professional journalists and on the internet. Since its creation in 1999, the Innocence Project has collected information that has led to the exoneration of eleven wrongfully convicted prisoners, five of whom had been on death row. The governor of Illinois imposed a moratorium on the death penalty based partly on data disseminated by the Innocence Project.

The Innocence Project students spent five years investigating the McKinney case. They located and interviewed witnesses who testified at McKinney's murder trial, and who had asserted that McKinney was at the scene at the time of the killing and/or was the trigger man. Many of those witnesses were themselves convicted felons. Several of them, in talking to the students, recanted their trial testimony. Some said they had simply lied on the witness stand. One witness told the students that the actual shooter was one of the other trial witnesses who had testified against McKinney.

The students ultimately shared the evidence they had collected with the Center on Wrongful Convictions of Northwestern's Bluhm Legal Clinic (the CWC). The CWC is staffed by law school faculty, practicing attorneys, and law students. It was the CWC that filed McKinney's petition seeking to vacate his conviction, or in the alternative, to grant him a new trial supported by the witness statements collected by the journalism students.

Upon being served with McKinney's petition, the state began an investigation of its own to test the veracity of the newly submitted evidence. As a result of its investigation, the state contended it uncovered several instances in which the students had improperly sought to influence the witnesses they interviewed.

According to the State's Attorney, several of the witnesses identified in McKinney's petition recanted the statements they had given to the Innocence Project students. One witness, Tony Drakes, said that after getting a statement from him, the student's investigator stated he would pay for Drakes's cab ride from the interview. Drakes contended the investigator gave the driver sixty dollars for a ride that the cab driver estimated would cost twenty dollars. Drakes said the investigator told the taxi driver to give Drakes the extra forty dollars. Drake told the state investigators that the statement he gave to the students was false.

One of the reinterviewed witnesses—who was in prison at the time of the student interview—said the female students had flirted with him. He said he simply told the students what he thought they wanted to hear.

The Contentions of the Parties:

Based on its concern for the students' interview techniques, the state issued subpoenas to Northwestern University seeking the journalism class' notes, interviews, tapes, emails, student grades, and course evaluations.

In response, the university filed a motion to quash the subpoenas, arguing primarily (1) that since the Innocence Project participants were "journalists," their work was subject to the shield law privilege, and (2) the students' and the university's rights to privacy precluded production of the students' grades as well as documents setting out how students were evaluated for the class.

The university denied that the students had acted inappropriately in gathering the evidence, and argued that the witnesses made false statements to the *state's* investigators. It asserted the public policies that the press shield laws were meant to protect applied to student journalists. The university asked the court to deny the state's request for the documents.

On the other hand, the state claimed (1) the students working on the Innocence Project acted as investigators regarding the Lundahl murder and not as "reporters," and (2) the Illinois shield law does not apply to that portion of the state's subpoena directed at the student evaluations.

According to the state's brief, "None of the students or the professor who worked on the criminal investigation of the Lundahl murder wrote a single story. . . In essence, the purpose of the class was to investigate and gather evidence, not to gather or report news." The state contended none of the materials the students produced were given to a news service or reporter until two years after the investigation concluded, and none of the students actually wrote a story for the press.

The state argued that even *if* the students were covered under the Illinois shield law, they waived that privilege by selectively giving material to McKinney's defense attorneys (the CWC) *prior* to any publication of the material. One of McKinney's attorneys stated she had obtained "a significant amount of materials" from the students.[54] The state asserted:

> The School cannot, on the one hand, show the materials
> relating to the McKinney case to attorneys and then, on
> the other hand, subsequently object to the disclosure of

---

[54]   *The New York Times* article "A Watchdog Professor, Now Defending Himself,"
       June 17, 2011, by David Carr and John Schwartz

such materials to the State. In short, the School waived the reporter's privilege to the extent that the privilege had any application to this case.

As to the request for production of the Innocence Project students' grades and the teachers' criteria for determining grades, the state argued this material was relevant to potential bias, motive, and possible personal interest when providing evidence to the court. In effect, the state was contending students may have felt (in order to get a good grade in the class) that their interviews and investigation had to produce something useful to the particular case they were working on. This argument was not made from whole cloth. One former trial witness who was interviewed by the students concluded from the students' comments that the content of his statement to them would potentially help the students get a good grade in the class. Illinois's attorneys contended:

> . . . the State must be allowed to examine not only the evidence submitted [with the petition] but also the circumstances surrounding the manner in which the evidence was obtained, including the interest, bias and motive of those who created the evidence.

The Applicable Law:

The Illinois Reporter's Privilege Act restricts access to information obtained by the press in the course of their reporting duties.[55] It was enacted to protect the First Amendment rights of a free press. (Forty-nine states have such laws along with the District of Columbia. There is no federal press shield law.) The Illinois shield law seeks to prevent reporters from being compelled "to become investigators for the State or anyone else."[56]

---

[55] 735 ILCS 5/8-901 to 8-909.

[56] From the court decision: *In re Subpoena Duces Tecum to Arya*, 226 Ill.App. 3d at 861-2.

Under Illinois law, to be covered by the state shield law, Northwestern University's journalism students must be found to be reporters regularly engaged on a full- or part-time basis in the business of collecting, writing, or editing news, and that this engagement results in the publication of news through a news medium.

Illinois law defines a "reporter" as:

> . . . [A]ny person regularly engaged in the business of collecting, writing or editing news for publication through a news medium on a full-time or part-time basis; and includes any person who was a reporter at the time the information sought was procured or obtained.

It is not necessary for a person claiming the protection of the shield law to actually have the status of a salaried employee of a publication or even regularly or frequently publish their work. To be protected by the shield law, the information acquired does not have to be in some way confidential (such as from an anonymous source) and can include information that would be available to the general public as long as it was acquired by the "reporter." The privilege applies whether the project would be characterized as either neutral or adversarial in nature. The statute is applied broadly in order to achieve its important First Amendment public purpose.

What's your verdict? (1) Were the investigative journalism students covered by the Illinois press shield law?

If you answer that question "no," the state prevails, and the school must turn over the subpoenaed material. If you answer that question "yes," you must answer a second question:

(2) Did the students, nevertheless, waive that protection by turning over their material to McKinney's attorneys (the CWC)? If you answer

that question "no," Northwestern's motion to quash the state's subpoena is granted. If you answer "yes," the state prevails and receives the documents it asked for.

STOP HERE AND DECIDE THE CASE
BEFORE GOING FURTHER

The Court's Decision

Held: The judge first ruled that, as journalism students, the participants in the Innocence Project *were* covered by the Illinois shield law. On the second question, the court found the students had *waived* the protections of the shield law by turning over their findings to the CWC before they published the material.

Based upon these findings, the judge denied Northwestern University's motion to quash the state's subpoenas. The university was ordered to turn over the items requested.[57] Sharing their work product with the CWC, the judge said, made the students not journalists but investigators for the defense, and the materials at issue were subject to discovery by the state.

It is important to note the judge's decision is not binding on any other court in Illinois or elsewhere. It applies only to the McKinney case. The decision was made at the trial level, and therefore has no precedential effect.

Postscript: After years of work by the Northwestern Innocence Project, the CWC, and the State's Attorney, McKinney's petition for post-conviction relief due to actual innocence was never ruled upon. Before the court could decide the matter, Anthony McKinney died in prison at age fifty-three in August of 2013. His petition had been pending for five years. Subsequently, a posthumous petition for clemency was filed on McKinney's behalf, but it was denied by the governor.

---

[57]   A written order by the judge could not be located for this book. The information about the judge's ruling was provided in a telephone interview in early 2021 with the author and one of the attorneys who filed a brief in the matter. The attorney said that in criminal matters judges often rule orally from the bench without a full written order, which appears to be what this judge did in ruling on the motion to quash the subpoenas.

Heuring v. State of Indiana

Indiana Supreme Court Case No. 19S-CR-528 (2020)

The Issue:

If someone attaches an unmarked object to your car without your knowledge, are you guilty of a "theft" if you remove it from the car?

Officers Matt Young and Jarret Busing of the Warrick County Sheriff's Department had suspicions about a local citizen, Derek Heuring. They believed he was dealing methamphetamines. In the summer of 2018, following up on their suspicions, they applied for a warrant to attach a GPS tracking device to Heuring's 1999 Ford Expedition. The warrant was issued, and a small magnetic black metal box (measuring six inches by four inches and containing electronics that would transmit the car's location to satellites) was secretly attached to the car. There was no label or printing of any kind on the outside of the box to identify the sheriff's department as the source of the unit.

The tracking unit provided the officers with the location of Heuring's vehicle over a ten-day period. Then it went silent.

The officers contacted a technician employed by the unit's manufacturer to see if the lack of data from the box could be explained. The tech was able to discern that the box's battery appeared to register a full charge. He said that the satellite was not getting a signal. Heuring's car had been seen at both his home and parked in a barn on his father's property. Thus, the officers knew that the monitor was in range. Ten days after the unit went silent, they decided to retrieve it to determine the cause for the lack of data, but the black box was no longer attached to the vehicle.

The officers concluded that Heuring had stolen the GPS device.

They applied for and obtained search warrants for both Heuring's home and his father's barn, claiming they had probable cause to believe a "theft" had taken place.

In the course of searching the barn, the officers found the tracking device in a bathroom locker. When other officers simultaneously commenced a search of Heuring's home pursuant to the search warrant, they saw in plain view "three lines of a crystal substance" and a long glass pipe containing "a white substance." A handgun was seen in a backpack sitting on the floor.

They immediately returned to the magistrate and applied for search warrants seeking evidence of illegal drug use. In executing this second round of search warrants at Heuring's home, they found two bags of methamphetamines, a container of pills, digital scales, razor blades, and a gun.

The officers sought the *original* warrants to investigate potential evidence of a theft of the GPS device only. The subsequent warrants to search for drugs were issued solely based upon items that were seen pursuant to the search based on the original warrants.

Heuring was arrested and charged with drug dealing and theft.

Motion to Suppress Evidence:

Heuring's attorneys filed a motion to preclude all of the evidence obtained by use of the search warrants from being presented in the case—a motion to suppress. They argued that the officers did not have probable cause to suspect a theft in the first instance because the officers had no facts to support the claim that a theft ever took place. Nor could they demonstrate that Heuring knew that the box belonged to law enforcement since it was unmarked.

The state countered that removing a device from a car where its placement has a legal basis deprives the police of its use and constitutes a crime. It might be true, the state said, that if a private citizen had placed the device on the car, Heuring's removal of it would not be illegal. But the device at issue in this case was placed there pursuant to a legal warrant, which made it the rightful and legal property of the police.

The trial court denied the suppression motion and allowed Heuring to take an immediate appeal (before trial). The Indiana Court of Appeal affirmed the trial court's denial of Heuring's motion. Heuring then appealed to the Indiana State Supreme Court.

The Applicable Law:

Heuring's challenge to the admissibility of the evidence is based upon the Fourth Amendment to the United States Constitution as well as Article 1, Section 11 of the Indiana Constitution. Both of these provisions require that search warrants be based upon probable cause. Such cause must be set out under oath in the facts within the warrant application that is provided to the magistrate who has been asked to approve the warrant. Probable cause exists when there is a "fair probability that contraband or evidence of a crime will be found in a particular place." While courts give great deference to a magistrate's decision to grant a search warrant, if upon review probable cause has been found to be clearly lacking, then a search based on the warrant would be illegal, and any evidence discovered would be inadmissible at trial under the "exclusionary rule."

The object of the search must be linked to criminal activity. It is not enough, for example, for an officer simply to say that she has suspicions about what is going on in someone's home. Facts must be set out indicating a specific potential crime.

"Theft," according to Indiana law, requires a showing that someone: "(1) at least 'knowingly' exerted 'unauthorized control over property of another person' and (2) did so 'with intent to deprive the other person of any part of its value or use.'" In other words, there must be an intent to take something that one knows belongs to another.

What's your verdict? Should all the evidence obtained as a result of the search warrants be admitted during Heuring's trial, or should his motion to suppress all the evidence be granted?

STOP HERE AND DECIDE THE CASE
BEFORE GOING FURTHER

The Court's Decision follows on the next page.

The Court's Decision

Held: The search warrants were invalid because the affidavits did not establish probable cause that the GPS device was stolen. The lower courts' rulings were reversed, and the evidence seized was deemed inadmissible for trial.

In a unanimous opinion, the justices of the Indiana Supreme Court asserted that if probable cause was to be established, the affidavits must have shown that someone took the GPS device from Heuring's vehicle knowing that it belonged to the sheriff's department and without proper consent from the department. But the justices wrote that there was no evidence in the affidavits provided to the magistrate that Heuring knew the GPS device belonged to law enforcement:

> The affidavits, however, are devoid of the necessary information to make such a showing [of probable cause]. Instead, they support a fair probability only that Heuring – or someone – found a small, unmarked black box attached to the vehicle, did not know what (or whose) the box was, and then took it off the car.

The most the officers had was a "hunch" that someone took the device to deprive the sheriff's office of its property. But, the justices said, a hunch does not come close to meeting the probable cause standard.

The justices did not question Officer Busing's *subjective* good faith in seeking the search warrants, but the magistrate can issue a warrant only when there is *objective* good faith, a neutral review of the facts as presented. Otherwise, any officer's hunch of criminal activity could justify the police conducting searches of persons, houses, papers, and other property. The officers' failure to show that Heuring—if in fact he was the one who detached the box from the car—knew he was stealing an object belonging to the police department. That failure was fatal to the state's request that the evidence be admitted.[58]

During the presentation of the oral arguments before the Indiana Supreme Court, one of the justices commented:

> If somebody wants to find me to do harm to me and it's not the police and they put a tracking device on my car and I find a tracking device and I dispose of it after stomping on it 25 times, I would hope they would not be able to go to a local prosecutor and somehow I'm getting charges filed against me for destroying someone else's property.[59]

If the GPS theft-related warrant was faulty, as the court found it was, then the subsequent search warrants (for the drug-related items) that flowed from the GPS warrant were also invalid. The inadmissibility of the evidence from the subsequent set of warrants was based upon a principle known as "fruit of the poisonous tree." The "poisonous tree" was the faulty warrant issued based upon allegations that the tracking device had been the subject of a theft.

Cases like this are obviously troubling for the justices. The court's decision includes the following:

> We are also aware that exclusion of the evidence here may result in criminal behavior going unpunished. Yet, "there is nothing new in the realization that the Constitution sometimes insulates the criminality of a few in order to protect the privacy of us all."

---

58 There are exceptions to the "exclusionary rule" that in some cases will allow the admission of evidence seized without a proper showing of probable cause in the warrant process. However, the justices found that no such exceptions applied in this case.

59 From an article appearing on the Ars Technica website (2019)

Samuels v. McCurdy, Sheriff
267 U.S. 188 (1925)

The Issue:

You obtained it legally. After you obtained it, the government passes a law to make it illegal to own it. Based on the new law, can the state confiscate that which you legally purchased?

This case presents an interesting set of circumstances that arose in 1925 during the prohibition era.

Sig Samuels liked his liquid refreshment. The resident of Dekalb County, Georgia, had stocked his house with whiskies, wines, beers, cordials, and liquors—all for personal use only. At the time he purchased these items, it was legal to do so.

In 1917, after Samuels had purchased the beverages, the State of Georgia passed a law that stated, in part:

> It shall be unlawful for any corporation, firm, person or individual to receive from any common carrier, corporation, firm, person or individual, or to have, control or possess, in this state, any of said enumerated liquors or beverages whether intended for personal use or otherwise . . .

The statute authorized the county sheriff to seize, condemn, and destroy liquor held in violation of the statute without first giving the owner a hearing before a neutral judge. The law did not, however, make it illegal to *drink* liquor, only to possess it.

After the statute went into effect, law enforcement officers seized the liquor from Samuels's home with the intention of destroying the illegal beverages.

Samuels's Challenge:

Samuels sued to restrain the county authorities from destroying the alcohol and to regain possession of his confiscated items. He challenged the confiscation of his alcoholic beverages on two grounds: (1) the 1917 Georgia statute was an *ex post facto* law,[60] and (2) the seizure and destruction of the liquor without first requiring a court hearing violated Samuels's due process rights.

The Applicable Law:

Article I, Section 9, Clause 3 of the United States Constitution prohibits Congress from passing *ex post facto* laws. The Constitution also prohibits the *states* from passing such laws. A law that increases the fine for running a red light and was made applicable to those red light violators who had committed their offense *before* passage of the law would be an example of an *ex post facto* law. The Constitution would prohibit making the penalty for running a red light greater *after* the offense was committed than it was at the time of the offense. Rather, the fine in place when the driver violated the ordinance should apply.

The Fourteenth Amendment to the Constitution provides that one's property may not be taken without "due process of law," the principle

---

[60] An *ex post facto* law is one that makes illegal a prior act that was legal when committed, or increases the penalties for an infraction after it has been committed, or changes the rules of evidence to make a conviction easier.

that an individual cannot be deprived of life, liberty, or property without appropriate legal procedures and safeguards.

What's your verdict? (1) Was the Georgia statute unconstitutional as an *ex post facto* law? (2) Were Samuels's due process rights violated by the seizure and destruction provisions of the statute? If you answer "yes" to either or both of those questions, Samuels's confiscated liquor is returned to him. If you answer "no" to both those questions, the sheriff can proceed with destroying the bottles.

STOP HERE AND DECIDE THE CASE
BEFORE GOING FURTHER

The Court's Decision follows on the next page.

The Court's Decision

Held: The statute at issue was not an *ex post facto* law and did not violate Samuels's due process rights.

In an 8-to-1 decision, the Supreme Court found that the Georgia statute was not an *ex post facto* law because it did not punish a past offense. Rather, the majority ruled, "The penalty it imposes is for continuing to possess the liquor after the enactment of the law." The majority noted that even though Samuels purchased the liquor when it was legal to do so, "the state did not thereby give any assurance, or come under an obligation, that its legislation upon that subject would remain unchanged."

Regarding Samuels's due process claims, the Court said that the confiscation of the alcohol was an appropriate exercise of "the police power of the states as [a] reasonable mode of reducing the evils of drunkenness." Furthermore, the justices held that the state was not required to compensate Samuels for the loss of his property

The majority also held that Samuels's due process rights were not violated by the 1917 law since his lawsuit (filed after the confiscation) stopped the proceedings until a court could hear his claims. The fact that the confiscation of the liquor took place *before* Samuels's lawsuit did not create a due process problem for the majority.

In his dissent, Justice Butler expressed his disagreement with the majority decision, writing:

> Any suggestion that the destruction of such private supply lawfully acquired and held for the use of the owner in his own home is necessary for or has any relation to the suppression of sales or to the regulation of the liquor traffic or to the protection of the public from injury would be fanciful and without foundation.

Christian Legal Society Chapter v. Hastings College of Law

561 U.S. 661 (2010)

The Issue:

Does the Hastings College of Law's official campus student organization recognition policy violate the freedom of religion protections of the First Amendment?

This dispute over the denial of official recognition of a religious group by an institute of higher learning gave rise to a spirited debate among the justices. One striking aspect of this case is the evidence the Supreme Court chose *not* to consider in making its ruling.

The Christian Legal Society (CLS) created a student chapter at Hastings College of Law, a school that operates under the University of California public school system. CLS requires its members to sign a Statement of Faith and live within its stated principles. The Statement of Faith includes the following:

Trusting in Jesus Christ as my Savior, I believe in:

- One God, eternally existent in three persons, Father, Son, and Holy Spirit.

- God the Father Almighty, Maker of heaven and earth.
- The Deity of our Lord, Jesus Christ, God's only Son conceived of the Holy Spirit, born of the virgin Mary; His vicarious death for our sins through which we receive eternal life; His bodily resurrection and personal return.
- The presence and power of the Holy Spirit in the work of regeneration.
- The Bible as the inspired Word of God.

CLS interprets its bylaws to exclude from membership anyone who engages in "unrepentant homosexual conduct," or otherwise holds religious convictions that conflict with the Statement of Faith.

After organizing on the Hastings campus, CLS applied to the law school for status as a Registered Student Organization (RSO). RSO status provides an organization with several benefits. Only approved RSO groups may meet on university grounds; have access to multiple channels for communicating with students and faculty (i.e., posting messages on designated bulletin boards, sending mass emails to the student body, and distributing material through the Student Information Center); participate in the annual student organizations fair; use the logo of the law school; and apply for financial assistance, which comes from mandatory student fees. To qualify for RSO consideration, an organization must agree to comply with Hastings's Nondiscrimination Policy that prohibits various forms of discrimination, including those based upon religion, national origin, disability, age, sex, and sexual orientation. An RSO must allow any student to participate as a member and as an officer of the group regardless of one's status or beliefs.

Hastings denied CLS's application. The school found that CLS's bylaws and its required affirmation of the Statement of Faith did not comply with the school's open-access policy. This was the first and only time that a group's application for RSO status was rejected since the RSO rules were created.

The law school has approximately sixty registered RSOs, including Hastings Democratic Caucus, Hastings Republicans, Hastings Jewish Students Association, Hastings Association of Muslim Students, Black

Law Students Association, Korean American Law Society, and the Middle Eastern Law Students Association. There are also prolife and prochoice RSO-qualified groups.

CLS's Challenge to Hastings's Policy:

CLS filed suit against Hastings Law School alleging CLS's rejection as an RSO was a violation of the First and Fourteenth Amendments. The group asserted the denial was an abridgment of its rights to free speech, association, and free exercise of religion.

Hastings argued that its policy was viewpoint-neutral, and therefore is not barred by the First Amendment. The law school noted the Hastings Democratic Caucus (an RSO) cannot bar students holding Republican beliefs. It also pointed out that since RSOs can get financial assistance from monies generated by mandatory student fees, the school's all-comers policy precluded a student from funding an organization that the student would not be allowed to join.

By rejecting CLS's application for RSO status, Hastings was not denying the club's right to organize and hold meetings on the campus. While without RSO status it would not get the official funding, preferential use of the meeting rooms, or use of the official campus communication facilities (such as the campus newsletter), CLS would, nevertheless, be free to exclude any person from its membership for any reason, and still access Hastings's facilities for its meetings and activities, and use certain chalkboards and campus bulletin boards for announcing its events. Hastings pointed out that there were many groups that maintain a presence at the university without official recognition, such as fraternities and sororities, social clubs, and secret societies.

Hastings asserted four specific justifications for its all-comers policy:

1. The policy is reasonable because it ensures that leadership, educational, and social opportunities are available to all students.
2. It is necessary to enforce the school's Nondiscrimination Policy.

3. It encourages diverse views, tolerance, cooperation, learning, and the development of conflict-resolution skills in the university setting.
4. The policy is necessary if the law school is to comply with the State of California's laws on discrimination.

CLS contended that the all-comers policy would allow students who hold beliefs that are contrary to its statement of purpose to infiltrate the organization and completely alter its goals and purposes. For example, under Hastings's policy, CLS would be required to allow Buddhists to become members, even though Buddhists do not believe in the same religious tenets as set out in the Statement of Faith. CLS would be required to accept sexually active gay students into its midst despite the group's core belief that sexual activity should be confined to a married man and woman. If enough Buddhists or gays joined the group, they could significantly change the very heart of the organization.

CLS also pointed out that it welcomes any and all students to the activities it sponsors. Thus, its Bible studies classes, speaker forums, and dinners have no restrictions on attendance. The restrictions only come into play when determining voting membership and leadership positions in the club.

CLS sought a court-ordered injunction prohibiting Hastings from denying it an exception to the RSO policies. The US District Court denied the petition and found in favor of Hastings. CLS's appeal to the Ninth Circuit Court of Appeals was also denied. CLS appealed to the United States Supreme Court.

The Applicable Law:

CLS's claims are founded upon the First and Fourteenth Amendments (both of which are applicable to the states as well as the federal government). The relevant portions of those amendments state:

First Amendment: "Congress shall make no law respecting an establishment of religion, or prohibiting the free exercise thereof; or abridging the freedom of speech . . . or the right of the people peacefully to assemble . . ."

The Fourteenth Amendment: " . . . No State shall . . . deny any person within its jurisdiction, the equal protection of the laws."

The Supreme Court has previously ruled that a college may not ban a group from recognized status because of the group's *viewpoint.* Thus, Hastings would not be able to refuse RSO status to the CLS solely because of its Christian-based philosophy. But the Court had not previously addressed circumstances in which a college has refused official recognition stemming from a school's "all-comers" policy.

The "right of association" is not a right explicitly set forth in the Constitution. However, the courts have held that the right to *expressive association* (the right to associate for purposes of speaking) is nevertheless an implicit protected constitutional right.

To further complicate this issue, the courts have also held forced inclusion of unwanted persons by a group improperly infringes on the group's ability to advocate for its particular viewpoint. Thus, a student Republican club, for example, may limit its members to those agreeing with its political philosophy. However, the Republican club may not exclude members based on their religion because one's religious beliefs do not impact the group's ability to advocate its political views. Does allowing non-Christians (or at least those not willing to endorse the Statement of Faith) interfere with CLS's advocacy rights? Does the fact that the Constitution specifically prohibits religious discrimination justify treating religious groups differently from political groups?

All these issues must be considered in the unique context of the university setting. Campuses should be catalysts for diversity, differing political philosophies, and hearty debate. Yet the university must be allowed some administrative regulation over campus activities.

What's your verdict? Is Hastings College of Law's all-comers policy, as applied to the Christian Legal Society Chapter, a violation of the Constitution?

STOP HERE AND DECIDE THE CASE
BEFORE GOING FURTHER

The Court's Decision follows on the next page.

The Court's Decision

Held: No, Hastings College of Law's all-comers policy as applied to the Christian Legal Society was not a violation of the Constitution.

In a 5-to-4 decision, the Supreme Court said that "Compliance with Hastings' all-comers policy, we conclude, is a reasonable, viewpoint-neutral condition on access to the student-organization forum." The Court stated:

> CLS, it bears emphasis, seeks not parity with other organizations, but a preferential exemption from Hastings' policy. The First Amendment shields CLS against state prohibition of the organization's expressive activity, however exclusionary that activity may be. But CLS enjoys no constitutional right to state [subsidy] of its selectivity.

In other words, Hastings (the state) cannot prohibit CLS from meeting or advocating a Christian lifestyle. However, the state cannot be forced to use its funds and facilities to advance the organization's philosophy insofar as it is incompatible with the all-comers policy for RSO approval.

Previous cases have held "freedom of association" includes the right *not* to associate. An organization cannot be forced to accept members who are opposed to its views. But in those cases, the schools provided only one option for the organizations: accept everyone. There was no alternative. In the case of Hastings's policy, the CLS was free to restrict its membership to those who complied with its faith-based qualifications, just not as an RSO. In other words, the CLS *did* have an available option to form and to meet, even though its policies did not comport with the all-comers RSO policy.

The majority wrote: "Hastings' (sic) all-comers requirement draws no distinction between groups based on their message or perspective.

An all-comers condition on access to RSO status, in short, is textbook viewpoint neutral."

From Hastings's vantage point, it is CLS's *conduct* in excluding students not willing to abide by the Statement of Faith, not its Christian viewpoint, that stands between the group and RSO status.

As to CLS's concern for possible "hostile takeovers," the majority said concerns about such "saboteurs" were strictly hypothetical and not sufficiently probable to serve as a basis for overturning the all-comers policy. The Court noted that someone interested in hijacking the organization's purpose and subverting it would not likely gain sufficient support within the organization to ever be elected to a leadership position.

In his concurring opinion, Justice Stevens asserted:

> In this case, petitioner excludes students who will not sign its Statement of Faith or who engage in "unrepentant homosexual conduct" . . . The expressive association argument it presses, however, is hardly limited to these facts. Other groups may exclude or mistreat Jews, blacks, and women – or those who do not share their contempt for Jews, blacks, and women. A free society must tolerate such groups. It need not subsidize them, give them its official imprimatur, or grant them equal access to law school facilities.

The dissenting justices argued CLS was denied recognition because of the viewpoint, not the conduct, CLS sought to express through its membership qualifications. In his dissenting opinion, Justice Alito argues CLS members are entitled to the right of expressive association, and the all-comers policy abridges that right:

> The State of California surely could not demand that all Christian groups admit members who believe that Jesus was merely human. Jewish groups could not be required to admit anti-Semites and Holocaust deniers. Muslim

groups could not be forced to admit persons who are viewed as slandering Islam.

One of the most surprising turn of events during the course of this case arose out of a stipulation that the parties executed and filed with the Supreme Court. A good argument could be made that the stipulation significantly altered the potential outcome of this case.

During litigation and appeals, the courts look to the parties to resolve as many disputed issues by agreement as they can. Parties often submit a list of stipulated or non-controverted facts to the court in which they agree that the facts included in the list are true, binding, and may be accepted as evidence without further foundation. For example, a defendant charged with driving the getaway car in a robbery might join with the prosecution in a written stipulation that the defendant owned the car he was driving when arrested. The state would still have to prove it was used in the robbery, but it would not have to bring evidence into court establishing ownership and the defendant could not challenge ownership.

One of CLS's arguments in its appeal to the Supreme Court was that Hastings applied the Nondiscrimination Policy in an unfair and discriminatory manner in regard to RSO groups. For example, the policy prohibits any restriction on membership due to religious belief or sexual orientation. But the policy does not specifically prohibit restrictions based on political philosophy. Would it, therefore, violate the Nondiscrimination Policy if a political group insisted that its leaders support its purposes and beliefs?

The evidence in the litigation demonstrated a willingness—at least until CLS's application—on Hastings's part to allow RSO groups to restrict membership. The Hastings Democratic Caucus opened its doors to any full-time student "*so long as they do not exhibit a consistent disregard and lack of respect for the objective of the organization.*" (italics in the original) Any student could join the Vietnamese American Law Society *provided* they did not "exhibit a consistent disregard and lack of respect for the objective of the organization." The Silenced Rights group limited voting membership to those students committed to the group's mission of "spread[ing] the pro-life message." An environmental club was not required to admit students who did not believe in global warming. An animal rights group was not required to extend membership to students who supported using animals to test cosmetics.

In fact, there was a conflict within Hastings's own pleadings as to the coverage of the Nondiscrimination Policy. At one point, early in the litigation, Hastings admitted the school permits political, social, and cultural student organizations to select officers and members dedicated to their organizations' ideals and beliefs.

However, a couple of months after making that admission, Hastings asserted it interpreted the Nondiscrimination Policy "as requiring that student organizations wishing to register with Hastings allow any Hastings student to become a member and/or seek a leadership position in the organization." The conflict between Hastings's seemingly contradictory positions was never explained. And although Hastings claims its all-comers policy had been in effect since 1990, the school could not produce any evidence that the policy was ever put into writing.

After these discrepancies in its pleadings were illuminated during the litigation, Hastings took action to enforce a more consistent application of the policy. It began contacting campus organizations and asking them to change their bylaws, if necessary, to reflect the all-comers policy.

CLS asserts, in practice, the Hastings Nondiscrimination Policy was unfairly applied to religious organizations, and perhaps only Christian organizations at that. The all-comers policy was, CLS argued, merely a pretext to justify what was, in practice, viewpoint discrimination.

However, the Supreme Court refused to consider CLS's assertions about the disparate application of Hastings's Nondiscrimination Policy because of the stipulation both sides had signed while briefing the case. The parties had stipulated that: "Hastings requires that registered student organizations allow *any* student to participate, become a member, or seek leadership positions in the organization." (emphasis in original)

CLS's credible evidence that Hastings applied its Nondiscrimination Policy in a discriminatory fashion and that the policy was only interpreted by Hastings as an all-comers policy *after* CLS challenged it in court contradicted the stipulation. So it was not considered by the justices. Although CLS did make the disparate treatment assertion in its briefs to the Supreme Court, the majority said they could not consider the evidence or arguments on that issue because of the stipulation. To be sure, in hindsight, the lawyers representing CLS must have regretted signing off on the stipulation.

The Court's handling of CLS's disparate treatment evidence is a good example of an instance where a stipulated fact does not necessarily apply to the actual situation. It is true that sometimes the "facts" presented in a court of law are not really the "facts" in the real world. Would it have made a difference in the way you decided this case if you could have considered the evidence the Supreme Court ruled was precluded by the stipulation?

Food Lion Inc. v. Capital Cities ABC, Inc.

951 F.3d 505 (4th Cir. 1999)

The Issue:

When reporters who want to investigate a company's business practices are hired by the target company based on false information the reporters intentionally listed on their employment applications, can the employer sue the reporters and the reporters' employer for fraud?

There is something exciting about seeing undercover video capturing a "Gotcha!" moment. Over the years, corporate malfeasance and discrimination that otherwise might not have been revealed have been captured by hidden cameras. This case examines the potential liability of undercover video investigators when the subject of the videos strikes back in court.

Lynn Dale and Susan Barnett were reporters for the ABC Television Network's show *PrimeTime Live*. In 1992, the producers of that program received information involving potential unsanitary practices at Food Lion grocery stores. The reports involved allegations that employees were mixing out-of-date beef with fresh beef, bleaching rank beef to cover up the odor, and redating expired products before placing them back in the case for sale.

Dale and Barnett suggested to the producers that they, as reporters, could best investigate these claims by actually becoming Food Lion employees. With the approval of their supervisors, they applied for jobs, each at a different Food Lion. Dale and Barnett submitted applications with false identities, fake references, fictitious local addresses, fabricated educational backgrounds, and nonexistent employment positions. Naturally, the applicants did not mention that they were currently employed with ABC.

After reviewing the applications, a South Carolina Food Lion hired Barnett as a deli clerk, and a North Carolina store hired Dale as a meat wrapper trainee. Barnett quit after two weeks and Dale after one week.

While going about their work, Dale and Barnett surreptitiously recorded on concealed cameras and microphones about forty-five hours of footage. The film depicted employees treating, wrapping, and labeling meat; cleaning machinery; and discussing the practices of the meat department. Footage was obtained from the meat cutting room, the deli counter, the employee break room, and a manager's office. Despite the "extracurricular" activities of the two reporters, they apparently still performed their regular duties well. Shortly before Dale quit, she was complimented by her supervisor, who said that Dale "would 'make a good meat wrapper.'" When Barnett quit, her supervisor recommended that Barnett be rehired if she sought reemployment with Food Lion.

In November of 1992, *PrimeTime Live* aired excerpts from the forty-five hours of tape on its national broadcast. Viewers were treated to scenes of Food Lion employees repackaging and redating fish that had passed the expiration date, grinding expired beef with fresh beef, and applying barbeque sauce to chicken past its expiration date to mask the smell and sell it as fresh in the gourmet food section. In addition, there were interviews with former Food Lion employees in which they confirmed these practices at stores across several states.

Food Lion filed a lawsuit against ABC as well as the *PrimeTime Live* producers and both reporters. (These parties who were on the receiving end of Food Lion's lawsuit will be referred to collectively as the "defendants.")

The Trial:

In an interesting and imaginative twist, the chain did not sue the defendants for defamation or slander. Indeed, the "truth" of the *PrimeTime Live* broadcast was never at issue, and the facts of the story were not challenged by Food Lion in the case it brought. Instead of focusing on the broadcast itself, Food Lion chose to base its lawsuit on the *methods used to obtain the video*. This case study deals with the following two claims made by Food Lion:[61]

(1) Fraud on the part of the defendants

(2) Breach of the duty of loyalty by Dale and Barnett

1. Fraud

Food Lion asserted that Dale and Barnett (with the authorization of ABC and *PrimeTime Live*) fraudulently applied for employment. The store contended that when the two reporters filled out the employment applications they not only provided false information, but they also applied knowing that they were never intending to actually work for Food Lion any longer than it took them to complete the surreptitious filming. Food Lion stated that had it known the reporters entered false information on the applications and that the reporters never really intended to be Food Lion employees in any real sense, the stores never would have hired them. In addition, the stores would not have spent time training them for their positions or paid them for the time worked, since a significant portion of their time at the store apparently was utilized on the investigation for the *PrimeTime Live* project, not quite the jobs for which they were actually hired.

Therefore, Food Lion claimed they were entitled to damages for the wages paid the two reporters, the cost of their training, and the administrative costs associated with their employment (screening applications, interviewing, completing forms, and entering data into the payroll system).

---

[61] There were other claims made by Food Lion, but the focus here is on the two primary ones.

2. Breach of the duty of loyalty

Food Lion argued that the interests of the reporters were adverse to the interests of Food Lion, the employer to whom the reporters were unfaithful.

Dale and Barnett argued that they did not compete with Food Lion's grocery business, misappropriate any of its profits, or breach any of its legitimate corporate confidences. Therefore, there was no breach of any duty of loyalty. The defendants said that pointing out uncomfortable truths about activities at the stores does not make one necessarily "disloyal."

At the trial of this case, the jury found all the defendants liable to Food Lion on the fraud claim, and Dale and Barnett liable for breach of the duty of loyalty. The defendants appealed to the United States Fourth Circuit Court of Appeals.

The Applicable Law:

To begin, we will take a brief look at two kinds of employment.

Most employees are designated as "at-will" employees. This means that: (1) the employee may quit the job at any time for any reason or no reason at all, and (2) the employer may terminate the employee at any time for any reason or no reason at all. This reciprocal arrangement provides both parties to the employment agreement equal opportunity to terminate the arrangement at any time.[62]

The other most common type of employment agreement is under a contract that sets out the term of employment and the specific causes under which the parties can terminate the agreement. If either party breaks the terms of the agreement, that party would be in breach of

---

[62]   Employers are, however, barred from terminating even "at-will" employees for reasons that would violate federal law and the US Constitution, such as on the basis of race or age discrimination.

contract and the other party to the contract could seek judicial relief—monetary damages or some other form of court order.

Many would argue that a contractual agreement of employment (the second of the examples above) provides both worker and employer with greater security. To others, the ability of either party to terminate the agreement at any time for any reason is an attractive feature.

In this case involving Food Lion, reporters Dale and Barnett would be considered "at-will" employees of Food Lion. The reporters *or* Food Lion could have terminated the employment relationship at any time for any reason. One of the documents signed by Dale and Barnett before being hired stated: "I also understand and agree that if employed, employment is for an indefinite period of time, and that I have the right to terminate my employment at any time for any reason, as does the Company."

Now we will look at the two legal claims involved.

1. Fraud

To prove "fraud," Food Lion must establish that the defendants: (a) made false representations of material (important) facts, (b) that they knew the representations were false, (c) they intended Food Lion to rely on those false representations, and (d) Food Lion actually sustained some type of injury or damage as a result of relying on the false representations. Under the facts of this case, it is *undisputed* that the defendants made representations during the hiring process that they knew were false *and* they intended for Food Lion to rely on those misrepresentations in order to hire them.

Thus, the only element of fraud that you need to consider in your decision is (d), whether or not Food Lion sustained damages as a result of its reliance on the false statements.

2. Breach of the duty of loyalty

In both North and South Carolina, where the two Food Lion stores involved were located, the courts have held that an employee owes a duty of loyalty to the employer. Prior court holdings have established three circumstances in which employees may be liable to the employer for disloyalty: (1) when employees themselves compete directly with the employer, either on their own or for another rival company, (2) when employees steal from the employer, or (3) when employees disclose the employer's confidences (such as confidential marketing strategy or customer data).

In deciding whether Dale and Barnett should be held liable for breach of the duty of loyalty, you should consider whether the facts apply to one of those three circumstances. However, since you sit as a justice on a court of appeals in this case, you may find that the reporters' actions breached the duty of loyalty on some basis that the courts have not previously considered but which you believe justifies applying the duty of loyalty to the facts of this situation.

What's your verdict? (1) *Fraud*: Did Food Lion sustain damages as a result of its reliance on the false statements? If you answer this question "yes," then all the defendants are guilty of fraud. If you answer this question "no," then Food Lion does not succeed on its fraud claim against the defendants.

(2) *Duty of Loyalty*: Did Dale and Barnett breach their duty of loyalty to Food Lion? If you answer this question "yes," then Dale and Barnett will be liable for damages that resulted from that breach. If you answer the question "no," then Food Lion fails to prevail on its breach of loyalty claim.

STOP HERE AND DECIDE THE CASE
BEFORE GOING FURTHER

The Court's Decision follows on the next page.

The Court's Decision

HELD: (1) *Fraud:* Food Lion did not sustain any damages as a result of its reliance on the misrepresentations of ABC, *PrimeTime Live*, Dale, or Barnett. Thus, Food Lion's favorable trial verdict on the fraud claim was set aside.

(2) *Breach of the Duty of Loyalty:* Dale and Barnett breached their duty of loyalty to Food Lion. Thus, Food Lion's favorable trial verdict on the breach of duty of loyalty claim was affirmed.

1. Fraud

In a 3-to-0 decision,[63] the court of appeals found that since Dale and Barnett were "at-will" employees and could quit at any time for any reason, Food Lion had no justification for relying on a belief that the employees would work for any period of time. *Any* employer who hires employees on an "at-will" basis risks loss in expending funds for administering the application process, setting up payroll, and paying wages to the employee if the employee decides to leave sooner rather than later.

In addition, the evidence showed that the two reporters had obviously performed the tasks for which they were hired and for which they were paid since both received favorable performance reviews from their supervisors.

Thus, even though it was undisputed that Dale and Barnett made false representations in order to gain employment, Food Lion failed to prove the fourth element required for fraud: that Food Lion suffered damages *as a result of relying on the misrepresentations.*

---

[63] This case was decided by a three-judge panel of the United States Court of Appeals for the Fourth Circuit.

2. Breach of the Duty of Loyalty

With the same 3-to-0 vote of the justices, the court of appeals found that Dale and Barnett were liable for damages for breach of the duty of loyalty. The justices held that "The interests of the employer (ABC) to whom Dale and Barnett gave complete loyalty were adverse to the interests of Food Lion, the employer to whom they were unfaithful."

Interestingly, they did not find that the two reporters violated any of the three circumstances the courts had previously held could result in a loyalty breach. Instead, the justices said, notwithstanding the fact that Dale and Barnett did not violate any of the three formerly established grounds, their conduct violated the duty of loyalty.

The district court (the initial trial court) had pointed out in the course of its ruling that it was the first court to hold that conduct like that of Dale and Barnett would entail a breach of duty of loyalty. The court of appeals justices, in confirming the decision of the district court, stated, "We believe the district court was correct to conclude that [the South and North Carolina courts] would decide today that the reporters' conduct was sufficient to breach the duty of loyalty and trigger tort liability."[64]

How then did the defendants emerge in regard to the damages they had to pay to Food Lion? Pretty well actually.

The damages awarded Food Lion in the trial court for fraud totaled $1,402 for compensatory damages and $315,000 in punitive damages (extra damages to punish and deter the defendants). These damages were thrown out because of the appellate court's decision.

---

[64] In litigated cases, the defendant's liability is usually based on one of two types of theories: (1) contractual, based on a violation of a written or oral contract in which damages are limited to the financial losses stemming from the violation, or (2) tort, conduct injuring another in which damages may include personal pain and suffering, medical expenses, emotional distress, other financial losses stemming from the wrongful conduct, and (under some limited circumstances) damages to punish and deter future bad conduct. In this case, both fraud and breach of the duty of loyalty are tort claims.

The damages awarded Food Lion in the trial court for breach of loyalty were $1.00 against *each* of the reporters for a total of $2.00 in damages.[65] Food Lion was entitled to the $2.00 from the defendants Dale and Barnett after the court of appeals sustained that claim.

Currently we hear a lot of news reports about "whistleblowers." Public policy says that whistleblowers should not be punished for pointing out illegal or otherwise wrongful conduct by their employers lest corruption might go unpunished. Weren't Dale and Barnett "whistleblowers"? By finding them liable for breach of the duty of loyalty did the court of appeals possibly dissuade other whistleblowers from speaking out? If so, is that good for society? On the other hand, is it good for society to give unfettered access to the workplace to employees making undercover films? How do we balance these two societal interests? Perhaps the jury's answer to that question was in its awarding only $2.00 in damages on the breach of loyalty claim.

---

[65] Juries sometimes find that the defendants were liable for the wrongful conduct that was alleged they committed, but nevertheless believe there was no *substantial* injury involved and so return a verdict for nominal damages. For the party bringing the claim, it is more of a "moral" win than a financial one.

Rucho v. Common Cause

139 S.Ct. 2484 (2019)

The Issue:

Is it constitutional for state legislators to intentionally establish voting district borders in a manner that gives an advantage to one political party over another?

Drawing voting districts in a partisan manner predated the colonies obtaining their independence. It was a practice that was well known to those who drafted our Constitution. They chose to hand control over establishing district boundaries to the state legislatures.

In 1812, Federalists in Massachusetts argued that the Democratic-Republicans, led by Governor Elbridge Gerry, had created grossly misshapen, illogical, and unnatural borders for voting districts to preserve their party's seats in Congress. One of the districts drawn by Governor Gerry and his supporters, it was noted, looked like a "salamander." Thus, the term "gerrymandering" was coined.

Gerrymandering is accomplished by two primary methods: cracked and packed. "Cracked" is when the party doing the gerrymandering sees to it that the opposing party's supporters are disbursed among multiple districts so that the opposing party's supporters are in the minority in each district. "Packed" is when the party doing the gerrymandering sees to it that the opposing party's supporters are bundled into a highly concentrated group in one district (so they win that district by a large margin) while diluting the opposing party's numbers in the surrounding districts, thus "wasting" many votes that would have improved the opposing party's chances in those other districts.

The main issues with respect to gerrymandering are: (1) When does political gerrymandering go too far, and how much partisan dominance is too much? (2) Is it the role of the judiciary to adjudicate disputes over the drawing of districts?

Two separate cases were brought by residents of Maryland and North Carolina as well as the public interest group Common Cause (subsequently referred to collectively as "plaintiffs"). Both cases challenged their states' congressional districting maps. The plaintiffs' claim was that the manner in which the districts at issue were drawn constituted unconstitutional partisan gerrymandering.

In 2011, Maryland Democrats dominated the state legislature and held the governor's office as well. Governor O'Malley, who oversaw the redistricting process at that time, said he wanted "to create a map [of congressional districts] that was more favorable for Democrats over the next ten years." The governor later testified that he only needed to "flip" one district to do so. The targeted district had been in the Republican column for nearly two decades. In something akin to the old shell game, districts were redrawn so that 360,000 voters were removed from the targeted district and 350,000 voters were moved into it. The plan resulted in a loss of 66,000 registered Republicans in the district, and a gain of 24,000 registered Democrats. The formerly solid Republican district now became a Democratic one.

The US District Court in Maryland found in favor of the plaintiffs, the challengers, and enjoined the state from executing the plan. The state appealed.

In 2016, the Republican-controlled North Carolina General Assembly instructed its mapmaker to use political data to draw a map that would produce a congressional delegation of ten Republicans and three Democrats. They sought this result despite the fact that in 2012 Democratic congressional candidates received more votes on a statewide basis than did Republican candidates. One of the Republican members of the redistricting committee stated: "I think electing Republicans is better than electing Democrats. So I drew this map to help foster what I think is better for the country." In setting the districts, several criteria were used, including one brazenly labeled "Partisan Advantage," which said that the committee would make all reasonable efforts to construct districts to maintain the current partisan Republican composition.

The federal district court that heard the North Carolina case ruled in favor of the plaintiffs, the voters who challenged the state's districting plan. One particular concern voiced by the district court was that gerrymandering was likely to persist in subsequent elections, so that the elected representatives from the "safe" party might not feel any need to respond to the concerns of constituents of the disfavored party. The district court based in North Carolina asserted that "the voters should choose their representatives, not the other way around." State Senator Robert Rucho was one of the Republican cochairs of the North Carolina Assembly's redistricting committee and was sued in his representative capacity.

The North Carolina and Maryland cases were consolidated for presentation to the United States Supreme Court.

The Trial:

The plaintiffs asserted multiple constitutional violations. Between the two states involved, the plaintiffs claimed the redistricting plans: (1) violated the Equal Protection Clause of the Fourteenth Amendment by intentionally diluting the electoral strength of Democratic voters in North Carolina and Republican voters in Maryland; (2) violated the First Amendment by retaliating against candidates on the basis of their political beliefs; (3) violated Article I, Section 2 of the Constitution, which mandates that members of the House of Representatives be chosen by the people of the states, claiming that the gerrymandering usurped the right of the people to elect their preferred candidates; and (4) violated the Elections Clause (Article I, Section 4) by exceeding the states' delegated authority to set the time, place, and manner for congressional elections.

The plaintiffs further argued that courts are perfectly capable of resolving such disputes. If the courts refuse to do so, the plaintiffs said, citizens are left without any remedy for their constitutional harms.

The two states, on the other hand, argued that the Constitution does not require proportional representation. In addition, they contended the federal courts are neither equipped nor authorized to apportion political power as a matter of fairness. The case presents a political question better handled by the legislature, they argued, and asserted that it is impossible to set a judicial standard for deciding *how much partisan dominance* is too much.

Furthermore, the states asked if the redistricting plan really created a constitutional crisis in the first place. After all, changing the gerrymandered districts in a less partisan manner would likely have produced only one more Democratic district in North Carolina and one more Republican district in Maryland.

The Applicable Law:

The initial issue that you must address is whether these two cases involve disputes that the courts should entertain in the first place.

Article III of the United States Constitution—the article that establishes the judicial branch of the government—limits federal courts to deciding "cases" and "controversies." This has been interpreted over the years to mean that the cases addressed by the courts must be seen as capable of *actually being resolved* through the judicial process. Sometimes "the law is that the judicial department has no business entertaining the claim of unlawfulness – because the question is entrusted to one of the political branches or involves no judicially enforceable rights."[66] In such a case the claim is said to present a "political question" and to be nonjusticiable—outside the courts' competence and therefore beyond the courts' jurisdiction.[67]

---

[66] *Viet v. Jubelirer,* 541 U.S. 267, 277 (2004) (plurality opinion)

[67] *Baker v. Carr,* 369 U.S. 217 (1962)

In essence, the question is whether the plaintiffs' claims deal with *legal* rights, and therefore can be resolved by applying *legal* principles. Or are they *political* questions best resolved by the other two branches of the government?

If the dispute involved in this case *is* one that the courts should address, then the next step is to consider the constitutionality of the gerrymandering activities of the two states.

Article I, Section 4 of the Constitution is referred to as the "Elections Clause." It provides: "The times, places, and manner of holding elections for Senators and Representatives, shall be prescribed by each State by the Legislature thereof; but the Congress may at any time by law make or alter such regulations . . ."

The Fourteenth Amendment to the Constitution guarantees all citizens "the equal protection of the law." The language of this amendment is at issue since the plaintiffs contend that partisan gerrymandering improperly dilutes the weight of the votes of the party out of power, and thus denies those voters the equal protection that the amendment commands.

The plaintiffs asserted that the manner in which the districts were created also abridged their First Amendment rights to free speech. They contended that the districts were drawn in such a manner as to punish the speech of the weaker party's candidates.

Article I, Section 2 of the Constitution may also come into play in resolving the case. It provides that the "Members of the House of Representatives shall be composed of members chosen every second year by the people of the several states . . ." The plaintiffs argued that partisan gerrymandering interferes with "the people" voting for those representatives.

What's your verdict? (1) Were the disputed claims the proper subject of federal court resolution, or does the case present a political dispute that would be improper for the courts to involve themselves in? If you believe the courts have the authority to rule on the disputes, then proceed to the second question. If you believe this dispute was not subject to court resolution, then the two state district court decisions are reversed—thus favoring the states—and that ends your deliberation.

(2) Was the admittedly partisan gerrymandering by the states of Maryland and North Carolina unconstitutional? If you answer that question "yes," then the redistricting plans of the two states are thrown out. If you vote "no," then the plans remain in effect.

STOP HERE AND DECIDE THE CASE
BEFORE GOING FURTHER

The Court's Decision follows on the next page.

The Court's Decision

Held: Partisan gerrymandering claims present political questions beyond the reach of the federal courts (nonjusticiable). Both the Maryland and North Carolina district court decisions were overturned.

In a 5-to-4 decision, the majority held that federal courts are neither equipped nor authorized to apportion political power to achieve "fairness." Any attempts to address partisan gerrymandering are for the political branch—Congress and the legislatures of the various states. Chief Justice Roberts wrote the majority opinion, joined by justices Thomas, Alito, Gorsuch, and Kavanagh. Justice Kagan wrote a dissenting opinion joined by justices Ginsburg, Breyer, and Sotomayor.

The majority questioned whether "fairness" was something that could even be decided in redistricting cases since there were so many variables at play. "There are no legal standards discernible in the Constitution for making such judgments, let alone limited and precise standards that are clear, manageable, and politically neutral."

The Supreme Court noted that several states had passed laws or state constitutional amendments prohibiting partisan gerrymandering. Thus, there was a remedy for those who felt disenfranchised by partisan gerrymandering; they could advocate to get the state legislatures to address the issue. That is where the dispute belonged, not the court.

A strong dissent was authored by Justice Elena Kagan. She argued that the degree of partisan apportionment in the two states involved in this case amounted to the creation of "rigged elections." The courts were the only avenues available to the victims of such rigging in order to protect the viability of their votes.

By drawing districts to maximize the power of some voters and minimize the power of others, a party in office at the right time can entrench itself there for a decade or more, no matter what the voters would prefer. Just ask the people of North Carolina and Maryland. . . ."

She noted that the justices in the majority did not deny any of the harms that partisan gerrymandering creates. She points out, for example, that the majority agrees that gerrymandering is "incompatible with democratic principles." To leave resolution of issues related to gerrymandering to the political process is to abdicate the courts' role in our system of government.

And yes, as the majority states, partisan gerrymandering has been with us since before our independence. But Justice Kagan pointed out, "[B]ig data and modern technology—of just the kind that the mapmakers in North Carolina and Maryland used—make today's gerrymandering altogether different from the crude line-drawing of the past."[68]

---

[68] Gerrymandering based on faulty data in the founding days of our nation often led to the opposite result from what was intended. They even had a name for those mistakes: dummymanders.

Carey (Cook County State's Attorney) v. Brown

447 U.S. 455 (1980)

The Issue:

May the government restrict protestors from picketing in front of private residences?

Protestors have discovered that picketing, marching, and chanting outside the residence of someone with whom they have a disagreement is an effective way of drawing both the media's attention to their cause and bringing the disputed issues to the forefront of the occupant of the targeted dwelling. The protestors insist such activities are protected speech under the First Amendment to the United States Constitution. Meanwhile, neighbors of the targeted residences are often inconvenienced and annoyed by the protestors interfering with the tranquility of their neighborhood. As a result, various governmental bodies have passed laws attempting to manage residential picketing. This case involves one such attempt.

In September of 1977, responding to the mayor of Chicago's refusal to support bussing of schoolchildren to achieve racial integration, protestors from a civil rights organization called Committee Against Racism picketed outside the mayor's home.

The plaintiffs, who had been among the picketers, were arrested under an Illinois law that generally prohibited picketing at residences or dwellings but exempted peaceful protesting at locations where the residence also served as a place of business. (The home of the mayor was not considered a place of business.)

The plaintiffs pled guilty and were sentenced to periods of supervision from six months to one year.

The Lawsuit:

The plaintiffs did not challenge their arrests. Rather, they subsequently brought a lawsuit in federal court against the State of Illinois (by suing Bernard Carey, the Cook County State's Attorney at that time) in which they sought both a finding that the statute under which they were arrested was unconstitutional and an injunction prohibiting state officials from enforcing it. The plaintiffs took this prospective approach as they wished to continue their picketing in residential neighborhoods in the future.

The district court denied the plaintiffs' petition, but the court of appeals reversed the district court, holding that the statute violated the Equal Protection Clause found within the Fourteenth Amendment.

Illinois appealed the case to the United States Supreme Court.

The Applicable Law:

The statute at issue in this case is challenged under both the First and Fourteenth Amendments to the Constitution. As a "free speech" issue, the First Amendment is applicable. The Fourteenth Amendment provision involved here—referred to as the Equal Protection Clause—provides that everyone is entitled to an equal and nondiscriminatory application of the law. The plaintiffs claim that the Illinois statute at issue violates provisions of both amendments.

The statute reads as follows:

It is unlawful to picket before or about the residence or dwelling of any person, except when the residence or dwelling is used as a place of business. However, this Article does not apply to a person peacefully picketing his own residence or dwelling and does not prohibit the peaceful picketing of a place of employment involved in a labor dispute or the place of holding a meeting or assembly on premises commonly used to discuss subjects of general public interest.

In a prior case, the Supreme Court had addressed similar constitutional issues to those addressed in this case, and said that a municipality "may constitutionally impose reasonable time, place, and manner regulations on the use of its streets and sidewalks." But a municipality may not discriminate in setting those restrictions based on the *content* of the expression.[69]

Illinois contends its statute serves a legitimate purpose of accommodating the competing rights of homeowners to enjoy their privacy and the rights of employees to demonstrate over labor disputes. It asserts that there is a relevant distinction between a site that is solely used as a residence and one that serves as both a residence and a business. As the state put it:

By "inviting" a worker into his home and converting that dwelling into a place of employment . . . the resident has diluted his entitlement to total privacy. In other words, he has "waived" his right to be free from picketing with respect to disputes arising out of the employment relationship, thereby justifying the statute's narrow labor exception at those locations.

In an equal protection analysis of the dispute, a prime consideration is whether there is an appropriate governmental interest suitably furthered by the differential treatment of residential picketing.

---

[69]   Hudgens v. NLRB, 424 U.S. 507 (1976) (Citations omitted)

As an example, we can look to a prior Supreme Court case also involving picketing.[70] In that matter, the court upheld a Louisiana statute that prohibited picketing in front of a government building that was used as a courthouse *if* the content of the picketing could be seen as an intent to influence the judiciary. However, the court noted that if the mayor had an office in the courthouse and the picketers were addressing issues related to the mayor's duties, then the picketing would be allowed even though the difference in treatment was based on the content of the message sought to be delivered. The Court found that there was an important government interest in not having the judiciary pressured by public opinion.

What's your verdict? Was the statute barring all residential picketing except that related to a labor dispute unconstitutional?

STOP HERE AND DECIDE THE CASE
BEFORE GOING FURTHER

---

[70]   Cox v. Louisiana, 379 U.S. 559 (1965)

The Court's Decision

Held: The Illinois statute is unconstitutional under the Equal Protection Clause of the Fourteenth Amendment.

In a 6-to-3 decision, the United States Supreme Court held that the statute made an impermissible distinction between peaceful labor picketing and other peaceful picketing. It found that the distinction was based on the "content" of the speech at issue, favoring one type of message over another. Thus, the justices said, permissibility of residential picketing is dependent solely on the nature of the message being conveyed. Labor picketing is no more deserving of First Amendment protection than other topics of public protest.

The dissenting justices argued that there was a rational basis for differentiating between picketing a place solely used as a residence versus a residence also used as a business. The justices in the minority denied the Equal Protection Clause was at issue because, they asserted, the differentiation in this case was based on how a residence was being used versus the message of the picketers. Justice Rehnquist (an associate justice at that time), believing the statute to be constitutional, wrote in his dissenting opinion, "equal protection does not require that 'things which are different in fact . . . be treated in law as though they were the same.'"

Postscript: Subsequently, in 1988, the Supreme Court heard and decided the case of *Frisby vs. Shultz* (487 U.S. 474), which involved anti-abortion picketing at the home of a local doctor who performed abortions. Wisconsin had passed a law that banned *all picketing in front of residential homes without any exceptions.* Two anti-abortion picketers challenged the statute as a violation of their First Amendment rights. In a 6-to-3 decision, the Supreme Court found that the statute was "content neutral" and served a "significant governmental interest." Most importantly, unlike our Illinois statute, the Wisconsin anti-residential-neighborhood-picketing law was applied uniformly without regard to the content of the protests or the status of the targeted residences.

United States v. Bryant

136 S.Ct. 1954 (2016)

The Issue:

Can tribal court convictions serve as a basis for an increase in one's sentence in subsequent federal court proceedings?

For Native Americans, there is a dual system of government. In recognition of their original sovereignty over the Americas, Congress has granted established tribes the right to their own laws and enforcement mechanisms for crimes that occur on their lands. However, Congress also maintained its right to exercise jurisdiction over the tribes as well. Issues arising from this dual system of governance sometimes lead to conflicts between tribal-based justice and rights provided by the United States Constitution. This case is one such dispute over the constitutional right to counsel in a criminal trial.

Michael Bryant Jr. was a member of the Northern Cheyenne Tribe residing on the tribe's reservation in Montana. His criminal record reflects over 100 tribal court convictions for domestic assault.

Native American women experience the highest rate of domestic violence compared to all other groups in the United States. Statistics also demonstrate that the severity of the abuse often escalates over time. American Indian and Alaska Native women are raped or sexually assaulted at a rate 2.5 times higher than other women in the United States.

In 1968, Congress passed the Indian Rights Act. The act governs tribal court proceedings. Safeguards applicable to defendants in tribal courts are similar—but not identical—to rights addressed in the Constitution. In tribal courts, the right to appointed counsel for those that cannot afford to hire an attorney only applies to defendants charged with a crime that carries a potential punishment of *more than one year*.

To address the problem of domestic assaults, Congress passed legislation providing for an increased term of imprisonment for a defendant convicted of domestic assault on Indian land upon a showing that the defendant had previously been convicted of the same type of crimes; i.e., a "habitual offender." Bryant had been convicted numerous times in the tribal courts for such assaults. In each prior case, Bryant received a sentence of less than one year of imprisonment. Due to the short-term sentences that applied to his tribal court charges, in his prior domestic assault cases Bryant had not been eligible for appointed counsel.

Based upon his multiple domestic assault convictions in the tribal courts, a federal grand jury indicted Bryant on two counts of domestic assault by a habitual offender. These proceedings took place in federal court rather than before the tribal court.

Federal Court Proceedings:

In his federal district court case, Bryant was appointed counsel as required by the Sixth Amendment to the Constitution. The prior tribal court convictions were used as a basis to enhance his sentence in the federal court proceedings. Bryant challenged the government's attempt to use those prior tribal court convictions as a basis for an enhanced sentence, arguing that he had not been afforded counsel in those tribal cases as, he asserted, he was entitled to under the Sixth Amendment. The district court denied his challenge and Bryant pleaded guilty but reserved the right to contest the sentence on appeal.

The Ninth Circuit Court of Appeals agreed with Bryant's argument and set aside the federal court conviction. While acknowledging Bryant's failure to have counsel appointed for him in the *tribal court proceedings* was valid because the Sixth Amendment right to counsel does not apply in tribal courts, the Ninth Circuit ruled that when proceedings moved to the federal district court the Sixth Amendment *did* apply. Thus, use of the uncounseled tribal court convictions to enhance the sentence in the federal court violated Bryant's Sixth Amendment rights. The appellate court noted that those uncounseled tribal court convictions would not have survived constitutional review if they had taken place in either state or federal court.[71] Federal prosecutors appealed the Ninth Circuit decision to the United States Supreme Court.

The Applicable Law:

While federal law generally governs Indian country, in crimes involving Indian-against-Indian, Congress has generally barred federal court jurisdiction, relying instead on the tribal courts to handle those cases. However, Congress was displeased with the fact that convictions for domestic abuse on Indian land result in only a one year or less term of imprisonment. Out of this concern, Congress enacted the federal domestic assault in Indian country by a habitual offender felony statute. This law gave the federal courts jurisdiction to prosecute repeat offenders.

Bryant was charged in federal court under the following statute:

> Any person who commits a domestic assault within . . . Indian country and who has a final conviction on at least 2 separate prior occasions in Federal, State, or Indian tribal court proceedings for offenses that would

---

[71] The Eighth and Tenth Circuits have, on the other hand, held that uncounseled tribal court convictions can be used in sentence enhancement proceedings. This conflict between the circuits is one reason the Supreme Court chose to hear Bryant's case.

be, if subject to Federal jurisdiction any assault, sexual
abuse, or serious violent felony against a spouse or
intimate partner . . . shall be fined . . . [or] imprisoned
for a term of not more than 5 years, or both . . .[72]

Many state and federal criminal statutes allow for an enhancement
or increase in a convicted defendant's time in jail if the defendant had
one or more prior convictions for the same or similar offense. The term
of imprisonment for a defendant found guilty of a burglary, for example,
might be increased from ten to twenty years if the individual had a prior
burglary conviction.

The Sixth Amendment to the United States Constitution guarantees
an indigent defendant the right to have "the assistance of counsel for
his defense" paid for by the government in "all criminal prosecutions"
in which, if found guilty, the defendant could receive a sentence of
imprisonment for *any* amount of time.

However, in recognition of the separate sovereigns (Indian country
and the United States) that preexisted the Constitution, tribes have
traditionally been excluded from the constitutional provisions in the Bill
of Rights. In the case of *Plains Commerce Bank v. Long Family Land &
Cattle Co.*, the Supreme Court ruled: "The Bill of Rights, including the
Sixth Amendment right to counsel, therefore, does not apply in tribal
court proceedings."[73]

A conflict arises between the Constitution and the Indian Rights
Act in cases where a recidivist defendant in the tribal courts faces a
potential increase in potential sentencing in the federal courts because
of prior convictions. The constitutional issue stems from the fact that
Bryant did not receive appointed counsel in the earlier tribal hearings
because his possible sentences were less than one year.

---

[72] 18 U.S.C. Section 117(a)

[73] 554 U.S. 316, 337 (2008)

What's your verdict? Does the use of Bryant's uncounseled tribal court convictions as a basis for sentence enhancement in subsequent federal court proceedings violate his Sixth Amendment right to counsel?

STOP HERE AND DECIDE THE CASE
BEFORE GOING FURTHER

The Court's Decision

Held: Because Bryant's tribal court convictions occurred in proceedings that complied with federal law and were valid when entered, use of those convictions as a basis for sentence enhancement in the subsequent federal prosecution does not violate the Constitution.

In a unanimous decision, the court reasoned that enhancement statutes do not affect the earlier uncounseled convictions but only penalize the last offense committed by the defendant. Bryant's tribal court proceedings complied with the Indian country laws and were therefore valid convictions. There was no reason, the majority said, why the tribal court convictions could not be used as a basis for giving the federal district court discretion to increase the term of imprisonment in the latest proceedings.

The Supreme Court reversed the Ninth Circuit court's decision and ordered the original federal district court enhanced sentence reinstated.

Postscript: It took so many years for Bryant's case to work its way through the appellate process that by the time the Supreme Court decided the case he had completed his trial-court-ordered enhanced prison sentence. Thus, if Bryant had *won* in the Supreme Court, it might have clarified the law for future cases, but the decision would have come too late to have made any difference in the time Bryant spent behind bars.

Carpenter v. United States

138 S.Ct. 2206 (2018)

The Issue:

Can the government obtain a consumer's cell phone records from the cell phone provider without first obtaining a search warrant?

Cell phone towers trace the location of your phone constantly, whether you are actually using one of the phone's functions or not. Wireless communication companies store the data for analysis and sale to third parties. Law enforcement can use it to trace anyone's movements throughout the day. The question arises, therefore: can a consumer assert a Fourth Amendment privacy right to preclude dissemination of this information? Applying the Constitution to new technologies once again sharply divides the Supreme Court.

Timothy Carpenter was one of several individuals arrested pursuant to Detroit police officers' suspicions that Carpenter's group was responsible for robbing a series of Radio Shack and T-Mobile stores.

Having obtained the cell phone number of the wireless phone Carpenter was using, the government requested and obtained a court order requiring two companies that supplied the cell phone service to release the location data they had collected from the phone.

The Trial:

Using information collected over a four-month period, the government was able to identify 12,898 "location points" cataloging Carpenter's movements—an average of 101 data points per day. Those data points showed that Carpenter was in the vicinity of four of the robberies at issue at the time they took place. He was charged with six counts of robbery and six counts of carrying a firearm during a federal crime of violence.

At trial, Carpenter objected to the cell phone evidence and moved to suppress it. Carpenter claimed that the obtaining and subsequent use of the records at issue violated his Fourth Amendment rights. The district court denied his motion. He was convicted of all but one of the firearms counts, and sentenced to more than one hundred years in prison.[74]

Carpenter appealed his conviction, and specifically challenged the denial of his motion to suppress the cell phone location records. The Sixth Circuit Court of Appeals affirmed Carpenter's conviction, holding that Carpenter lacked a "reasonable expectation of privacy" in the cell phone company business records at issue, and therefore, a warrant based on probable cause was not necessary. Carpenter took his appeal to the United States Supreme Court.

How did his cell phone records assist in his conviction? The majority opinion in the case describes the technology at issue as follows:

> Cell phones continuously scan their environment looking for the best signal, which generally comes from the closest cell site. Most modern devices, such as smartphones, tap into the wireless network several times a minute whenever their signal is on, even if the owner is not using one of the phone's features. Each time the phone connects to a cell site, it generates a time-stamped record known as cell-site location information (CSLI).

---

[74] Considering the type of evidence that was used to convict him, the fact that a T-Mobile store was one of his "victims" is, in no small way, ironic.

Depending on the number and density of cell phone towers, a phone's location can be determined within a range of fifty meters. Absent disconnecting the phone from the network provider, there is no way to avoid leaving behind a trail of location data. Cell phone providers collect, store, analyze, and even sell this location-related information.

The Applicable Law:

That Fourth Amendment, upon which Carpenter relies in challenging the cell phone evidence, provides:

> The right of the people to be secure in their persons, houses, papers, and effects, against unreasonable searches and seizures, shall not be violated, and no warrants shall issue, but upon probable cause, supported by oath or affirmation, and particularly describing the place to be searched, and the persons or things to be seized.

Carpenter's cell phone records were obtained under the Stored Communications Act.[75] This act only requires the government to demonstrate to the court "reasonable grounds" that the records compiled by the cell phone companies will assist in an ongoing investigation. If the court finds those grounds exist, a subpoena is issued to the cell phone provider for the CSLI records.

On the other hand, when a search is conducted that falls under the protections of the Fourth Amendment, a judge must issue a warrant for the records only after the government demonstrates "probable cause"—a higher standard than "reasonable grounds"—that a crime is taking or has taken place. Courts have held that "some quantum of individualized suspicion" must be provided the court before a search may be undertaken. The Stored Communications Act, however, only requires the government to show that the evidence "might be pertinent

---

[75]   18 U.S.C. Sec. 2703(d)

to an ongoing investigation – a 'gigantic' departure from the probable cause rule."

Another important issue in analyzing this case involves the "third party" possession of the data at issue. A warrant is not required in every instance involving third-party records. Rather, a warrant is required only in the rare case where the suspect has a "legitimate privacy interest in records held by a third party." The legal principle involved is that when one voluntarily provides information to a third party, the privacy interest in that information is forfeited.

No one denies that the records the government obtained belonged to the cell phone providers (third parties) instead of Carpenter. Carpenter did not compile the data; he did not own the data; he did not have any say as to how long the records were kept; he could not demand that the records be modified or destroyed; his own access to the records was restricted; and the carrier could sell to private businesses the very same data it had provided to the government.

As technology has advanced, the issue of privacy rights over third-party data has been the subject of heated debate. For example, a pen register—a device that records the outgoing phone numbers dialed on a landline telephone—placed on a suspect's phone by the government was held *not* to be a search requiring a warrant based on probable cause. The Supreme Court said that when the caller dialed a phone number she voluntarily conveyed the dialed numbers to the phone company's equipment, and that the caller assumed the risk that the telephone company would reveal that information to law enforcement.

Likewise, bank records, credit card records, vehicle registration records, hotel records, employment records, and utility records may all be obtained by subpoena without meeting the higher standards of a warrant. The courts have ruled that an individual does not have a reasonable expectation of privacy regarding this data.

On the other hand, by obtaining CSLI information, the government can track a person's movements with relative precision. Is that the type of "Big Brother" activity that the Fourth Amendment was meant to protect us from?

What's your verdict? Did Carpenter have a "reasonable expectation of privacy" in the cell phone companies' records such that a warrant based on "probable cause" was required before releasing the records to the government? If you answer that question "yes," then the court's decision is reversed, and the cell phone data is inadmissible against Carpenter. If you answer that question "no," then Carpenter's conviction (based in part on the cell phone data) is confirmed.

STOP HERE AND DECIDE THE CASE
BEFORE GOING FURTHER

The Court's Decision

Held: Carpenter's Fourth Amendment rights were violated. The government should have first obtained a warrant supported by probable cause before acquiring the records.

In a 5-to-4 decision the Supreme Court ruled that Carpenter did have a reasonable expectation of privacy in the cell phone provider data. The justices acknowledged that advancements in technology may require an adjustment in the court's perspective when it comes to privacy rights:

> [F]ew could have imagined a society in which a phone goes wherever its owner goes, conveying to the wireless carrier not just dialed digits, but a detailed and comprehensive record of the person's movements. We decline to extend [holdings in prior cases] to cover these novel circumstances.

The dissenters argued that there was no Fourth Amendment violation in the government's obtaining Carpenter's cell phone data. They noted that prior decisions failed to find a reasonable expectation of privacy (thus, no warrant required) in obtaining telephone numbers dialed, checking account records, and credit card data. Yet these materials can reveal one's personal affairs, opinions, habits, and associations—what one has purchased; how much money he or she makes; the political and religious organizations in which they participate; whether they have visited a psychiatrist, abortion clinic, or AIDS treatment center; whether they go to gay or straight bars; and who their closest friends and family members are. Whereas the CSLI records involved in this case "only" provided the general whereabouts of the cell phone user over a given time.

The dissenters also argued that the Fourth Amendment itself should not apply to CSLI records because the amendment only addresses searches and seizures of "persons, houses, papers, and effects." The third-party records of the cell phone provider would not come within the parameters of the amendment's declared subject matter, they asserted.

As a result of the Supreme Court finding that there was a constitutional violation regarding the location points evidence, the court overturned Carpenter's conviction and sent it back to the lower court for further review consistent with the decision.

Carpenter's moment of victory, however, was short lived. Upon remand, the Sixth Circuit Federal Court of Appeals applied what was is known as the "good faith" exception to the exclusionary rule. The Sixth Circuit ruled that because the police obtained the cell phone data *reasonably believing* that they were complying with a valid law (the Stored Communications Act), the evidence they obtained was admissible. The Stored Communications Act was ruled unconstitutional only *after* the government had obtained the challenged data. The Supreme Court has held that evidence obtained in violation of the Constitution (usually excluded) may be admitted if the law enforcement agents acted in good faith in obtaining it. So even though the law under which the incriminating evidence was obtained was deemed unconstitutional, the Sixth Circuit Court ruled that the evidence could still be used against Carpenter, and his one-hundred-year sentence was reinstated.

Dauber v. The Utility Company
Los Angeles County Superior Court (1993)

The Issue:

Is a utility company responsible for the injuries sustained in a fall by a woman whose heel got caught in one of the utility company's grates imbedded in the sidewalk?

Can't a lady in her senior years dress with style anymore? She can. But it might be hazardous to her health. This is a personal injury matter for monetary damages.[76]

Esther Dauber always liked to look her best when she was out and about. At sixty-eight years of age, it may have taken her a little longer to get ready for an outing, but as anyone who passed her on the sidewalk could tell, she took a great deal of pride in her appearance. She was, what we might call, "old school" when it came to manners and respect for elders.

On a clear, sunny day, Mrs. Dauber headed out to the local grocery store. She parked her car at the curb next to a parking meter. After exiting her car, she walked over to the meter to insert her coins. Having deposited her parking fee, she attempted to take a step back and proceed with her shopping.

---

[76] This *is* a real case, but for reasons set out in the Appendix the names of the parties have been changed.

Instead, one of the heels of her shoes became lodged between the slots of a six-inch diameter round iron grate that had been installed in the sidewalk. As she started to lose her balance, the grate pivoted within the round frame that was holding it, and Mrs. Dauber, with her shoe still stuck in the grate, fell to the ground. She suffered a fracture of her right hip.

The grate was a cover for an underground concrete vault owned by The Utility Company. Inside the vault were meters for the surrounding businesses. The grate was situated about six inches from the base of the parking meter.

The Trial:

In her subsequent lawsuit against the utility company, Mrs. Dauber contended the company was negligent in placing such a metal grate at the base of a parking meter. She presented expert testimony that as one approaches a parking meter the focus is drawn to the top of the meter. A reasonable person would be unlikely to note the grate at the base of the meter. Her expert stated that the utility company should not have put a grate with slots at that location, or at least not have placed it right at the base of the meter. He said the company could have used a solid plate lid for the cover if it had to be placed at that exact spot. It would have been reasonable for the utility company to have considered the fact that women wearing high-heeled shoes could become entangled in the grate. The site of Mrs. Dauber's fall was an accident waiting to happen, according to her property expert.

The gas company responded by pointing out that Mrs. Dauber had been wearing shoes with a high "stiletto" heel. Stiletto heels taper quickly from the top to a diameter of about one centimeter (slightly less than half an inch) at the base of the heel. The Utility Company claimed she assumed the risk of wearing such shoes as there are grates all over the city into which that type of heel can slip. The company argued that she was required to maintain a heightened sense of awareness of her surroundings when she wore that type of shoe.

The company also defended itself by noting that the grate was open and obvious, and was a common type of utility vault lid without a history of prior problems of the kind involved in this case. It was, the company said, not reasonable to require that grates such as the one at issue completely preclude anything from slipping into the slots.

On cross-examination, the company admitted that it had no women on the staff that designed the grates for sidewalk use, and that they subsequently replaced the grate at the site of Mrs. Dauber's fall with a solid lid.

The hip surgery to repair the unstable fracture consisted of placing a steel rod and pins in her femur. At the time the case went to trial, her medical expenses were about $50,000, with future rehabilitation still required.

The Applicable Law:

This is a "premises liability" case, the issue being whether a reasonable person would or would not have found the placement and design of the metal lid to have been a danger to the public. Unlike in a criminal trial, the burden of proof for plaintiff Dauber requires that she prove her case by a "preponderance of the evidence" (as opposed to the higher criminal standard of "beyond a reasonable doubt").

A jury sitting on such a case would be instructed on the law as follows:

> Plaintiff Dauber claims that she was harmed because of the way the defendant, The Utility Company, constructed and maintained the utility vault at issue in this case. To establish this claim, she must prove all of the following:
>
> 1. The defendant was negligent in the design or maintenance of the site at issue.
> 2. The plaintiff was harmed.
> 3. The defendant's negligence was a substantial factor in causing the plaintiff's harm.

The judge would have defined "negligence" as follows:

> Negligence is the failure to use reasonable care to prevent harm to oneself or to others.
>
> A party (plaintiff, defendant, or both) can be negligent by acting or by failing to act. A party is negligent if they do something that a reasonably careful person or corporation *would not do* in the same situation or fails to do something a reasonably careful person or corporation *would do* in the same situation.
>
> You must decide how a reasonable party would have acted under the circumstances presented in this case.

The defendant asserted it was the plaintiff who was primarily at fault for her own injuries. This claim would give rise to the following instruction:

> The Utility Company claims that Mrs. Dauber's own negligence contributed to her harm. To succeed on this claim, the defendant most prove by a preponderance of the evidence:
>
> 1. The plaintiff was negligent.
> 2. The plaintiff's negligence was a substantial factor in causing her harm.

What's your verdict? Who was *primarily* at fault for Mrs. Dauber's injuries: the plaintiff, Mrs. Dauber, or the defendant, The Utility Company?

STOP HERE AND DECIDE THE CASE
BEFORE GOING FURTHER

The Court's Decision

Held: The jury found in favor of The Utility Company.

The jury believed that Mrs. Dauber "assumed the risk" of just the type of accident that happened by wearing the stiletto heels. Otherwise, the jury surmised, a property owner could be held liable for any small opening in the sidewalk or other surface.

Mrs. Dauber had previously offered to settle her case against The Utility Company for $200,000. The Utility Company had offered Mrs. Dauber $25,000 just before the commencement of trial.

A jury in a civil case is not allowed to hear about any settlement discussions. The courts encourage settlements. If juries were allowed to hear about prior settlement discussions, the parties would not likely attempt to settle a case before trial. Thus, Mrs. Dauber's jury was unaware of the demands and offers.

Schenck v. United States
249 U.S. 47 (1919)

The Issue:

To what extent should constitutional guarantees be set aside in times of war?

Although this freedom of speech case may not be familiar to you, chances are you have heard the sentiment first expressed in this case that the First Amendment does not protect "a man in falsely shouting fire in a theatre."

World War I started on July 28, 1914, and ended four years later, on November 11, 1918. During this period, the United States government initiated a draft of military-age male adults to conscript them into the army. In addition, in 1917 Congress passed the Espionage Act, which made it illegal to obstruct recruitment and enlistment efforts.

General Secretary of the US Socialist Party Charles Schenck believed that the draft was a violation of the Constitution because, he argued, the Constitution does not give the government the right to enroll adults into the military against their will. He said that the forced conscription of men violated the Thirteenth Amendment, which prohibits involuntary servitude. His constitutional claim was based upon the following portion of that amendment: "Neither slavery nor *involuntary servitude*, except as punishment for a crime . . . shall exist

within the United States, or any place subject to their jurisdiction."
(emphasis added)

Forced conscription into the military, he said, was a form of "involuntary
servitude," because the government was forcing age-eligible males into a
job working in the military whether they wanted the job or not.

Schenck took his protest public by distributing thousands of flyers
to draft-eligible men, calling for them not to "submit to intimidation,"
and asserting that if one does not resist the draft "you are helping to
deny or disparage rights which it is the solemn duty of all citizens and
residents of the United States to retain." And while he did suggest that
people *resist* the draft, at no point did he actually urge people to *refuse*
to respond to a draft notice.

When hostilities started, President Woodrow Wilson wanted
to utilize a strictly volunteer army. But the call for volunteers fell
substantially short of what was minimally necessary. In May of 1917,
the United States government authorized the raising of a national army
through conscription.[77] The government contended that the mandatory
draft was authorized within Congress's constitutional powers to declare
war and raise and support armies.

The distribution of his flyers led to Schenck's arrest under the
Espionage Act of 1917. The United States asserted that Schenck's
flyers interfered with the recruiting and enlistment programs that were
established in the 1917 Selective Service Act and, therefore, violated the
Espionage Act.

The Trial:

Schenck was found guilty of the Espionage Act charges. His
appeal of the conviction ended up before the United States Supreme
Court. Schenck asserted three basic arguments as to why the Supreme

---

[77]   At the end of the war—November 1918—the Selective Service Act of 1917 was
      cancelled. Although there have been subsequent draft laws, there has not been
      a draft in the US since 1973, when Congress allowed the then existing draft
      authorization to expire.

Court should overturn his conviction. (1) It was a violation of his First Amendment free speech rights in that he was being prosecuted for speaking out against the draft. (2) The Espionage Act refers only to interfering with the "recruitment or enlistment" activities of the government. Schenck said that the mandatory draft was not a form of either "recruitment or enlistment" since those two practices imply a voluntary, rather than mandatory, action. (3) The government did not present evidence that any harm actually resulted from the distribution of his flyers. The Espionage Act of 1917 says the actions at issue must be injurious to the United States in order to be susceptible to prosecution.

The government countered those assertions: (1) The government has the right to not only raise an army but also to restrict activities during a time of war for the security of the country, including some restrictions on freedom of speech. The First Amendment's protections are not absolute and without limits. For example, one can be sued for making damaging false statements about someone. (2) The draft *was* a form of recruitment and enlistment as it provided for the personnel to fight the war. (3) The government did not have to present evidence that any recruits actually refused to serve after reading one of Schenck's flyers. It only had to provide evidence that urging resistance to the draft created a danger to the security of the nation.

The Applicable Law:

The passages in the Constitution that pertain to Congress' right to raise an army are found within Article 1, Section 8, the section that sets forth the powers granted to Congress. Paragraph 12 states that Congress has the authority "[t]o raise and support armies." Paragraph 13 provides the authority to "maintain a navy." And paragraph 14 gives Congress the power "[t]o make rules for the [governing] and regulation of the land and naval forces."

The First Amendment provides, in part, "Congress shall make no law . . . abridging the freedom of speech." In referring to this provision that some say is the bedrock of democracy, Benjamin Franklin stated:

Freedom of speech is a principal pillar of a free government: When this support is taken away, the constitution of a free society is dissolved, and tyranny is erected on its ruins. Republics . . . derive their strength and vigor from a popular examination into the action of the magistrates.[78]

Schenck's distribution of the flyers led to his being charged with violating Section 3 of the Espionage Act of 1917:

Sec. 3 . . . [W]hoever, when the United States is at war, shall willfully cause or attempt to cause insubordination, disloyalty, mutiny, refusal of duty, in the military or naval forces of the United States, or shall willfully obstruct the recruiting or enlistment service of the United States, to the injury of the service or of the United States, shall be punished by a fine of not more than $10,000 or imprisonment for not more than twenty years, or both.

Note that you are not being called upon to decide if Schenck's Thirteenth Amendment "involuntary servitude" arguments about the draft are correct or not. The issue is whether his distribution of the anti-draft flyers was conduct that could be punished under the Espionage Act. It was his urging resistance to the draft and not his reasons for doing so that led to his conviction.

What's your verdict? Should Schenck's conviction under the Espionage Act of 1917 be reversed.

STOP HERE AND DECIDE THE CASE
BEFORE GOING FURTHER

---

[78]   Benjamin Franklin, "On Freedom of Speech and the Press," *Pennsylvania Gazette,* 17 November 1737

The Court's Decision follows on the next page.

The Court's Decision

Held: Schenck's prosecution under the Espionage Act was a proper exercise of the government's wartime authority and did not violate Schenck's First Amendment rights.

In a unanimous decision, the court held that Schenck's anti-draft pamphlets may have been acceptable in "ordinary times," but not when the country was embroiled in a war that required the services of men in uniform. The majority opinion stated ". . . [T]he character of every act depends upon the circumstances in which it is done." And then the court added the often-cited free speech limitation reference: "The most stringent protection of free speech would not protect a man in falsely shouting fire in a theatre and causing a panic."

Another often-cited standard for deciding free speech disputes was included in the court's decision. It was in ruling against Schenck that the court said,

> The question in every case is whether the words used are used in such circumstances and are of such a nature as to create a *clear and present danger* that they will bring about the substantive evils that Congress has a right to prevent. (emphasis added)

Schenck's distribution of the flyers did create a "clear and present danger" to the security of the country, the court found.

The court also rejected Schenck's argument that urging resistance to the mandatory draft was not the same as interfering with recruitment and enlistment efforts. In dismissing that challenge, the court said ". . . [R]ecruiting is gaining fresh supplies for the forces, as well by draft as otherwise."

Justice Oliver Wendell Holmes wrote the 1919 majority opinion in *Schenck*, setting forth the "clear and present danger" standard of review in free speech cases. This standard would be cited by the courts for the next fifty years. But in 1969, the Court replaced it with a more stringent test, which holds that the state can only limit speech that incites "imminent" unlawful action. We will never know if this higher standard would have made a difference in Charles Schenck's case.

Minnesota v. Carter

119 S.Ct. 469 (1998)

The Issue:

Does a person have a constitutionally protected "right of privacy" in regard to government surveillance when they are a guest in another's person's home?

Most Americans are aware that the Constitution provides safeguards against state intrusion into our homes. Picture this: you are sitting in your living room watching the evening news when you suddenly notice there is a police officer at your window peering inside your house. A little disconcerting, right? Keep that scenario in mind when you consider the case that follows.

An Eagan, Minnesota, police officer walked over to a ground floor apartment and looked through a gap in the closed blinds. He observed Carter, Johns, and Thompson (the apartment's tenant) bagging cocaine. The officer later said he looked in the window because of a tip from a confidential informant who allegedly had seen the cocaine packaging operation through the same window. The officer then called in a request for a search warrant to be obtained, but before one could be prepared, Carter and Johns got in a car and left the apartment complex.

Shortly thereafter, they were pulled over by police, who found a loaded handgun, a scale, and forty-seven grams of cocaine in plastic sandwich bags. The police returned to the apartment with a warrant and searched the premises, where they found cocaine residue on the kitchen table. Carter, Johns, and the tenant were arrested on drug trafficking charges.

The Trial:

Carter and Johns lived in Chicago. Neither of them had ever been in this apartment before. They had been using Thompson's apartment to bag cocaine for two and a half hours prior to their arrest. (Thompson was given one-eighth of an ounce of the cocaine for providing Carter and Johns the use of the apartment.)

At his trial, Carter challenged the admission of the cocaine and other evidence, arguing that the officer's initial observation (from which everything else flowed) was an unreasonable search in violation of the Fourth Amendment. Carter's motion to suppress the evidence was denied and he was found guilty of state drug charges. Carter appealed.

The Minnesota State Supreme Court overturned Carter's conviction, holding that he had a *legitimate expectation of privacy* in the invaded place, and that the officer's window observation constituted an unreasonable search. As a result, the state court said, all of the seized evidence was inadmissible.[79] The decision was then appealed to the United States Supreme Court.

The Applicable Law:

The Fourth Amendment to the Constitution reads as follows:

> The right of the people to be secure in their persons, houses, papers, and effects, against unreasonable searches and seizures, shall not be violated, and no Warrants

---

[79] In considering this case, you should *assume* that the officer's observation *was* an unreasonable search.

shall issue, but upon probable cause, supported by Oath
or affirmation, and particularly describing the place to
be searched, and the persons or things to be seized.

The primary issue to be resolved in this case is whether or not
Carter, as a visitor to the apartment, could reasonably have expected
that he had a protected right of privacy in the apartment during the
drug transaction. One might argue the fact that the officer had to view
the apartment interior through *drawn blinds* proves Carter had such a
privacy expectation. On the other hand, since he had only been in the
unit for a short time and was packaging drugs as a business venture,
one might argue he did not have a *reasonable* expectation that he was
entitled to a right of privacy under the circumstances.

If Carter is held to have had a reasonable expectation of privacy in
the apartment, he would be entitled to have all of the evidence gained
in searching the car and apartment thrown out. If he is held *not* to have
been entitled to a reasonable expectation of privacy, it would not matter

if the search was reasonable or not since he would not be a person who was eligible to challenge the search.[80]

It is up to the court to determine if the persons charged did, in fact, have a reasonable expectation of privacy. The extent to which the Fourth Amendment protects people may depend upon where those people are located. An overnight guest, for example, may have a legitimate expectation of privacy in someone else's home while spending the night there. But does the same go for someone who stops in for just a brief visit? When does a "home" become a "business"? The courts have held that expectations of privacy in commercial premises are different from, and indeed less than, those in a home.

What's your verdict? Was it reasonable for Carter to assume he had a right of privacy inside the apartment? If you answer this question "yes," then the evidence would be thrown out. If you answer the question "no," then Carter has no basis for challenging the evidence, and his original conviction would be reinstated.

STOP HERE AND DECIDE THE CASE
BEFORE GOING FURTHER

---

[80] The rights of the actual *tenant*—Thompson, in this case—to challenge the evidence differed from Carter's rights as the apartment was the tenant's *home* which gives rise to special constitutional protections. Thompson was, therefore, tried separately from Carter and Johns.

The Court's Decision

Held: The Supreme Court held that it was not reasonable for Carter to believe he had a right of privacy during the cocaine packaging operation, and therefore the evidence could be admitted and used against him.

In a 6-to-3 decision, the Supreme Court majority found that the purely commercial nature of the transaction, the relatively short period of time that Carter and Johns were on the premises, and the lack of any previous connection between them and the tenant all led to a conclusion that Carter did not have a Fourth Amendment privacy claim. His conviction was reinstated.

Consider this in light of the court's decision: Do individuals who work for a living out of their homes (regardless of the nature of that work) forfeit their right to a reasonable expectation of privacy in their homes?

Foucha v. Louisiana
504 U.S. 71 (1992)

The Issue:

If a criminal defendant is found *not guilty by reason of insanity* and then committed to a psychiatric hospital, what are the state's constitutional options once that defendant is no longer considered "insane"?

Terry Foucha entered the home of a married couple intending to steal from them. He pointed a gun at the couple, chased them out of their house, and fired on police officers who confronted him when he fled. He was subsequently apprehended and charged with aggravated battery and illegal discharge of a firearm. In October of 1984, he was committed to a psychiatric hospital after the trial court determined that:

> . . . Foucha was not guilty by reason of insanity, finding that he "is unable to appreciate the usual, natural and probable consequences of his acts; that he is unable to distinguish right from wrong; that he is a menace to himself and others; and that he was insane at the time of the commission of the . . . crimes, and that he is presently insane."

Foucha's Application for Release:

Four years later, Foucha applied to the court to be released from the mental institution in which he had been confined. A defendant found guilty of the same charges brought against Foucha could be imprisoned for thirty-two years. At the time Foucha applied for his release, he had been held for less than one-third of that potential statutory sentence.

A medical panel found that Foucha had recovered from the drug-induced mental illness from which he suffered upon initial confinement. They stated he was now in "good shape" mentally. However, the same panel stated that Foucha had an antisocial personality—a condition that is neither a mental disease nor treatable. The panel stated they could not "certify that he would not constitute a menace to himself or others if released." Evidence that Foucha had been involved in several altercations during his time at the psychiatric hospital was presented by the state in opposing Foucha's request for release. The state contended that although he may no longer be insane, he was nevertheless "dangerous."

Upon review, the Louisiana Supreme Court held that it was *not* a violation of Foucha's Fourteenth Amendment right to due process to permit continued confinement based on dangerousness alone. Foucha appealed to the United States Supreme Court.

The Applicable Law:

The "due process" clause found in the Fourteenth Amendment to the US Constitution provides that everyone is entitled to a fair and consistent application of the law and the legal process. The amendment forbids an arbitrary application of the laws.

Foucha was adjudicated insane under what is called the M'Naghten test, which is applied to the defendant's state of mind *at the time he committed the offense at issue.* Thus, a defendant could be determined to be insane at the time he commits the offense but not at the time of trial and still be found not guilty by reason of insanity. The M'Naghten test provides:

> If the circumstances indicate, that, because of a mental disease or mental defect the offender was incapable of distinguishing between right and wrong with reference to the conduct in question, the offender shall be exempt from criminal responsibility.

In Louisiana, a defendant in a criminal case found not guilty by reason of insanity is committed to a psychiatric hospital unless the defendant proves that he is *not* dangerous. Subsequently, a defendant may be held in the psychiatric hospital for as long as he is determined to be mentally ill *and* dangerous. After six months of confinement in the hospital, the defendant can request a hearing to demonstrate that he is no longer insane. Even if found no longer to be mentally ill, under Louisiana law, if he is found to be "dangerous" he may be returned to the hospital. This period of forced hospitalization may be more or less than the law provides as a term of imprisonment for the offenses with which the defendant was originally charged.

On the other hand, persons who have been found guilty of a criminal act can be held no longer than their sentence, regardless of whether or not they are believed to be "dangerous" at the end of the time set by the sentence.

One of the most famous cases involving the insanity defense involved John Hinckley Jr., who attempted to assassinate President Ronald Reagan in March of 1981. Hinckley was found not guilty by reason of insanity. In 1987, he filed the first of many applications for release from the facility in which he was being held, arguing he was no longer insane. He was held in the psychiatric hospital until September of 2016. At that time, a judge determined he was no longer a threat to himself or others. Hinckley was, however, placed under numerous restrictions at the time of his release, including being forbidden to contact Jodie Foster, the actress he said he had tried to impress when he attempted to kill the president. In September of 2021, the court removed all the remaining restrictions that had been in effect and Hinckley became a free man once again.

What's your verdict? Is continued confinement based on "dangerousness" alone a violation of the Due Process Clause of the Fourteenth Amendment in the case of a person who was found not guilty by reason of insanity?

STOP HERE AND DECIDE THE CASE
BEFORE GOING FURTHER

The Court's Decision follows on the next page.

The Court's Decision

Held: Foucha may be held only as long as he is *both* mentally ill *and* dangerous, but no longer. The judgment of the lower courts was reversed.

In a 5-to-4 decision, the Supreme Court said that since Louisiana does not contend that Foucha was mentally ill, the basis for holding him in a psychiatric facility had disappeared and the state was no longer entitled to hold him based on dangerousness alone. Freedom from bodily restraint by the government is at the core of the Due Process Clause of the Fourteenth Amendment. "As Foucha was not convicted, he may not be punished," the majority wrote.

Criminals actually found guilty at trial and sent to prison do not have to prove they are no longer dangerous in order to be released at the end of their sentence; the Court noted:

> Yet it is surely strange to release sane but very likely dangerous persons who have committed a crime knowing precisely what they were doing, but continue to hold indefinitely an insanity detainee who committed a criminal act at a time when, as found by a court, he did not know right from wrong.

The dissenting justices asserted that a verdict of "not guilty by reason of insanity" is neither equivalent nor comparable to a verdict of "not guilty" standing alone. Instead, not guilty by reason of insanity means the defendant committed the crimes with which he has been charged. Thus, the state possesses the constitutional authority to incarcerate Foucha for the protection of society. The dissenters noted: "Surely, the citizenry would not long tolerate the insanity defense if a serial killer can convince a jury that he is not guilty by reason of insanity and then is returned to the streets immediately after trial by convincing a different court that he is not, in fact, insane."

Cruzan v. Director, Missouri Department of Health

497 U.S. 261 (1990)

The Issue:

Does the United States Constitution allow for what is in common parlance referred to as a "right to die"?

Nancy Beth Cruzan was left in a persistent vegetative state as a result of a 1983 automobile accident.[81] Her car had rolled over into a ditch. When paramedics got to her they had to restart her heart. They estimated that she had not been breathing for about fifteen minutes. Although she displayed some motor reflexes thereafter, medical personnel could not detect any indications of cognitive function.

For the next eight years, all her sustenance was provided through a gastrostomy tube that was surgically implanted into either her stomach or small intestine. Her body was rigid, all four limbs were severely contracted, and her fingernails were cutting into her wrists. She

---

[81] In its footnote #1, the majority opinion in this case provides a definition of persistent vegetative state: "A body which is functioning entirely in terms of its internal controls. It maintains temperature. It maintains heart beat and pulmonary ventilation. It maintains digestive activity. It maintains reflex activity of muscles and nerves for low level conditioned responses. But there is no behavioral evidence of either self-awareness or awareness of the surroundings in a learned manner."

occasionally vomited and suffered seizures. She breathed without the assistance of a ventilator. The State of Missouri paid for all her medical care in a state hospital. The sole purpose of her medical treatment was to keep her alive metabolically. There was no known medical treatment that could have "cured" her.

Eventually, Cruzan's parents (as Nancy's "surrogates") asked the hospital doctors to terminate Nancy's life-support systems. But the staff refused to do so without court approval.

A coalition of euthanasia and abortion opponents challenged the right of the parents and the hospital to allow Cruzan to die. They argued that every life has value, even one in a vegetative state. Bringing about her death by removing the feeding tube, they asserted, devalued all life.

The Parents' Petition:

The parents filed an action in court to order the health care providers at the state hospital to disconnect the feeding tube. At the hearing on their petition, a former roommate testified that Nancy, at age twenty-five, had once expressed a wish not to continue her life unless she could live it "at least halfway normally." Otherwise, she would not want to be kept alive by extraordinary means. The trial court found this testimony sufficient to grant the parents' request to terminate nutrition and hydration for their daughter. The state appealed. The Missouri State Supreme Court overruled the trial court and held in favor of the state rejecting the parents' request to terminate treatment.

The Applicable Law:

It is a well-established rule of law "that the Due Process Clause of the Fourteenth Amendment confers a significant liberty interest in avoiding unwanted medical treatment."

"Informed consent" to allow medical procedures is a bedrock of civil law. Likewise, a patient has the right to refuse consent to such procedures.

Over the years, medical knowledge and medical technology have advanced to the point that a patient's life can be extended indefinitely when in the past the patient would have died shortly after failure of the heart, lungs, and/or cognitive function. As a result, conflicts have developed between medicine and law.

Missouri requires that a surrogate prove a person's intent regarding life-ending preferences by clear and convincing evidence. On the other hand, no proof is required to support a finding that the incompetent person would wish to *continue* treatment.

> Here, Missouri has in effect recognized that, under certain circumstances, a surrogate may act for the patient in electing to have hydration and nutrition withdrawn in such a way as to cause death, but it has established a procedural safeguard to assure that the action of the surrogate conforms as best it may to the wishes expressed by the patient while competent. Missouri requires that evidence of the incompetent's wishes as to the withdrawal of treatment be proved by clear and convincing evidence. The question, then, is whether the United States Constitution forbids the establishment of this procedural requirement by the State.

A definition provided for the "clear and convincing standard of proof" is found in footnote #11 in the majority opinion. It states: "[P]roof sufficient to persuade the trier of fact that the patient held a firm and settled commitment to the termination of life supports under the circumstances like those presented."

Missouri claims its statutory requirements are justified pursuant to its significant interest in preserving human life. One test for analyzing the constitutionality of the Missouri statute was set out in a 1978 Supreme Court case that held that "if a requirement imposed by the State 'significantly interferes with the exercise of a fundamental right, it cannot be upheld unless it is supported by sufficiently important state interests and is closely tailored to effectuate only those interests.'"

One consequence of the Missouri procedure is that it denies a family member or other surrogate from terminating life support in the case of an incompetent patient who has never made his or her wishes known. In such a case, a patient in a vegetative state would have to be maintained on hydration and nutrition sources until the patient's body finally gives up. Is that requirement a violation of the patient's due process rights?

The State of Missouri has recognized a surrogate's right to act for an incompetent patient, including the withdrawal of nutrition and hydration. Missouri's living will statute provides for certain safeguards. Without a living will drawn up consistent with its statute, Missouri requires other clear and convincing evidence of the patient's desires in terms of life-saving care.

In this case, the Missouri courts found that the testimony of Nancy's parents, her sister, the friend of hers who had testified, and Nancy's court-appointed guardian (to the effect that Nancy would have wanted the hydration and nutrition withdrawn) did not meet the "clear and convincing" evidence of Nancy's wishes to specifically terminate sustenance that would result in her death. The courts said that the testimony was not specific to withdrawing life-sustaining treatment in the event Nancy was in a vegetative state.

While the State of Missouri does not set out exactly what kind of evidence it *would* consider clear and convincing, it appears from the briefs filed in this case that only a living will or equivalent form of directive from the patient while competent would suffice. Cruzan's representatives point out that too few people actually execute such documents, and thus Missouri's standard of proof is unreasonable. As Justice Sandra O'Connor has noted, "Few individuals provide explicit oral or written instructions regarding their intent to refuse medical treatment should they become incompetent."

What's your verdict? Should Cruzan's parents, on their daughter's behalf, be allowed to refuse her further life-sustaining treatment?

STOP HERE AND DECIDE THE CASE
BEFORE GOING FURTHER

The Court's Decision follows on the next page.

The Court's Decision

Held: The Supreme Court ruled that the State of Missouri's procedures designed to preserve human life were constitutional.

In a 5-to-4 decision, the court said that in a conflict between the state's interest in protecting the "sanctity of life" and the potential countervailing interest on the part of the patient in the "quality of life," the state's interest was superior. The Court expressed a concern that there was no guarantee that family members would always act in the best interests of incompetent persons.

The majority held that a state may require an increased burden of proof regarding the patient's wishes about life-saving techniques since a mistaken decision on that issue in favor of the state would mean the maintenance of the *status quo,* while a mistaken decision resulting in termination of such techniques would result in the death of the patient. The former allows for correction of errors in the decision, while the latter does not.

The dissent challenges the majority on exactly what is the *status quo* that the state believes it is protecting. The *status quo* that the state wants to maintain includes feeding tubes for hydration and nutrition. The dissent points out, however, that the *status quo* could just as easily be considered as the patient's condition before those medical treatments were placed; i.e., the natural result of not having the external hydration and nutrition. "To decide otherwise that medical treatment once undertaken must be continued irrespective of its lack of success or benefit to the patient in effect gives one's body to medical science without their consent."

The dissent also noted that concern for a possible "mistaken decision" has never been a factor in granting a *competent* person's wish to terminate life-saving treatment. Therefore, it is an abridgment of the equal protection of the law to have that concern enter into the decision for an incompetent person.

In his dissenting opinion, Justice Brennan stated: "Nancy Cruzan has a fundamental right to be free of unwanted artificial nutrition and hydration, which right is not outweighed by any interest of the State . . ." Brennan asserted that the "biased procedural obstacles imposed by the Missouri Supreme Court impermissibly burden that right."

Postscript: Two months after the Supreme Court ruled on the Cruzan case, her parents asked the Missouri courts to set another hearing, arguing that they had new evidence regarding Nancy Cruzan's likely preference for ending her life rather than continuing in a vegetative state. Three of Nancy's former coworkers testified at the second hearing that they recalled Nancy saying that she would never want to live "like a vegetable." Nancy's court-appointed guardian did not oppose the parents' reasserted request. Missouri did not challenge the request either.[82] As a result, the judge ruled there was clear and convincing evidence of Nancy's wishes and gave permission to remove the feeding tube.

Nancy Cruzan died on December 26, 1990, twelve days after the court's latest ruling and the removal of her feeding tube. Her death came eight years after the auto accident and six months after the Supreme Court had decided her case. She was thirty-three years old.

Perhaps the most important "lesson" to come from this case is the need for each and every adult to execute a living will or power of attorney for health care (in accordance with appropriate state laws) to ensure that medical providers and family members know what one's wishes are in regard to life-extending medical care and one's "right to die."

---

[82]   Missouri did not challenge this second petition by the parents because it was satisfied with the earlier ruling by the Supreme Court that its statute was constitutional.

Good News Club v. Milford Central School

533 U.S. 98 (2001)

The Issue:

Did a school district violate the free speech rights of a religious-oriented club by denying it access to school facilities?

In the laboratory of public debate, stand back when mixing religion, public schools, and the Constitution, since an explosion of passion and opinion is very likely to result. It is in this dynamic area of law where you must make a decision.

The State of New York has authorized local school boards to open their facilities to public groups according to certain guidelines. Milford Central School (with students in kindergarten through twelfth grade) created a community-use policy for its facilities. Two of the policy's stated purposes are relevant in this case: (1) to provide a location for "instruction in any branch of education, learning or the arts" and (2) to provide "social, civic and recreational meetings and entertainment events, and other uses pertaining to the welfare of the community, provided that such uses shall be nonexclusive and shall be opened to the general public." The policy prohibits use "by any individual or organization for religious purposes."

Many of the early settlers immigrated to America to escape religious persecution in their home countries. Freedom to practice one's religion was important to the drafters of the Constitution. It is interesting to note, therefore, that neither "God" nor "religion" are mentioned anywhere in the original document. But some of the drafters refused to sign off on the Constitution without some protection of personal rights, including freedom of speech and religion. They would vote to ratify it only if those rights were specifically protected. Thus, the drafters added the first ten amendments, which we know as the Bill of Rights.

The Good News Club is a private Christian organization for children ages six to twelve. The Milford, New York, club requested permission of the school board to utilize the Milford Central School's cafeteria for after-school meetings. During the application process, the club provided the school board with a sample lesson plan in which the students are to be told:

> The Bible tells us how we can have our sins forgiven by receiving the Lord Jesus Christ. It tells us how to live to please Him . . . [I]f you received the Lord Jesus as your Savior from sin, you belong to God's special group – His family.

The lesson plan instructs the teacher to "lead a child to Christ," and to "[e]mphasize that this verse is from the Bible, God's Word" and is "important – and true – because God said it." In another part of the lesson plan, the students are told to bow their heads and close their eyes. Then the instructor is to say:

> If you have never believed on the Lord Jesus as your Savior and would like to do that, please show me by raising your hand. If you raised your hand to show me you want to believe in the Lord Jesus, please meet me so I can show you from God's Word how you can receive His everlasting life.

In what was certainly "bad news" for the Good News Club, the school board superintendent denied the club's request, asserting that the club's activities were "the equivalent of religious worship," and as such, their meeting in the school cafeteria would violate the terms of use for the facilities.

The Good News Club challenged Milford Central School's denial of its facilities by filing suit against the school.

The Trial:

The trial court ruled in favor of the superintendent and the Milford Central School. The club appealed to the Second Circuit Court of Appeals, which upheld the trial court's decision in favor of the school district, asserting that Milford's applying its facility use policy in this case was *constitutional subject discrimination, not unconstitutional viewpoint discrimination*" (emphasis added) The Good News Club then appealed to the United States Supreme Court.

The Applicable Law:

Because Milford Central School is a government entity, its decision to deny the Good News Club use of the cafeteria requires the facts to be analyzed according to two constitutional provisions, both of which are found in the First Amendment to the Bill of Rights. The relevant portion: "Congress shall make no law respecting an establishment of religion, or prohibiting the free exercise thereof; or abridging the freedom of speech . . ."

In this case, one must first decide if the school's denial of its facilities breached the club's free speech rights.

Milford's opening of its facilities to the public created a *limited* public forum. As such, it is not required to allow persons to engage in every type of speech. It can reserve its forum to certain groups or certain topics. However, its power to restrict speech is not without limits. The restrictions cannot pick and choose the "viewpoint" in the presentations of the allowed topics. In deciding the free speech issue in this case, one must decide whether the school's refusal to allow the club to meet on its campus was based on the club's choice of topic (permitted discrimination) or was it based on the club's viewpoint (nonpermitted discrimination).

If you find the refusal to allow the club to use the cafeteria did *not* violate the club's free speech rights, then the analysis ends, and the Good News Club does not receive permission to use the facilities. If, however, Milford's denial of its facilities *did* violate the free speech rights of the club, a second step is required before deciding the case: whether the school is, nevertheless, entitled to deny access to the Good News Club pursuant to the First Amendment's Establishment and/or Free Exercise clauses.

These religion-oriented provisions were placed within the First Amendment since the Founding Fathers were concerned about government becoming too entrenched in religious issues. Thus, it prohibits Congress from making any "law respecting an establishment of religion." On the other hand, other drafters of the Constitution did not want the government to interfere with citizens' rights to practice their particular religion, and so added a provision barring the government from "prohibiting the free exercise thereof." In addressing these clauses, the courts have held that the government may not give its stamp of approval to religious beliefs. It may not become so involved in religious activity that it appears the government endorses any particular religious forum. The government may limit the use of its facilities even though it is limiting free speech if the use of the facilities would reasonably lead people to believe that the governmental entity was endorsing and/or promoting a particular religion.

If allowing the Good News Club to present its program in the school's cafeteria would violate either or both the Establishment Clause and/or Free Exercise Clause, then the verdict must be in favor of Milford despite the fact that there would be a limiting of the club's free speech. However, if denying access would improperly deny the club's free speech rights, and denying access would not violate either or both the

Establishment Clause or Free Exercise Clause, then the Good News Club prevails, and Milford must allow it to use its cafeteria.

Many of the cases before the Supreme Court dealing with religious practices or symbols arise from this inherent tension regarding the degree of government involvement in matters related to religion.

What's your verdict? (1) Did the Milford Central School violate the free speech rights of the Good News Club when it excluded the club from meeting after hours at the school? If your answer to that question is "no," the case ends in favor of Milford. You need not go any further in your analysis. Only if you answered the question "yes," should you address the second issue.

(2) Is the school allowed to deny use of its facilities to the club anyway because the school's allowing the club to use its facilities would violate either or both the Establishment Clause and/or Free Exercise Clause? If you answer that question "yes," the case ends in favor of Milford Central School. If you answer that question "no," the case ends in favor of the Good News Club.

STOP HERE AND DECIDE THE CASE
BEFORE GOING FURTHER

The Court's Decision follows on the next page.

The Court's Decision

Held: (1) Milford *did* violate the club's free speech rights when it excluded the club from meeting after hours at the school. (2) Use of the facilities by the club *would not* violate either the Establishment or Free Exercise clauses. Thus, the verdict was in favor of the Good News Club.

In a 6-to-3 opinion, the Supreme Court ruled that Milford's denial of the Good News Club's application violated the club's free speech rights. Justice Clarence Thomas wrote, "When Milford denied the Good News Club access to the school's limited public forum on the ground that the club was religious in nature, it discriminated against the club because of its religious viewpoint in violation of the Free Speech Clause of the First Amendment."

Milford Central School allowed public use of its facilities by groups that address the *subject matter* of morals and character development. The majority found the Good News Club did exactly that and that Milford violated the First Amendment free speech rights of the club by discriminating on the basis of the club's *viewpoint* that it was through prayer and reading the Bible that participants were taught morals and character development. In the context of a "limited public forum," a speaker may not be excluded just because the speaker approaches the topic for discussion from a religious viewpoint. The Court's opinion states:

> What matters for purposes of the Free Speech Clause is that we can see no logical difference in kind between the invocation of Christianity by the club and the invocation of teamwork, loyalty, or patriotism by other associations to provide a foundation for their lessons.

Having found a violation of the club's free speech rights, the Supreme Court then went on to the second issue: Was there was an Establishment or Free Exercise Clause violation? It held there was not.

The classes at issue were to be held after school, were not sponsored by the school, and were open to the public, not just church members. The majority said it was unlikely anyone would perceive Milford's allowing the club to use its facilities as the school's endorsement of religion.

In arguing that the club's use of the school's facilities *would* violate the First Amendment, Milford noted that this case was different from prior decisions regarding a religious use of school facilities since the Good News Club directed its activities to elementary school students who are more impressionable and might feel more coerced to participate than would high school or college students. However, the Supreme Court majority answered this claim by noting that the students needed parental consent to participate, and therefore there was adequate protection for the impressionable feelings of the younger students.

The justices who voted in the minority argued that the club's program was essentially an evangelical service of worship.

Sarah Dole v. Allan Greenway; San-Fran Cab Co.

San Francisco County Superior Court (2017)

The Issue:

Who had the "right of way" in this personal injury case: the taxicab or the bicyclist?

The woman who brought this action, Sarah Dole, was twenty-five years old and a resident of San Francisco. (She is the plaintiff.) On the day of the incident, she was riding her bike through the streets of the city. The weather was clear and the traffic was moderate in density. Eventually, she found herself pedaling behind a taxicab driven by Allen Greenway and operated by the San-Fran Cab Company. (They are the defendants.[83]) The plaintiff was riding within a marked bicycle lane as she and the cab approached an intersection regulated with a traffic light. As the two of them entered the intersection, the taxicab began a right-hand turn and struck the plaintiff, knocking her to the pavement.

Dole suffered a fractured sacrum and developed pain in her coccyx. She was treated non-surgically at a hospital and was released the next day. She subsequently followed up with her doctor several times. After five doctor visits she was advised that no other treatment could relieve

---

[83] This *is* a real case, but for reasons set out in the Appendix the names of the parties have been changed.

her pain. She is able to ride her bike, walk, run, and sit; however, long periods of sitting and riding her bicycle cause discomfort.

The bicyclist sued both Greenway and San-Fran Cab Co. claiming they were negligent and were the cause of her injuries.

The Trial:

The plaintiff testified that she had intended to proceed straight through the intersection. She said that she checked to see if the taxicab intended to make a right turn by looking at his turn signal. It was not blinking. Just as she entered the intersection (on a green light), she started to pass the taxi on the taxi's right-hand side assuming the cab was going to drive straight through the intersection. Instead, the cab began a right-hand turn and hit her bike.

The defendants contend that the plaintiff was negligent and the primary cause of her own injuries as she illegally passed the taxicab on the right as she pedaled through the intersection. Defendant Greenway admitted to the police that he turned on his right turn signal at the last second and did not look over his right shoulder prior to turning. He alleged that the plaintiff was speeding on her bicycle and that if she intended to pass him, she should have passed the taxicab on the left side, rather than the right side.

The Applicable Law:

We all know that when a car is going to make a left or right turn it is required to give a signal (by either blinkers or hand signals) of its intentions in sufficient time to adequately warn vehicles traveling behind it.

But what is required of bicyclists passing a vehicle? May a bicyclist pass on the right as it overtakes a car? The rule on this varies from state to state and even city to city. As our case took place in San Francisco, the California Vehicle Code applies. One of the vehicle codes applicable to our facts states:

(a) [A]any person operating a bicycle upon the roadway at a speed less than the normal speed of traffic moving in the same direction at that time shall ride within the bicycle lane, except that the person may move out of the lane under any of the following situations:

(1) When overtaking and passing another bicycle, vehicle, or pedestrian within the lane or about to enter the lane if the overtaking and passing cannot be done safely within the lane . . .

(4) When approaching a place where a right turn is authorized.[84]

Another vehicle code section applicable to bicycles says

(a) Any person operating a bicycle upon a roadway at a speed less than the normal speed of traffic moving in the same direction at that time shall ride as close as practicable to the right-hand curb or edge of the roadway except under any of the following situation:

(4) When approaching a place where a right turn is authorized.[85]

The SF Bicycle Coalition has a website that informs bicyclists of the Rules of the Road. Its website states: "Although bike lanes are often on the right side of the road, people biking and driving are required to pass on the left."

---

[84]   Vehicle Code, Operation of Bicycles, Section 21208.

[85]   Vehicle Code, Operation of Bicycles, Section 21202.

What's your verdict? Who was *primarily* at fault in this case? The taxi driver for striking the bicyclist in the course of his right turn? Or the bicyclist, who was passing the taxi on the right side?

STOP HERE AND DECIDE THE CASE
BEFORE GOING FURTHER

The Court's Decision

Held: The jury found the taxicab driver and the taxi company primarily at fault for the plaintiff's injuries.

However, the jury also found that Sarah Dole was partially at fault. They attributed 65 percent fault to the taxi and 35 percent fault to the bicyclist.

Prior to the trial, the plaintiff had demanded $50,000 to settle the case, but withdrew the offer after thirty days when it was not accepted by the defendants. Later, the defendants offered $50,000 to settle the matter (just before the commencement of the trial), but the plaintiff rejected it.

The jury awarded $162,672 to the plaintiff, including $8,832 in past medical expenses, $3,840 in lost earnings, $50,000 for pain and suffering, and $100,000 for future pain and suffering. The amount awarded to the plaintiff for pain and suffering—past, present, and future—was reduced by 35 percent, the amount of fault the jury found she bore for the accident.

Kansas v. Hubbard

Supreme Court of Kansas No. 113,888 (2018)

The Issue:

Is a police officer's belief that she smells raw marijuana coming from the open front door of an apartment a legal basis for searching the occupants and the residence?

In order for a law enforcement officer to obtain a search warrant, the officer must present a sworn affidavit to a neutral judge or magistrate with sufficient facts to demonstrate probable cause for suspecting that a crime is being or has been committed. But the courts have allowed a search to take place without a warrant where it appears to the officer that evidence of the crime will be gone by the time a warrant is obtained. In these instances, *following the search*, the officer must demonstrate the necessary probable cause in order for any evidence obtained to be admitted at the trial of the charged individual. In this case, the officers' basis for the warrantless search was their belief that they smelled raw marijuana emanating from a residence.[86]

Officer Kimberly Nicholson was in her patrol car conducting surveillance of a convenience store. She ran a standard license check on

---

[86] "Raw marijuana," meaning marijuana that had not yet been smoked or burned in any way.

a vehicle parked there, and determined that several weeks earlier the car had been stopped with a man named Irone Revely driving. Nicholson also noted that there was an outstanding arrest warrant for Irone's brother, Chayln Revely. Officer Nicholson confirmed that Irone was driving the vehicle and began following the car when it left the store, believing the *passenger* in Irone's vehicle was Chayln.

Nicholson continued to follow the vehicle, waiting for the driver to commit a traffic violation that would entitle her to pull the vehicle over and confirm the passenger's identity. No violation occurred.

She followed the car until it parked at an apartment complex, where she too parked her patrol car. Irone's passenger got out and ran into one of the rental units. As Irone walked toward the apartment, Nicholson stopped him and asked if his passenger had been Chayln. Irone continued walking to the apartment without responding to Nicholson. At this point in time, Officer Nicholson was joined by Officer Ronald Ivener.

A short time after Irone had entered the apartment, the "passenger" came out and spoke to the officers. As it turned out, he was not Chayln, but rather Lawrence Hubbard. Hubbard acknowledged he lived in the apartment.

The exchange between Nicholson and Hubbard took place approximately two feet from the door of the apartment. Officer Nicholson later testified she "smelled a strong odor of raw marijuana emanating from the apartment" when Hubbard went back into the apartment after talking to her. The officer then knocked on the door. Both Irone and Hubbard came out of the unit and spoke to Nicholson about her suspicions. The men stated they did not smell anything. Hubbard expressed his frustration with Office Nicholson "confusing" him with Irone's brother, Chayln. He claimed Nicholson had been guilty of racial profiling, since the only thing Hubbard and Chayln had in common was that they were Black males.

When Irone and Hubbard reentered the apartment, Nicholson stated she again smelled raw marijuana coming from the unit.

The two officers then instituted what is called a "security sweep," a precursor to obtaining an actual search warrant. This action entails a search of the unit to account for all persons within the unit, and a visual search of objects in plain sight in order to locate any guns or other threats to the safety and security of the officers while awaiting the delivery of an actual search warrant. The occupants were asked to step outside. None of the occupants had the smell of marijuana about them as they passed by the officers. Various drug paraphernalia, a handgun, and a locked safe in a closet were noted during the security sweep.

When the search warrant arrived, a full search of the unit was conducted. The officers pried open the door of the safe they had previously located in the closet. Inside the safe they found twenty-five grams of raw marijuana stored in a Tupperware container. Elsewhere in the apartment, they came upon unused bongs and a partially burnt cigarillo with a small amount of marijuana on it.

As a result of the items discovered in the searches, Hubbard was arrested and charged with misdemeanor possession of marijuana and possession of drug paraphernalia.

The Trial:

Hubbard filed a motion to have the evidence thrown out because, he argued, Nicholson's and Ivener's statements that they smelled raw marijuana while standing outside Hubbard's apartment did not provide a sufficient showing of probable cause for the warrantless security sweep, nor for the issuance of the subsequent search warrant. Hubbard contended there was no marijuana smell but only cigarette smoke and incense. Hubbard's defense attorney argued "'no reasonable person' would be able to detect an ounce of cannabis in a container, inside a safe, inside a closet thirty feet away from a closed apartment door."[87]

Hubbard also challenged the officers' trial testimony. He contended they did not have sufficient credentials and background to render relevant opinions on the smell of marijuana, yet the state had referred to them as "experts."

---

[87] From an article on *High Times* website, December 11, 2018.

Hubbard argued the searches violated his rights under the Fourth Amendment to the United States Constitution. Once such a challenge is filed, it becomes the state's burden to demonstrate the searches at issue were lawful.

In opposing Hubbard's motion to suppress the evidence, the State of Kansas argued that the officers' police training and field experience provided a sufficient basis for their testimony.

> Ivener said his training was at the police academy, and that "[t]hey did a pass-around of raw marijuana . . . so you can recognize the odor of it." Nicholson testified to similar training but added she had detected the smell of raw marijuana between 200 and 500 times.

It was not necessary, the state argued, for the officers to be qualified specifically as "experts" to be able to testify about the smell of raw marijuana.

The court denied Hubbard's motion to suppress the evidence collected during the searches. Hubbard appealed the ruling. The issue ultimately came before the Kansas Supreme Court.

The Applicable Law:

The Fourth Amendment guarantees the right "of the people to be secure in their persons, houses, papers, and effects, against unreasonable searches and seizures." Hubbard relied upon the "exclusionary rule" to have the contested evidence tossed out:

> . . . [T]he judicially created exclusionary rule prevents evidence obtained through an illegal search or seizure from being admitted at trial. . . . This exclusionary rule "safeguards Fourth Amendment rights by preventing the use of unconstitutionally obtained evidence in criminal proceedings against victims of illegal searches."

For the exclusionary rule to apply, there first must be a constitutional violation.

The results of a warrantless search can be admissible at trial if it was shown (1) there was probable cause for the search in the first place and (2) there were certain exigent circumstances justifying an immediate search (the "security sweep"). Exigent circumstances can arise when the law enforcement officer reasonably believes there is a realistic threat that the evidence or contraband will be lost, destroyed, or removed in the time it would take to obtain a warrant for the search.

Hubbard argued the officers did not have enough evidence to demonstrate probable cause for the searches. He asserted that the officers' alleged ability to smell marijuana coming from the apartment did not give rise to a fair probability that the place to be searched contains contraband or evidence of a crime, and therefore no probable cause was established.

The first issue that must be addressed is whether an opinion about marijuana requires one to be an expert in such matters.

Testimony by a witness at trial can come from a layperson or it may be elicited from experts. Laypersons are not usually allowed to express opinions drawn from what they see or hear, especially if to render such opinions requires special training and experience. For example, if you are driving down the road and witness a car whizzing by that is later involved in an accident and subsequently you are called as a witness at trial, you may be able to testify that you had just looked at your speedometer as the car passed and you knew you were going sixty-five miles per hour. Thus, you might be allowed to give your opinion that the vehicle at issue was going seventy-five miles an hour based on your everyday experience as a driver. But if you were asked how fast the vehicle was going based solely on photos of the damage done to the vehicles involved in the accident and their points of rest after the collision, you would not be allowed to give such testimony absent being an expert trained in the techniques of accident reconstruction.

Before experts are allowed to render an opinion, they must be shown to be qualified to do so. This is often accomplished outside the presence of the jury. The side against whom the proposed experts will be testifying is given an opportunity to challenge their credentials by asking questions about the field in which the expert proposes to testify and the experts' specific amount of experience and learning in that field.

However, in regard to lay witnesses, the courts have stated:

> If the witness is not testifying as an expert, the testimony in the form of opinions or inferences is limited to such opinions or inferences as the judge finds: (1) are *rationally based on the perception of the witness*; (2) are helpful to a clearer understanding of the testimony of the witness; and (3) are not based on scientific, technical or other specialized knowledge . . . (emphasis in original)

Over Hubbard's objections, Officers Nicholson and Ivener were allowed to testify as lay witnesses on the issue of smelling the raw marijuana. Hubbard argues their testimony was the subject of expert opinion. Had Hubbard's attorney been able to question the officers' credentials as experts, the attorney might have been able to ask some of the following questions:

> How much raw marijuana must be present in order for a human to be able to detect its odor? How close must the person be to the raw marijuana in order to detect its odor? Does it make a difference whether the raw marijuana is in a closed container or a closed container within a closed container? How long does the odor of raw marijuana linger? Does the temperature of the area in which the marijuana is detected matter? How about the humidity? Does the presence of an odor of burnt marijuana affect a person's ability to smell raw marijuana?

Instead, Nicholson and Ivener were allowed to testify without being qualified as experts about their ability to recognize the smell of raw marijuana.

What's your verdict? Should the evidence secured from the searches be admitted or should Hubbard's motion to suppress the evidence be granted?

STOP HERE AND DECIDE THE CASE
BEFORE GOING FURTHER

The Court's Decision

Held: The Kansas Supreme Court held that the officers' testimony that they smelled raw marijuana was admissible and provided sufficient probable cause to justify the searches of Hubbard's apartment.

In a 4-to-3 ruling, the court found the officers' training as police officers and Nicholson's experience in drug cases was sufficient to allow them to render an opinion about the smell of raw marijuana emanating from the open door of the apartment. The majority noted, "We are not dealing with sommeliers trying to identify a white wine as a Loire Valley Chenin Blanc."

The dissenters argued that the officers were, in reality, testifying as *experts* on the smell of raw marijuana. Therefore, the officers should have been subject to the defense questions about their qualifications as experts before testifying. The trial court's refusal to allow this type of examination, the dissenters asserted, was an error warranting reversal.

CASES CATEGORIZED BY ISSUE IN DISPUTE

Civil Cases for Damage

Civil Forfeiture

Death Penalty

Entrapment

Flag Desecration

Freedom of the Press

Freedom of Speech

Government Control of Interstate Commerce

Immigration

Labor Dispute

National Security

Right to Appointed Counsel

Right to Life

Religious Freedom

Second Amendment: Right to Bear Arms

Trademark Infringement

How likely are the customers of a bar called "The Velvet Elvis" to believe it is in some way affiliated with Elvis Presley and his estate?

Voting Rights

Appendix

A note about citations

Since lawyers are not the primary target audience for this book, a brief discussion as to how cases are "cited" in legal reporters may be in order. The citation for each of the cases set out in this book is located immediately below the name of the case.

When an appeals court issues a decision, it is published in multiple "official" court reporters. The commonly used method to cite these reports is to list the volume of the particular reporter, then the reporter abbreviation, followed by the page number of the first page of the particular decision within that volume of the reporter, and the year the decision was issued. For example, United States Supreme Court decisions are published in several different reporters. One of those reporters is called The United States Reports and is abbreviated in citations as "U.S." One of the Supreme Court cases discussed in this book, *Katz v. United States,* bears the citation "389 U.S. 347 (1967)." To read the full court decision and any dissents, one would go to volume 389 of the United States Reports and turn to page 347. There one would find the facts of the case, the 1967 majority decision, and any concurring or dissenting opinions. Another way to locate the full decision is to simply enter an internet "search" for the citation and call it up on a computer.

Here are the citations you will find referenced in this book:

United States Reports: As discussed above, the citation for this compilation of United States Supreme Court decisions will read "394 U.S. 731 (1969)," representing the volume number, page number, and the year the decision was issued.

Supreme Court Reporter: This set of United States Supreme Court decisions uses citations reading "139 S.Ct. 1960 (2019)," representing the volume number, page number, and year the decision was issued.

Federal Digest Reporter: These reporters set out case decisions from the federal district and circuit courts. Cases cited in this book are from the third edition of that reporter. A typical citation to this reporter will read "614 F.3d 1070 (9th Cir. 2010)," representing the volume number, page number, the circuit court number, and the year of the decision.

United States Court of Appeals: Some of the cases from the United States federal courts of appeals are referenced by the appellate court's file number rather than a citation from one of the various reporters. For example, a case from the United States Court of Appeals for the Sixth Circuit might have the citation listed as "No. 17-3427 (April 2018)," representing the case number and the month and year of the decision.

State Supreme Court Cases: In the case of a citation to a particular state's supreme court, the citation will list the court case number and the year of the decision, such as "Indiana Supreme Court 19S-CR-528 (2020)."

County Court Cases: Those decisions or verdicts that come from the local county court systems (other than civil damage cases) are usually referenced simply by a case number and the year of the decision or verdict. In those cases, the county court is identified below the case title, and will look something like this: "Grant County Superior Court Cause No. 27D01-1308-MI-92 (2020)."

Civil Damage Cases: For six of the seven civil cases for damages (as opposed to constitutional or criminal cases) in the book, I have referenced the county in which the case took place. For the remaining case, *Food Lion Inc. v. Capital Cities ABC, Inc*, I have provided the federal reporter cite because that particular case study is taken from an appeal case. In most of the civil damage cases, I have changed the names of the parties involved. I have culled the majority of the civil cases from summaries published in jury verdict reporters. These verdict reports are written by the attorneys involved—most often the victorious attorney—and I have no way of verifying what is stated in the verdict summary. Therefore, not wishing this book to lead to a civil case for damages against *me*, I decided the better of part of valor was to simply change the names of the parties involved, but only in the civil damage cases. (For a list of the civil damage cases, see "Cases Categorized by Issue in Dispute" section in the back of the book.)

There are frequent quoted excerpts from the case decisions throughout this book. When I have quoted directly from the court's opinion, I have not provided any further specific reference other than the case citation directly below the case caption. If, however, a quotation comes from a source other than the specific opinion for the case study at issue, I have acknowledged the source, usually in a footnote.

Acknowledgments

I don't get out much. So one of the best aspects of writing this book was interacting with some wonderful and helpful people. I would like to recognize a few.

First, I would like to thank Los Angeles attorney Sanford M. Gage. His decision to hire me was the single most significant event in my working life as a trial attorney. As of the spring of 1982, I had been practicing law for three years in Atlanta, Georgia. For a variety of reasons, I decided I wanted to move to the west coast. Because I had not passed the California Bar Exam, I had to apply for a law clerk's position. I checked the hiring ads in the Los Angeles legal newspaper. One of the listings was for Mr. Gage's firm. Unbeknownst to me, Mr. Gage was one of the most preeminent consumer trial attorneys in the entire State of California. He hired me as a law clerk in August of 1982. When I passed the California Bar Exam, he awarded me the honor of joining his excellent group of attorneys. I went from handling mostly minor injury cases and drafting simple wills in Georgia to litigating major complex litigation in Southern California.

The point is, working for Mr. Gage made me a better lawyer. I knew that whenever I walked in an opposing lawyer's office or into a courtroom and announced I was from Sanford Gage's firm representing the plaintiff, the lawyers and judges expected lawyering of the highest caliber. Knowing that Mr. Gage's reputation, in part, rested on my shoulders was both intimidating and energizing. I worked hard and worked long hours to try to be the best prepared lawyer in the room, not just for my own self-esteem but because I knew Mr. Gage expected nothing less. Had I not had the remarkable opportunity to work in his firm, I do not think I would ever have achieved whatever success I had as a trial lawyer. Most of the members of the firm called him "Sandy." I couldn't do it. To me he was and always will be Mr. Gage. (Okay, sometimes when I had to work a full weekend, both day and night, I might have called him some other "names," but never out loud!)

While at the Gage firm, I had the opportunity to work with one amazing paralegal, Karen Mezger. We stayed connected and shared personal and professional thoughts even after we both left the firm. She is a wonderful friend. Her legal mind and strong personality have been acknowledged by and been assets to all the lawyers for whom she has worked. As a paralegal, the only thing she couldn't legally do was try a case in a courtroom. But the legal arguments set out in the pleadings she drafted often made the difference between a client getting his or her day in court and having a case dismissed. I mention her here specifically to thank her for the assistance she gave me in drafting this book. Since I no longer have the benefit of a law firm's access to legal research, Karen was kind enough to send me cases from jury verdict reports and check the subsequent histories on some of the decisions I have cited. This is a better book thanks to Karen.

The list of attorneys to whom I owe a great debt in terms of my career would not be complete without also acknowledging Kirby G. Bailey, Stanley K. Jacobs, and Lyle F. Greenberg.

I was fortunate to have a few friends agree to read the manuscript as it progressed to get their input. I sincerely thank these kind souls for the time and attention they devoted to reading the manuscript: Kevin Cox, David Tseng, Nancy and Joel Pelser-Borowitz, and local Huntsville author Jacquelyn Procter Gray. In addition, I cannot thank the folks at Xlibris enough for their participation and patience in helping me navigate through this new realm of book publishing. I shudder to think what the contents would have looked like without their thorough editing.

To give the book a little "life" away from the text, I chose to add drawings depicting the action in some of the cases. I was lucky to find an illustrator on the other side of the pond who was easy to work with and understood the "mission." I must thank Simon Goodway of Brighton, England, the creator of all the drawings in the book. If you ever need an illustrator, I would highly recommend his services. You can contact him at simon@simongoodway.com. Tell him "Tom, the Alabama lawyer" sent you.

I am truly indebted to the Judicial Council of California for its gracious permission to allow me to use their copyrighted jury instructions in the civil damage cases in this book. The standard jury instructions published by the council allow for continuity and accuracy in informing juries of the laws that apply to the cases they hear. The Judicial Council instructions have been carefully drafted by special committees who look at the way the appeal courts have interpreted language and law. Using these standard approved instructions allows California lawyers to stand on firmer ground when suggesting the instructions judges provide jurors. In some cases, I paraphrased or slightly edited instructions for this book, but the core wording is that of the Judicial Council in most of the civil cases appearing here.

Occasionally, I have reached out to court clerks and attorneys involved to find out a little bit more about the cases I have selected. I thank them for taking my calls and responding to my emails. In particular, I would like to thank Kathy Maufas, Criminal Division Clerk's Office, Cook County, Illinois (*Illinois v. McKinney*); Atty. Steven A. Drizin, Center on Wrongful Convictions (*Illinois v McKinney*); Atty. David Gaudlin (*A.H. v. State*); Timothy A. Beacham, Shelby County, Tennessee, District Attorney's Office (*Payne v. Tennessee*); Atty. Wesley Hotott (*Timbs v. Indiana*); Atty. James H. Lohr (*Bearden v. Georgia*); and Atty. Steven C. Babcock, assistant federal defender, Montana (*United States v. Bryant*).

When tackling a project for which one has no prior experience (that would be me and this book), it's nice to have someone in your corner with whom you can kick ideas around, express frustrations, share the fun, and just be there for you. For that I thank my good friend (and retired Los Angeles attorney) Eric Rosenblatt. Eric has endured a couple of years of my talking about "the book I am writing." Well, Eric, here it is.

About the Author

Tom Borcher enjoyed a career as a trial attorney arguing for plaintiffs in civil jury trials in Los Angeles and Atlanta for thirty-five years before retiring in 2014.

Since leaving the world of litigation, he has been presenting a live program he calls *You Be the Judge* to many different types of audiences including civic groups, adult continuing education classes, high school students and church groups.

He served on the Board of Directors of the Southern California affiliate of the American Civil Liberties Union for many years, and was the president of its Hollywood Chapter at one time. He was a member of the Bar of the Supreme Court of the United States.

Besides the law, he also is a White House historian and has given his educational series entitled *Alligators in the East Room and Other White House Tales* to audiences around the country, including several presidential libraries.

He currently lives in Huntsville, Alabama, sharing a home with his parrot Jack.

Index

Jeppesen Dataplan Inc., 145–46, 150, 328
Jesus, 106
JLCT Inc., 65–68
Johns (apartment tenant), 284–85, 287–88
Judaism, 103–4

K

Kagan, Elena, 252–53
Kansas Supreme Court, 315, 318, 322
Kansas v. Hubbard, 315
Karem, Brian J., 76–80, 82
Karem v. President Donald J. Trump and White House Press Secretary Stephanie A. Grisham, 76
Katz, 131–34, 136, 138, 330, 333
Katz v. United States, 131, 333
Kavanaugh (justice), 196
Kennedy, Rob, 64–68
Kentucky, 13, 16, 180
Kentucky State Supreme Court, 181, 183, 186
Keystone Cops, 1
Kingsford Homeowners Association (HOA), 187–92
Kirchner, Stephen, 7–10, 325
Klingseisen, Josh, 7–10

L

law
ex post facto, 219–20, 222
shield, 203, 207–8, 210, 326
"son of Sam," 45–46, 48, 50
Layton, Frank, 155
Louisiana, 23, 25–26, 28–29, 257, 289, 291, 294, 324–25
Louisiana State Supreme Court, 24, 28, 290
Louisiana v. Tucker, 23
Lundahl, Donald, 203

M

Madison, James, 101
Madison, Vernon, 193–97
Malone, Nigel, 180
Marleau, Russell, 57
Marshal, Thurgood, 100
Marshall (justice), 100
Martin, Beverly, 187–88, 190
Martin v. Kingsford Homeowners Association, 187
Maryland, 167, 246, 250, 252–53
Massachusetts, 152–53, 245, 330
Massachusetts Supreme Judicial Court, 153–54, 158
McKinney, Anthony, 203–4, 206, 210, 326, 339
media, 35, 37, 76, 89
menorah, 102–4, 106–7
Milford Central School, 302–4, 306, 308, 327, 329
military, 158, 277–78, 280
Miller, Jack, 155
misrepresentations, 239, 242
Missouri, 295–98, 301
Missouri courts, 298, 301
Mohamed, Binyam, 145
Mohamed et al. v. Jeppesen Dataplan, Inc. and the United States of America, 145
money, 1, 44–48, 131, 172–73, 175, 179, 270
monies, 46, 48, 50, 225
monuments, 11–12, 14, 16–17
murder, 57–58, 100, 164–65, 169–70, 183, 194, 196, 203, 325

N

National Firearms Act, 155
National Voter Registration Act (NVRA), 141–42
Native Americans, 259

reasonable expectation of, 69–71, 74, 133, 266, 268–70, 286–88, 329
right of, 37, 268, 270, 284, 330
privileges, 58, 86, 88, 116, 206–8
probable cause, 70–71, 109–10, 132, 137, 212–14, 216–17, 266–70, 286, 315, 317, 319
proceedings, 148, 158, 196, 222, 260–61, 264
tribal court, 260–62, 264
Process Clause, 292, 294, 296
proof, 3, 21, 96, 274, 297–98, 300
property, 25, 32, 60, 66, 69–71, 75, 79, 86, 116, 136, 175, 179, 190–91, 216–17, 219–20
property owner, 66, 71, 175, 189, 276
property succession, 31
prosecution, 2, 46, 57, 62, 130, 164, 167, 182–83, 193, 232, 279, 326
prosecutor, 23, 58, 61–63, 115, 119, 165, 170, 182–83, 193
protections, 34, 78, 111, 153, 155, 175, 208, 210, 222, 267, 287, 294, 303
equal, 13, 25–26, 32, 34, 85–86, 116, 227, 249, 258, 300
protests, 84, 258, 278
provisions, 13, 53–54, 114, 195, 213, 255, 279
constitutional, 262, 304
public domain, 37, 150
punishment, 26, 80, 114, 118–19, 174, 195, 277, 325
cruel and unusual, 25, 166

R

Randy White (Warden) v. Roger Wheeler, 180
rape, 35–36, 97
rape victims, 35–38
Rawls, Jerry Lee, 57–63
raw marijuana, 315–18, 320

smell of, 315–18, 320–22
records, 34, 74, 109, 126, 162, 266–70
redistricting plans, 247–48, 250
Registered Student Organization (RSO), 224–25, 230, 233
regulations, 48, 222, 249, 256, 279
Rehnquist (justice), 258
religion, 12–13, 16, 101, 103–4, 161, 224–25, 227, 303, 306
endorsement of, 104, 309
establishment of, 13, 103, 227, 304–5
impermissible endorsement of, 104, 106
improper endorsement of, 101, 328
religious beliefs, 101, 107, 227, 232, 305
religious symbol, 107
reporters, 7, 35, 38, 76–79, 82, 206–8, 235–40, 242–44, 323, 326, 333–34
representations, 85, 89, 239, 242
representatives, 47, 200, 247, 249
restrictions, 226, 232, 256, 279, 291–92, 305
Revely, Chayln, 316
Revely, Irone, 316
revocation, 79, 82–83
Reynolds, Gregory, 120–22, 124, 148, 150
Reynolds v. Vitoni and Clark, 120
Riley, Michael, 69–70, 72, 74–75
robbery, 2–3, 6, 198, 232, 266
Roberts (justice), 252
Rodriguez, Yvonne, 8, 10
Rose Garden, 77

S

Sam (dog), 45–46
Samuels, Sig, 218–20, 222, 330
Samuels v. McCurdy, Sheriff, 218
sanction, 78–79, 82–83
San Diego Padres, 121
San-Fran Cab Company, 310